COLLECTIONS

BETWEEN TIMES

Program Authors
Richard L. Allington
Jesús Cortez
Patricia M. Cunningham
Sam Leaton Sebesta
Robert J. Tierney

Program Consultants
Molly S. McLaurin
Robert Slavin
Zena Sutherland

Instructional Consultant
John C. Manning

Critic Readers
Eneida M. Alcalde
Anita Moore Broms

Pupil Readers
Jason Benavides
Marcus Dixon
Caroline Galyean
Jill Haan
Megan Lestrange
Valerie Silk
Scott Taylor

Scott, Foresman and Company

Editorial Office:
Glenview, Illinois

Regional Offices:
Sunnyvale, California
Tucker, Georgia
Glenview, Illinois
Oakland, New Jersey
Carrollton, Texas

Acknowledgments

Text

Page 12: From *Babe: The Gallant Pig*, text by Dick King-Smith, illustrated by Mary Rayner, (British title: *The Sheep Pig*). Text copyright © 1983 by Dick King-Smith. Illustrations copyright © 1983 by Mary Rayner. Used by permission of Crown Publishers, Inc. and Victor Gollancz Ltd.

Page 41: "The Laughing Faces of Pigs" from *Barnyard Year* by Fred Lape. Copyright, 1949, 1950 by Fred Lape. Reprinted by permission of Harper & Row, Publishers, Inc.

Page 50: from *Time Cat: The Remarkable Journeys of Jason and Gareth* by Lloyd Alexander. Copyright © 1963 by Lloyd Alexander. Reprinted by permission of Henry Holt and Company, Inc. and Brandt & Brandt Literary Agents, Inc.

Page 73: "Dinosaur Air" from *Poems of Earth and Space* by Claudia Lewis. Text copyright © 1967 by Claudia Lewis. Reprinted by permission of the publisher, E. P. Dutton, a division of NAL Penguin Inc.

Page 82: reprinted with permission of Macmillan Publishing Company and McIntosh and Otis, Inc. from *Zeely* by Virginia Hamilton, illustrated by Symeon Shimin. Text, copyright © Virginia Hamilton 1967. Illus. Copyright © Macmillan Publishing Company 1967.

Page 125: "Unfolding Bud" by Naoshi Koriyama. Reprinted by permission from *The Christian Science Monitor*. Copyright © 1957 The Christian Science Publishing Society. All rights reserved.

Page 134: *Scott Joplin and the Ragtime Years* by Mark Evans. Copyright © 1976 by Mark Evans. Reprinted by permission of Jane Jordan Browne, Multimedia Product Development, Inc.

Page 163: "The Piper" by William Blake, 1789

Page 173: Excerpt from *The Supreme Court in America's Story* by Helen Stone Peterson. Copyright © 1976 by Helen Stone Peterson. Reprinted by permission of the author.

Page 181: Excerpt from *Incredible Constructions and the People Who Build Them* by Mel Boring. Copyright © 1984 by Melvin Boring. Reprinted by permission of Walker and Company, Inc.

Page 190: "Lincoln Monument: Washington" from *The Dream Keeper and Other Poems* by Langston Hughes. Copyright 1932 by Alfred A. Knopf, Inc. and renewed 1960 by Langston Hughes. Reprinted by permission of Alfred A. Knopf Inc. and Harold Ober Associates.

Page 193: Excerpt from *Auks, Rocks and the Odd Dinosaur* (Thomas Y. Crowell). Copyright © 1985 by Peggy Thomson. Reprinted by permission of Harper & Row, Publishers, Inc.

Page 208: "The Wise and Clever Maiden" by Helen A. Murphy reprinted by permission from *Children's Plays from Favorite Stories*, edited by Sylvia E. Kamerman. Copyright © 1959, 1970, 1978 by Plays, Inc.

Page 233: "Rebels from Fairy Tales" by Hyacinthe Hill. Reprinted by permission of the author.

Page 242: *The Secret Garden* by Frances Hodgson Burnett, 1911.

Page 281: "Echo" by Walter de la Mare. Reprinted by permission of The Literary Trustees of Walter de la Mare and The Society of Authors as their representative.

Page 290: Chapters 7, 8, and 9 from *The Agony Of Alice* by Phyllis Reynolds Naylor. Copyright © 1985 by Phyllis Reynolds Naylor. Reprinted with the permission of Atheneum Publishers, an imprint of Macmillan Publishing Company; and John Hawkins & Associates.

Page 321: "Abigail" by Kaye Starbird from *The Pheasant on Route Seven*. Copyright © 1968 by Kaye Starbird. Reprinted by permission.

Page 330: "Shrewd Todie & Lyzer the Miser," "The Elders of Chelm & Genendel's Key," and "When Shlemiel Went to Warsaw" from *When Shlemiel Went to Warsaw* by Isaac Bashevis Singer, illustrated by Margot Zemach. Copyright © 1968 by Isaac Bashevis Singer and Margot Zemach. Reprinted by permission of Farrar, Straus and Giroux, Inc.

Page 359: "They Have Yarns. . ." from *The People, Yes* by Carl Sandburg. Copyright 1936 by Harcourt Brace Jovanovich, Inc.; renewed 1964 by Carl Sandburg. Reprinted by permission of the publisher.

Acknowledgements continued on page 544

ISBN 0-673-73355-6

As a young person, there were two things I loved to do—I loved reading and I loved writing. My writing was encouraged by my parents and my teachers, but I would have written things down anyway. Another pleasure was discovering new books to take home from the library.

One person who had a great deal to do with my enjoyment of reading was the Story Lady. Twice a week, my class tramped over to the fieldstone library in my village in Ohio and there waiting for us was the Story Lady. We would walk down a flight of stairs to the basement where we sat down on a large, rag rug near a big, fat, warm furnace. Oh, it was cozy down there on a cold winter day! Sitting on a low chair facing us was the wonderful Story Lady.

She had beautiful black hair and dark eyes and usually she wore a bright shawl. For the next hour or so, she would read us tales from around the world. As I listened, I felt I actually entered into the world of the stories. Afterwards, I would go look for the book from which she read that day and I would sit down right then and there to read the story.

Recently, I went to visit my Story Lady. She still lives in my home town. I was happy to tell her that it was she who had so much to do with my becoming a writer and avid reader. I think I must have begun writing books not just because I enjoy writing good stories, but because I hoped I could become one of your story ladies, and you could become my readers. Now that's what I call happiness.

Virginia Hamilton

An excerpt from Newbery Medal-winner Virginia Hamilton's novel *Zeely* appears on page 79.

4

Babe

The Gallant Pig

Dick King-Smith
Illustrated by Mary Rayner

Farmer Hogget wins a piglet at an English country fair and takes it home to his wife, who longs for a pig to fatten for Christmas dinner. An intelligent and mannerly piglet, Babe has a few surprises for the Hoggets.

A Farm in Rural England

As you read *Babe: The Gallant Pig*, you'll find that the animals on Farmer Hogget's farm are not pets. The sheep are raised for their wool. Fly, the collie sheepdog, works hard herding sheep. A pig, such as Babe, becomes dinner.

The author, Dick King-Smith, sets his story in rural England. The characters' speech is the speech of the English countryside. For example, when Mrs. Hogget talks, she uses words such as "'tis" to mean "it is," "afore" to mean "before," "'twas" to mean "it was," and "'un" to mean "one." King-Smith writes these words as they sound in conversation. Words such as "'tis" are dialect, the way a language is

spoken in a certain region of a country. Rural
English dialect sounds different from the English
spoken on a farm in Vermont or the streets of
London. Using local dialect is one way the author
makes *Babe: The Gallant Pig* realistic.

Thinking About Animal Characters

Authors often give human qualities such as
speech, emotions, and thoughts to their nonhuman
characters. In *Babe: The Gallant Pig*, King-Smith has
the farm animals talk. They tell how they feel about
the events that take place around them. This helps
the reader experience those events from various
points of view. For more information about this kind
of story, look up *Animal Fantasy* in your Student's
Handbook.

As you're reading this excerpt on your own,
discover why Babe is called "gallant."

Babe
The Gallant Pig

"Guess my weight"

"What's the noise?" said Mrs. Hogget, sticking her comfortable round red face out of the kitchen window. "Listen, there 'tis again, did you hear it, what a racket, what a row, anybody'd think someone was being murdered, oh dearie me, whatever is it, just listen to it, will you?"

Farmer Hogget listened. From the usually quiet valley below the farm came a medley of sounds: the oompah oompah of a brass band, the shouts of children, the rattle and thump of a skittle alley, and every now and then a very high, very loud, very angry-sounding squealing lasting about ten seconds.

Farmer Hogget pulled out an old pocket watch as big around as a saucer and looked at it. "Fair starts at two," he said. "It's started."

"I knows that," said Mrs. Hogget, "because I'm late now with all these cakes and jams and pickles and preserves as is meant to be on the Produce Stall this very minute, and who's going to take them there, I'd like to know, why you are, but afore you does, what's that noise?"

The squealing sounded again.

"That noise?"

Mrs. Hogget nodded a great many times. Everything that she did was done at great length, whether it was speaking or simply nodding her head. Farmer Hogget, on the other hand, never wasted his energies or his words.

"Pig," he said.

Mrs. Hogget nodded a lot more.

"I thought 'twas a pig, I said to meself that's a pig that is, only nobody round here do keep pigs, 'tis all sheep for miles about, what's a pig doing, I said to meself, anybody'd think they was killing the poor thing, have a look when you take all this stuff down, which you better do now, come and give us a hand, it can go in the back of the Land Rover, 'tisn't raining, 'twon't hurt, wipe your boots afore you comes in."

"Yes," said Farmer Hogget.

When he had driven down to the village and made his delivery to the Produce Stall, Farmer Hogget walked across the green, past the fortune tellers, the games of chance, the ferris wheel and the band, to the source of the squealing noise, which came every now and again from a small pen in a far corner, against the churchyard wall.

By the pen sat the Vicar, notebook in hand, a cardboard box on the table in front of him. On the pen hung a notice—'Guess my weight. Ten pence a shot.' Inside was a little pig.

As Farmer Hogget watched, a man leaned over and picked it out of the pen. He hefted it in both hands, frowning and pursing his lips in a considering way, while all the time the piglet struggled madly and yelled blue murder. The moment it was put down, it stopped. Its eyes, bright intelligent eyes, met the farmer's. They regarded one another.

One saw a tall thin brown-faced man with very long legs, and the other saw a small fat pinky-white animal with very short ones.

"Ah, come along, Mr. Hogget!" said the Vicar. "You never know, he could be yours for ten pence. Guess his weight correctly, and at the end of the day you could be taking him home!"

"Don't keep pigs," said Farmer Hogget. He stretched out a long arm and scratched its back. Gently, he picked it up and held it before his face. It stayed quite still and made no sounds.

"That's funny," said the Vicar. "Every time so far that someone has picked him up he's screamed his head off. He seems to like you. You'll have to take a guess."

Carefully, Farmer Hogget put the piglet back in the pen. Carefully, he took a ten-pence piece from his pocket and dropped it in the cardboard box. Carefully, he ran one finger down the list of guesses already in the Vicar's notebook.

"Quite a variation," said the Vicar. "Anything from twenty pounds to forty, so far." He wrote down "Mr. Hogget" and waited, pencil poised.

Once again, slowly, thoughtfully, the farmer picked the piglet up.

Once again, it remained still and silent.

"Thirty-one pounds," said Farmer Hogget. He put the little pig down again. "And a quarter," he said.

"Thirty-one and a quarter pounds. Thank you, Mr. Hogget. We shall be weighing the little chap at about half past four."

"Be gone by then."

"Ah well, we can always telephone you. If you should be lucky enough to win him."

"Never win nothing."

As he walked back across the green, the sound of the pig's yelling rang out as someone else took a guess.

"You never do win nothing," said Mrs. Hogget over tea, when her husband, in a very few words, had explained matters. "Though I've often thought I'd like a pig, we could feed 'un on scraps, he'd come just right for Christmas time, just think, two nice hams, two sides of bacon, pork chops, kidneys, liver, chitterlings, trotters, save his blood for black pudding, there's the phone."

Farmer Hogget picked it up.

"Oh," he said.

"There. Is that nice?"

In the farmyard, Fly, the black-and-white collie, was beginning to train her four puppies. For some time now they had shown an instinctive interest in anything that moved, driving it away or bringing it back, turning it to left or right, in fact herding it. They had begun with such things as passing beetles, but were now ready, Fly considered, for larger creatures.

She set them to work on Mrs. Hogget's ducks.

Already the puppies were beginning to move as sheepdogs do, seeming to creep rather than walk, heads held low, ears pricked, eyes fixed on the angrily quacking birds as they maneuvered them about the yard.

"Good boys," said Fly. "Leave them now. Here comes the boss."

The ducks went grumbling off to the pond, and the five dogs watched as Farmer Hogget got out of the Land Rover. He lifted something out of a crate in the back, and carried it into the stables.

"What was that, Mum?" said one of the puppies.

"That was a pig."

"What will the boss do with it?"

"Eat it," said Fly. "When it's big enough."

"Will he eat us," said another, rather nervously, "when we're big enough?"

"Bless you," said his mother. "People only eat stupid animals. Like sheep and cows and ducks and chickens. They don't eat clever ones like dogs."

"So pigs are stupid?" said the puppies.

Fly hesitated. On the one hand, having been born and brought up in sheep country, she had in fact never been personally acquainted with a pig. On the other, like most mothers, she did not wish to appear ignorant before her children.

"Yes," she said. "They're stupid."

At this point there came from the kitchen window a long burst of words like the rattle of a machine gun, answered by a single shot from the stables, and Farmer Hogget emerged and crossed the yard toward the farmhouse with his loping stride.

"Come on," said the collie bitch. "I'll show you."

The floor of the stables had not rung to a horse's hoof for many years, but it was a useful place for storing things. The hens foraged about there, and sometimes laid their eggs in the old wooden mangers; the swallows built their nests against its roof beams with mud from the duck pond; and rats and mice lived happy lives in its shelter until the farm cats cut them short. At one end of the stables were two loose boxes with boarded sides topped by iron rails. One served as a kennel for Fly and her puppies. The other sometimes housed sick sheep. In there Farmer Hogget had put the piglet.

A convenient stack of straw bales allowed the dogs to look down into the box through the bars.

"It certainly looks stupid," said one of the puppies, yawning. At the sound of the words the piglet glanced up quickly. He put his head to one side and regarded the dogs with sharp eyes. Something about the sight of this very small animal standing all by itself in the middle of the roomy loose box touched Fly's soft heart. Already she was sorry that she had said that pigs were stupid, for this one certainly did not appear to be so. Also there was something dignified about the way it stood its ground, in a strange place, confronted with strange animals. How different from the silly sheep, who at the mere sight of a dog would run aimlessly about, crying "Wolf! Wolf!" in their empty-headed way.

"Hullo," she said. "Who are you?"

"I'm a Large White," said the piglet.

"Blimey!" said one of the puppies. "If that's a large white, what's a small one like?" And they all four sniggered.

"Be quiet!" snapped Fly. "Just remember that five minutes ago you didn't even know what a pig was." And to the piglet she said kindly, "I expect that's your breed, dear. I meant, what's your name?"

"I don't know," said the piglet.

"Well, what did your mother call you, to tell you apart from your brothers and sisters?" said Fly and then wished she hadn't, for at the mention of his family the piglet began to look distinctly unhappy. His little forehead wrinkled and he gulped and his voice trembled as he answered.

"She called us all the same."

"And what was that, dear?"

"Babe," said the piglet, and the puppies began to giggle until their mother silenced them with a growl.

"But that's a lovely name," she said. "Would you like us to call you that? It'll make you feel more at home."

At this last word the little pig's face fell even further.

"I want my mum," he said very quietly.

At that instant the collie bitch made up her mind that she would foster this unhappy child.

"Go out into the yard and play," she said to the puppies, and she climbed to the top of the straw stack and jumped over the rail and down into the loose box beside the piglet.

"Listen, Babe," she said. "You've got to be a brave boy. Everyone has to leave their mother, it's all part of growing up. I did it, when I was your age, and my puppies will have to leave me quite soon. But I'll look after you. If you like." Then she licked his little snout with a warm rough tongue, her plumed tail wagging.

"There. Is that nice?" she said.

 A little while later, Farmer Hogget came into the stables with his wife, to show her his prize. They looked over the loose box door and saw, to their astonishment, Fly curled around the piglet. Exhausted by the drama of the day, Babe lay fast asleep against his newfound foster parent.

"Well, will you look at that!" said Mrs. Hogget. "That old Fly, she'll mother anything, kittens, ducklings, baby chicks, she's looked after all of them, now 'tis a pig, in't he lovely, what a picture, good thing he don't know where he'll finish up, but he'll be big then and we'll be glad to see the back of him, or the hams of him, I should say, shan't we, wonder how I shall get it all in the freezer?"

"Pity. Really," said Farmer Hogget absently.

Mrs. Hogget went back to her kitchen, shaking her head all the way across the yard at the thought of her husband's softheartedness.

The farmer opened the loose box door, and to save the effort of a word, clicked his fingers to call the bitch out.

As soon as Fly moved the piglet woke and followed her, sticking so close to her that his snout touched her tail tip. Surprise forced Farmer Hogget into speech.

"Fly!" he said in amazement. Obediently, as always, the collie bitch turned and trotted back to him. The pig trotted behind her.

"Sit!" said Farmer Hogget. Fly sat. Babe sat. Farmer Hogget scratched his head. He could not think of anything to say.

"Why can't I learn?"

By dark it was plain to Farmer Hogget that, whether he liked it or not, Fly had not four, but five children.

All the long summer evening Babe had followed Fly about the yard and buildings, aimlessly, it seemed to the watching farmer, though of course this was not the case. It was in fact a conducted tour. Fly knew that if this foster child was to be allowed his freedom and the constant reassurance of her company for which he obviously craved, he must quickly learn (and clearly he was a quick learner) his way about the place; and that he must be taught, as her puppies had been taught, how to behave like a good dog.

"A pig you may be, Babe," she had begun by saying, "but if you do as I tell you, I shouldn't be a bit surprised if the boss doesn't let you run about with us, instead of shutting you up. He's a kind man, the boss is."

"I knew that," said Babe, "when he first picked me up. I could feel it. I knew he wouldn't hurt me."

"You wait . . ." began one of the puppies, and then stopped suddenly at his mother's warning growl. Though she said nothing, all four of her children knew immediately by instinct what she meant.

"Wait for what?" said Babe.

"Er . . . you wait half a sec, and we'll take you round and show you everything," said the same puppy hastily. "Won't we, Mum?"

 So Babe was shown all around the yard and the farm buildings, and introduced to the creatures who lived thereabouts, the ducks and chickens and other poultry, and the farm cats. He saw no sheep, for they were all in the fields.

Even in the first hour he learned a number of useful lessons, as the puppies had learned before him: that cats scratch and hens peck, that turning your back on the turkey cock means getting your bottom bitten, that chicks are not for chasing and eggs are not for eating.

"You do as I do," said Fly, "and you'll be all right."

She thought for a moment. "There is one thing though, Babe," she said, and she looked across at the back door of the farmhouse, "if I go in there, you stay outside and wait for me, understand?"

"Aren't pigs allowed in there?" asked Babe.

"Not live ones," said one of the puppies, but he said it under his breath.

"No, dear," said Fly. Well, not yet anyway, she thought. But the way you're going on, I shouldn't be surprised at anything. Funny, she thought, I feel really proud of him, he learns so quick. Quick as any sheepdog.

That night the loose box in which Babe had first been put was empty. In the one next door, all six animals slept in the straw together. Though he did not tell his wife, Farmer Hogget had not had the heart to shut the piglet away, so happy was it in the company of the dogs.

At first the puppies had not been equally happy at the idea.

"Mum!" they said. "He'll wet the bed!"

"Nonsense," said Fly. "If you want to do anything, dear, you go outside, there's a good boy."

I nearly said, "There's a good pup," she thought. Whatever next!

In fact, in the days that followed, Babe became so doglike, what with coming when Fly came and sitting when Fly sat and much preferring dog's food to anything else he was offered, that Farmer Hogget caught himself half expecting, when he patted the piglet, that it would wag its tail. He would not have been surprised if it had tried to accompany Fly when he called her to go with him on his morning rounds, but it had stayed in the stables, playing with the puppies.

"You stay with the boys, Babe." Fly had said, "while I see to the sheep. I shan't be long."

"What's sheep?" the piglet said when she had gone.

The puppies rolled about in the straw.

"Don't you know that, you silly Babe?" said one.

"Sheep are animals with thick woolly coats."

"And thick woolly heads."

"And men can't look after them without the help of the likes of us," said the fourth.

"Why do they need you?" said Babe.

"Because we're sheepdogs!" they all cried together, and ran off up the yard.

Babe thought about this matter of sheep and sheepdogs a good deal during the first couple of weeks of his life on the Hoggets' farm. In that time Fly's puppies, now old enough to leave home, had been advertised for sale, and Fly was anxious to teach them all she could before they went out into the world. Daily she made them practice on the ducks, while Babe sat beside her and watched with interest. And daily their skills improved and the ducks lost weight and patience.

Then there came, one after another, four farmers, four tall long-legged men who smelled of sheep. And each picked his puppy and paid his money, while Fly sat and watched her children leave to start their working life.

As always, she felt a pang to see them go, but this time, after the last had left, she was not alone.

"It's nice, dear," she said to Babe. "I've still got you."

But not for all that long, she thought. Poor little chap, in six months or so he'll be fit to kill. At least he doesn't know it. She looked at him fondly, this foster child that now called her "Mum." He had picked it up, naturally enough, from the puppies, and it pleased her to hear it, now more than ever.

"Mum," said Babe.

"Yes, dear?"

"They've gone off to work sheep, haven't they?"

"Yes, dear."

"Because they're sheepdogs. Like you. You're useful to the boss, aren't you, because you're a sheepdog?"

"Yes, dear."

"Well, Mum?"

"Yes, dear?"

"Why can't I learn to be a sheep-pig?"

"You'm a polite young chap"

After the last of the puppies had left, the ducks heaved a general sigh of relief. They looked forward to a peaceful day and paid no attention when, the following morning, Fly and Babe came down to the pond and sat and watched them as they squattered and splattered in its soupy green depths. They knew that the old dog would not bother them, and they took no notice of the strange creature at her side.

"They'll come out and walk up the yard in a minute," said Fly. "Then you can have a go at fetching them back, if you like."

"Oh yes, please!" said Babe excitedly.

The collie bitch looked fondly at her foster child. Sheep-pig indeed, she thought, the idea of it! The mere sight of him would probably send the flock into the next county. Anyway, he'd never get near them on those little short legs. Let him play with the ducks for a day or two and he'd forget all about it.

When the ducks did come up out of the water and marched noisily past the piglet, she half expected him to chase after them, as the puppies usually did at first; but he sat very still, his ears cocked, watching her.

"All right," said Fly. "Let's see how you get on. Now then, first thing is, you've got to get behind them, just like I have to with the sheep. If the boss wants me to go round the right side of them (that's the side by the stables there), he says 'Away to me.' If he wants me to go round the left (that's the side by the Dutch barn), he says 'Come by.' O.K.?"

"Yes, Mum."

"Right then. Away to me, Babe!" said Fly sharply.

26

At first, not surprisingly, Babe's efforts met with little success. There was no problem with getting around the ducks—even with his curious little seesawing canter he was much faster than they—but the business of bringing the whole flock back to Fly was not, he found, at all easy. Either he pressed them too hard and they broke up and fluttered all over the place, or he was too gentle and held back, and they waddled away in twos and threes.

"Come and have a rest, dear," called Fly after a while. "Leave the silly things alone, they're not worth upsetting yourself about."

"I'm not upset, Mum," said Babe. "Just puzzled. I mean, I told them what I wanted them to do but they didn't take any notice of me. Why not?"

Because you weren't born to it, thought Fly. You haven't got the instinct to dominate them, to make them do what you want.

"It's early days yet, Babe dear," she said.

"Do you suppose," said Babe, "that if I asked them politely . . . "

"Asked them politely! What an idea! Just imagine me doing that with the sheep—'please will you go through that gateway,' 'would you kindly walk into that pen?' Oh no, dear, you'd never get anywhere that way. You've got to tell 'em what to do, doesn't matter whether it's ducks or sheep. They're stupid and dogs are intelligent, that's what you have to remember."

"But I'm a pig."

"Pigs are intelligent too," said Fly firmly. Ask them politely, she thought. Whatever next!

 What happened next, later that morning in fact, was that Babe met his first sheep.

Farmer Hogget and Fly had been out around the flock, and when they returned Fly was driving before her an old lame ewe, which they penned in the loose box where the piglet had originally been shut. Then they went away up the hill again.

Babe made his way into the stables, curious to meet this, the first of the animals that he planned one day to work with, but he could not see into the box. He snuffled under the bottom of the door, and from inside there came a cough and the sharp stamp of a foot, and then the sound of a hoarse complaining voice. "Wolves! Wolves!" it said. "They never do leave a body alone. Nag, nag, nag all day long, go here, go there, do this, do that. What d'you want now? Can't you give us a bit of peace, wolf?"

"I'm not a wolf," said Babe under the door.

"Oh, I knows all that," said the sheep sourly. "Calls yourself a sheepdog. I knows that, but you don't fool none of us. You're a wolf like the rest of 'em, given half a chance. You looks at us, and you sees lamb chops. Go away, wolf."

"But I'm not a sheepdog either," said Babe, and he scrambled up the stack of straw bales and looked over the bars.

"You see?" he said.

"Well I'll be dipped," said the old sheep, peering up at him. "No more you ain't. What are you?"

"Pig," said Babe. "Large White. What are you?"

"Ewe," said the sheep.

"No, not me, you—what are you?"

"I'm a ewe."

Mum was right, thought Babe, they certainly are stupid. But if I'm going to learn how to be a sheep-pig I must try to understand them, and this might be a good chance. Perhaps I could make a friend of this one.

"My name's Babe," he said in a jolly voice. "What's yours?"

"Maaaaa," said the sheep.

"That's a nice name," said Babe. "What's the matter with you, Ma?"

"Foot rot," said the sheep, holding up a foreleg. "And I've got a nasty cough." She coughed. "And I'm not as young as I was."

"You don't look very old to me," said Babe politely.

A look of pleasure came over the sheep's mournful face, and she lay down in the straw.

"Very civil of you to say so," she said. "First kind word I've had since I were a little lamb," and she belched loudly and began to chew a mouthful of cud.

Though he did not quite know why, Babe said nothing to Fly of his conversation with Ma. Farmer Hogget had treated the sheep's foot and tipped a potion down its protesting throat, and now, as darkness fell, dog and pig lay side by side, their rest only occasionally disturbed by a rustling from the box next door. Having at last set eyes on a sheep, Babe's dreams were immediately filled with the creatures, all lame, all coughing, all, like the ducks, scattering wildly before his attempts to round them up.

"Go here, go there, do this, do that!" he squeaked furiously at them, but they took not a bit of notice, until at last the dream turned to a nightmare, and they all came hopping and hacking and maa-ing after him with hatred gleaming in their mad yellow eyes.

"Mum! Mum!" shouted Babe in terror.

"Maaaaa!" said a voice next door.

"It's all right dear," said Fly, "it's all right. Was it a nasty dream?"

"Yes, yes."

"What were you dreaming about?"

"Sheep, Mum."

"I expect it was because of that stupid old thing in there," said Fly. "Shut up!" she barked. "Noisy old fool!" And to Babe she said, "Now cuddle up, dear, and go to sleep. There's nothing to be frightened of."

She licked his snout until it began to give out a series of regular snores. Sheep-pig, indeed, she thought, why the silly boy's frightened of the things, and she put her nose on her paws and went to sleep.

Babe slept soundly the rest of the night, and woke more determined than ever to learn all that he could from their new neighbor. As soon as Fly had gone out on her rounds, he climbed the straw stack.

"Good morning, Ma," he said. "I do hope you're feeling better today?"

The old ewe looked up. Her eyes, Babe was glad to see, looked neither mad nor hateful.

"I must say," she said. "you'm a polite young chap. Not like that wolf, shouting at me in the middle of the night. Never get no respect from them, treat you like dirt they do, bite you soon as look at you."

"Do they really?"

"Oh ar. Nip your hocks if you'm a bit slow. And worse, some of them."

"Worse?"

"Oh ar. Ain't you never heard of worrying?"

"I don't worry much."

"No no, young un. I'm talking about sheep-worrying. You get some wolves as'll chase sheep and kill 'em."

"Oh!" said Babe, horrified. "I'm sure Fly would never do that."

"Who's Fly?"

"She's my m . . . she's our dog here, the one that brought you in yesterday."

"Is that what she's called? No, she bain't a worrier, just rude. All wolves is rude to us sheep, see, always have been. Bark and run and nip and call us stupid. We bain't all that stupid, we do just get confused. If only they'd just show a bit of common politeness, just treat us a bit decent. Now if you was to come out into the field, a nice well-mannered young chap like you, and ask me to go somewhere or do something, politely, like you would, why, I'd be only too delighted."

"Keep yelling, young un"

Mrs. Hogget shook her head at least a dozen times.

"For the life of me I can't see why you do let that pig run all over the place like you do, round and round the yard he do go, chasing my ducks about, shoving his nose into everything, shouldn't wonder but what he'll be out with you and Fly moving the sheep about afore long, why don't you shut him up, he's running all his flesh off, he won't never be fit for Christmas, Easter more like, what d'you call him?"

"Just Pig," said Farmer Hogget.

A month had gone by since the Village Fair, a month in which a lot of interesting things had happened to Babe. The fact that perhaps most concerned his future, though he did not know it, was that Farmer Hogget had become fond of him. He liked to see the piglet pottering happily about the yard with Fly, keeping out of mischief, as far as he could tell, if you didn't count moving the ducks around. He did this now with a good deal of skill, the farmer noticed, even to the extent of being able, once, to separate the white ducks from the brown, though that must just have

32

been a fluke. The more he thought of it, the less Farmer Hogget liked the idea of butchering Pig.

The other developments were in Babe's education. Despite herself, Fly found that she took pleasure and pride in teaching him the ways of the sheepdog, though she knew that of course he would never be fast enough to work sheep. Anyway the boss would never let him try.

As for Ma, she was back with the flock, her foot healed, her cough better. But all the time that she had been shut in the box, Babe had spent every moment that Fly was out of the stables chatting to the old ewe. Already he understood, in a way that Fly never could, the sheep's point of view. He longed to meet the flock, to be introduced. He thought it would be extremely interesting.

"D'you think I could, Ma?" he had said.

"Could what, young un?"

"Well, come and visit you, when you go back to your friends?"

"Oh ar. You could do easy enough. You only got to go through the bottom gate and up the hill to the big field by the lane. Don't know what the farmer'd say though. Or that wolf."

Once Fly had slipped quietly in and found him perched on the straw stack.

"Babe!" she had said sharply. "You're not talking to that stupid thing, are you?"

"Well, yes, Mum, I was."

"Save your breath, dear. It won't understand a word you say."

"Bah!" said Ma.

For a moment Babe was tempted to tell his foster mother what he had in mind, but something told him to keep quiet. Instead he made a plan. He would wait

for two things to happen. First, for Ma to rejoin the flock. And, after that, for market day, when both the boss and his mum would be out of the way. Then he would go up the hill.

 Towards the end of the very next week the two things had happened. Ma had been turned out, and a couple of days after that Babe watched as Fly jumped into the back of the Land Rover, and it drove out of the yard and away.

Babe's were not the only eyes that watched its departure. At the top of the hill a cattle truck stood half-hidden under a clump of trees at the side of the lane. As soon as the Land Rover had disappeared from sight along the road to the market town, a man jumped hurriedly out and opened the gate into the field. Another backed the truck into the gateway.

Babe meanwhile was trotting excitedly up the hill to pay his visit to the flock. He came to the gate at the bottom of the field and squeezed under it. The field was steep and curved, and at first he could not see a single sheep. But then he heard a distant drumming of hooves and suddenly the whole flock came galloping over the brow of the hill and down toward him. Around them ran two strange collies, lean silent dogs

that seemed to flow effortlessly over the grass. From high above came the sound of a thin whistle, and in easy partnership the dogs swept around the sheep, and began to drive them back up the slope.

Despite himself, Babe was caught up in the press of jostling bleating animals and carried along with them. Around him rose a chorus of panting protesting voices, some shrill, some hoarse, some deep and guttural, but all saying the same thing.

"Wolf! Wolf!" cried the flock in dazed confusion.

Small by comparison and short in the leg, Babe soon fell behind the main body, and as the reached the top of the hill he found himself right at the back in company with an old sheep who cried "Wolf!" more loudly than any.

"Ma!" he cried breathlessly. "It's you!"

Behind them one dog lay down at a whistle, and in front the flock checked as the other dog steadied them. In the corner of the field the tailgate and wings of the cattle truck filled the gateway, and the two men waited, stick and arms outspread.

"Oh hullo young un," puffed the old sheep. "Fine day you chose to come, I'll say."

"What is it? What's happening? Who are these men?" asked Babe.

"Rustlers," said Ma. "They'm sheep rustlers."

"What d'you mean?"

"Thieves, young un, that's what I do mean. Sheep stealers. We'll all be in that truck afore you can blink your eye.

"What can we do?"

"Do? Ain't nothing we can do, unless we can slip past this here wolf."

She made as if to escape, but the dog behind darted in, and she turned back.

Again, one of the men whistled, and the dog pressed. Gradually, held against the headland of the field by the second dog and the men, the flock began to move forward. Already the leaders were nearing the tailgate of the truck.

"We'm beat," said Ma mournfully. "You run for it, young un." I will, thought Babe, but not the way you mean. Little as he was, he felt suddenly not fear but anger, furious anger that the boss's sheep were being stolen. My mum's not here to protect them so I must, he said to himself bravely, and he ran quickly around the hedge side of the flock, and jumping onto the bottom of the tailgate, turned to face them.

"Please!" he cried "I beg you! Please don't come any closer. If you would be so kind, dear sensible sheep!"

His unexpected appearance had a number of immediate effects. The shock of being so politely addressed stopped the flock in its tracks, and the cries of "Wolf!" changed to murmurs of "In't he lovely!" and "Proper little gennulman!" Ma had told them something of her new friend, and now to see him in the flesh and to hear his well-chosen words released them from the dominance of the dogs. They began to fidget and look about for an escape route. This was opened

for them when the men (cursing quietly, for above all
things they were anxious to avoid too much noise) sent
the flanking dog to drive the pig away, and some of
the sheep began to slip past them.

Next moment all was chaos. Angrily the dog ran at Babe, who scuttled away squealing at the top of his voice in a mixture of fright and fury. The men closed on him, sticks raised. Desperately he shot between the legs of one, who fell with a crash, while the other, striking out madly, hit the rearguard dog as it came to help, and sent it yowling. In half a minute the carefully planned raid was ruined, as the sheep scattered everywhere.

"Keep yelling, young un!" bawled Ma, as she ran beside Babe. "They won't never stay here with that row going on!"

And suddenly all sorts of things began to happen as those deafening squeals rang out over the quiet countryside. Birds flew startled from the trees, cows in nearby fields began to gallop about, dogs in distant farms to bark, passing motorists to stop and stare. In the farmhouse below Mrs. Hogget heard the noise as she had on the day of the Fair. She stuck her head out the window and saw the rustlers, their truck, galloping sheep, and Babe. She dialled 999 but then talked for so long that by the time a patrol car drove up the lane, the rustlers had long gone. Snarling at each other and their dogs, they had driven hurriedly away with not one single sheep to show for their pains.

"You won't never believe it!" cried Mrs. Hogget when her husband returned from market. "But we've had rustlers, just after you'd gone it were, come with a huge cattle truck they did, the police said, they seen the tire marks in the gateway, and a chap in a car seen the truck go by in a hurry, and there's been a lot of it about, and he give the alarm, he did, kept screaming and shrieking enough to bust your eardrums, we should have lost every sheep on the place if 'tweren't for him, 'tis him we've got to thank."

"Who?" said Farmer Hogget.

"Him!" said his wife, pointing at Babe who was telling Fly all about it. "Don't ask me how he got there or why he done it, all I knows is he saved our bacon and now I'm going to save his, he's staying with us just like another dog, don't care if he gets as big as a house, because if you think I'm going to stand by and see him butchered after what he done for us today, you've got another think coming, what d'you say to that?"

A slow smile spread over Farmer Hogget's long face.

Babe trains with Farmer Hogget and Fly and before long becomes a highly skilled sheep-pig. Then a second disaster, even more terrible than the raid by sheep rustlers, threatens. Will Babe triumph once again?

Meet the Author: **Dick King-Smith**

It is not surprising that British author Dick King-Smith writes convincingly about farmyard life in *Babe: The Gallant Pig* and his other novels. King-Smith spent twenty years working as a farmer before turning to teaching and, since 1982, full-time writing. Both readers and critics find his animal fantasies funny and touching. King-Smith writes only for children. "I couldn't possibly write a modern sort of novel for grown people—I should get the giggles," he explains.

When asked to explain his writing, King-Smith says, "If there is a philosophical point behind what I write, I'm not especially conscious of it; maybe I do stress the need for courage, something we all wish we had more of, and I also do feel strongly for underdogs."

You'll find King-Smith's values, as well as his eye for telling details and his whimsical sense of humor, reflected in his novels *The Fox Busters, Pigs Might Fly, The Mouse Butcher, Magnus Powermouse,* and *The Queen's Nose.*

Responding To Literature

1. Many authors write about animals. Some write realistic stories and others write fantasies. Why do you think animal stories, such as *Babe: The Gallant Pig*, are appealing to most people?

2. At first, Mrs. Hogget plans to butcher Babe. By the end of the excerpt, she says she is going to save his bacon. Describe the events that cause Mrs. Hogget to change her mind.

3. Babe is a pig with many fine qualities. Why is he described as "gallant"?

4. In some ways the animals in the selection are like people. In other ways they are like animals. Think of Ma, the sheep. Which of her traits are human? In what ways does she behave like an animal?

5. In very few words Dick King–Smith creates two memorable and humorous characters, Mr. and Mrs. Hoggett. Why are the Hoggets such an amusing couple?

The Laughing Faces of Pigs

Eight young pigs in a row look at me from the trough,
eight laughing faces waiting for their food.
Am I so funny seen from a pig's eyes?
No, they'd look the same at any stick or beam.
Nothing can make a pig look sad; his face
is built wrong for it; his mouth curls up;
his eyes are formed into a grin; his nose
wrinkles with laughter at every move he makes.

Is it so many centuries of good nature,
no inhibitions, no worry of neighbor opinion,
that leaves its stamp upon the faces of his race?
Or does it go back further?
                     I sometimes think
the soil's good humor runs inside his veins.
Maybe the earth herself had a good belly laugh
the era that she first gave birth to pigs.

Fred Lape

41

Appreciating Author's Craft

Thinking About Animal Characters

Some authors make their animal characters feel, think, speak, and act exactly like humans. Other authors write about animals that have no human qualities at all. In either case, animal characters often help readers understand some things about human actions and values.

Many authors create animal characters with both human and animal traits. In *Babe: The Gallant Pig*, Dick King-Smith creates animal characters that act like animals but speak, feel, and think like humans. Here is an example in which Fly acts like a collie, but speaks as a concerned human mother might:

> "Then she licked his little snout with a warm rough tongue, her plumed tail wagging. 'There. Is that nice?' she said."

You can learn something about human mothers from these sentences about Fly.

Writing About Animal Characters

How would you help someone who had not read about Babe appreciate the plucky piglet? You could write a paragraph describing Babe. (For more ideas about writing, look at your Writer's Handbook.)

Prewriting To help you remember the characters' human and animal qualities, add to the chart by writing examples for Babe. In the second column, find words from the selection that describe Babe's animal qualities. In the last column, find words that show his human qualities.

Animal character	Animal qualities	Human qualities
Fly	runs, licks, chases sheep, trains pups	speaks, has warm heart, thinks sheep are stupid
Babe		

Writing Review Babe's human and animal qualities. Then write a paragraph describing Babe based on the information you listed on the chart. Use vivid words that describe Babe clearly, so that readers can almost imagine that a living, breathing pig is sitting before them.

Revising Read your draft to a partner and discuss the words you have chosen to describe Babe. Your partner may suggest that you change some words or sentences to make the description clearer and more accurate. Then revise your draft. Make sure that all the sentences in your paragraph describe Babe. Proofread for errors. Then write your final copy.

Presenting Read the paragraph to your classmates. Ask classmates who have read the excerpt which parts of the paragraph describe Babe clearly and which parts don't describe Babe accurately.

Extending Your Reading

Expressing Yourself
Choose one or more of these activities:

Make Babe a Star The book *Babe: The Gallant Pig* is about to become a major motion picture. Work with a partner to create a movie poster featuring Babe as the leading pig and supporting actors Fly, Ma, and the Hoggets. Remember: your poster can help make the movie a success.

Design a Prize Babe deserves a prize for saving Farmer Hogget's flock from rustlers. But what sort of prize? Make a drawing or model from clay or construction paper of something Babe would really enjoy.

Write a Post Card A delighted Babe has found out where his mother is living and decides to send her a post card. What will he write?

Find Out About Sheep Dogs What did Babe have to learn to become a sheep-pig? Go to the library and find information about how dogs are trained to herd sheep. Think of ways that training might have to be adapted for a pig. Discuss your ideas with a friend or classmate.

More Books About Clever Animals

The Aesop for Children illustrated by Milo Winter. Aeonian Press. Readers are sure to find favorites such as "The Fox and the Grapes" and "The Ant and the Grasshopper" in this collection of 128 fables.

Trouble in Bugland by William Kotzwinkle. David R. Godine, Publisher. A quick-witted insect, patterned after Sherlock Holmes, displays brilliant detective work. Inspector Mantis and his loyal assistant, Doctor Hopper, meet such villains as the Tarantula, the Termites of Banana, and the Robber Flies.

Lassie Come-Home by Eric Knight. Holt, Rinehart and Winston. This is the classic story of Lassie, a loyal and intelligent English collie, the boy who loves her, and the difficulties they face. Lassie's perilous journey will touch readers today just as it did almost fifty years ago when the book was first published.

Racso and the Rats of NIMH by Jane Leslie Conly. Harper & Row, Publishers. In this sequel to *Mrs. Frisby and the Rats of NIMH* (written by the author's daughter), Racso, a young city rat, joins the rats who escaped from NIMH and helps rescue the colony.

Ben and Me by Robert Lawson. Little, Brown and Company. A mouse named Amos sets the record straight about his friend Benjamin Franklin. In Amos's version of history, the tiny rodent reveals for the first time the source of Franklin's achievements— Amos himself.

Time Cat

by Lloyd Alexander
illustrated by Ben Otero

Introducing

Time Cat

Jason has the ordinary problems anyone might expect. He accidentally spills things. He fights with his younger brother. He feels sorry for himself when his mother sends him to his room. Just when it seems there is no escape from his daily problems, Jason finds help from an unexpected source—his cat Gareth.

Peru, 1555

Time Cat by Lloyd Alexander is a type of fantasy called time travel. In this form of fantasy, the author moves characters backward or forward through time and space by means of a clever device such as a fantastic machine, an ordinary object, or a mysterious animal. (For more information about this kind of story, look up *Fantasy* in your Handbook.) In *Time Cat* Alexander transports his two main characters more than four hundred years into the past to what is today the country of Peru, in South America.

Jason and Gareth arrive during the final days of the once-magnificent Inca civilization, which flourished centuries before the founding of the United States. The Incas had enjoyed a culture with great achievements in science, economy, and law. In 1524, Francisco Pizarro (pi zär′ō), a Spanish explorer, traveled to Peru. He was stunned by the great wealth of the Inca empire.

Eight years later Pizarro returned with an army to
conquer the Incas and their capital city of Cuzco (kü′skō),
seize their wealth of gold and silver, and make the
territory a colony of Spain, to be ruled by a Spanish
viceroy, or governor. Within a year Pizarro and his army
had done just that. The greedy soldiers then fought one
another for the spoils of victory. It is during this period
that Jason and Gareth meet the unhappy Don Diego and
the Inca ruler Sayri Tupac (sā′rē tü′pak).

Thinking About Multiple Settings
Every story has a setting, a time and place that events
take place. Authors often change the setting in their works
to introduce characters to new adventures and to give them
new problems to solve. In *Time Cat* Alexander abruptly
changes both the time and place of the original setting.

As you're reading this excerpt on your own, think
about the things Jason learns about the world and about
himself on his travels through time and space.

Time Cat

THE VISITORS Gareth was a black cat with orange eyes. Sometimes, when he hunched his shoulders and put down his ears, he looked like an owl. When he stretched, he looked like a trickle of oil or a pair of black silk pajamas. When he sat on a window ledge, his eyes half-shut and his tail curled around him, he looked like a secret.

He belonged to a boy named Jason, who loved him and believed Gareth could do anything in the world. As things turned out, Jason was right—not entirely, but almost.

It happened this way.

In the middle of a sunny afternoon, Jason sat in his room on the end of his bed, with his chin in his hands, and wished the past five minutes had never happened.

Downstairs, in that space of time, he had accomplished the following:

1/ Spilled paint on the dining-room table.

2/ Dropped his model airplane and stepped on it.

3/ Coated the inside of one pocket of his jacket with glue, when the tube he had been saving for emergencies had come uncapped.

4/ Torn his shirt.

5/ Punched his younger brother in the ribs for laughing at him.

6/ Talked back to his mother, who had not agreed his brother needed punching.

7/ Begun to cry, a thing Jason despised because he considered himself too old for it.

There had been other details he preferred to forget. In any

case, he had been told to go to his room, which he did, feeling put down and miserably sorry for himself.

Gareth, who had been drowsing on top of Jason's pillow, uncurled and climbed onto the boy's lap. Jason stroked the cat and ran his finger over Gareth's only white spot—on his chest, a T-shaped mark with a loop over the crossbar.

"Lucky Gareth," Jason sighed, lying back and closing his eyes, "I wish *I* had nine lives."

The cat stopped purring. "I wish I did, too," he said.

Jason started up in surprise. Not because Gareth had spoken. Jason had always been sure he could if he wanted to. It was what Gareth had said.

"You mean you really don't have nine lives?" Jason asked, disappointed.

"I'm afraid not," said the cat, in a very matter-of-fact way. "But, since you mention it, I'll tell you a secret. I only have one life. With a difference: I can visit."

"Visit?" Jason said.

"Yes," Gareth went on, "I can visit nine different lives. Anywhere, any time, any country, any century."

"Oh, Gareth!" Jason clapped his hands. "Can all cats do that?"

"Where do you think cats go when you're looking all over and can't find them?" Gareth replied. "And have you ever noticed a cat suddenly appear in a room when you were sure the room was empty? Or disappear, and you can't imagine where he went?"

"And you've actually gone to a lot of different countries?" Jason asked.

"No, not yet," Gareth said. "I've been waiting for—oh, I don't know, a special occasion, you might say. I never saw much sense in just going as a tourist. It's better to wait until there's some important reason."

"I guess you're right," Jason nodded. He looked over at Gareth. "I was wondering if you thought there might be a special occasion coming up soon?"

"There might be," said Gareth.

"Gareth, listen," Jason said eagerly, "if it were a special occasion and somebody else, somebody you liked, wanted very much to go, could you take him with you?"

Gareth did not answer immediately. He began looking like an owl and stayed that way for a while. Finally, he said, "Yes, I suppose I could."

"Would you take me?"

Gareth was silent again. "I could take you with me," he said, after a moment, "but I have to warn you of this. You'd be on your own, you wouldn't have any kind of protection. Neither of us would. Naturally, I'd help you every way I could; we'd be able to talk to each other, but only when no one else was around. Aside from that, what happens, happens. And you couldn't change your mind in the middle.

"Oh, there's something else. Whatever you did, you wouldn't dare be separated from me for any length of time. Otherwise, you'd never see home again. Now, if you accept the conditions . . ."

"Oh, Gareth, I accept!"

"Are you sure?" the cat asked. "Think carefully."

Jason nodded.

"Very well," said the cat. "Look into my eyes." And he gave Jason a long, slow wink.

DON DIEGO 🌀 Jason and Gareth stood in a cluttered room. Against one of the stone walls leaned a heavy musket; a couple of Spanish-style helmets, with round tops and curved brims, had rolled into a corner, along with a breastplate that needed polishing. Piles of what seemed to be laundry waited to be sent out; there were two left-footed boots, a sword that would have been most warlike had it been sharp. At a wooden table, his head in his arms, the owner of these items snored peacefully. However, as soon as Jason moved, the sleeper started up, blinking; except for the curled mustache and pointed beard, which didn't quite appear to belong to him, the man looked like a surprised fish.

"Who . . . what . . . ," he stammered. Noticing Gareth, the man suddenly began to beam delightedly. "Of course!" he cried. "The cat I ordered! But how did you get here so fast? I gave the letter to a messenger only six weeks ago. This is really amazing. All the way from Peru to Spain and back again." He stopped abruptly. "It is my cat, isn't it? There's no mistake about the delivery? One cat to be sent to Don Diego Francisco Hernández del Gato Herrera y Robles?"

All the while, Don Diego was patting Gareth fondly; and before Jason could answer, the Spaniard picked up Gareth and cradled him in his arms. "No, no," Don Diego said. "There couldn't be a mistake. No, I've waited too long. It must have cost a fortune! But it's worth it. Just to have a cat. Ah, a cat. Even the sound of the name is worth another fortune."

Don Diego wiped a tear from his eye. "Forgive me," he sniffled through his mustache. "But we are an emotional family, on my mother's side. Oh, it's been so lonely here," he added. "I didn't ask to be in the army, but my family, on my father's side, didn't know what else to do with me. And they spent so much money buying me a captain's commission I can't disappoint them."

"Bought you a commission?" Jason asked.

Don Diego looked at him, puzzled. "Naturally," he said. "How else would a gentlemen start off in the army? But I didn't think it would turn out like this. I'll tell you one thing." Don Diego looked over his shoulder and dropped his voice to a whisper, "The whole business has gone wrong from the beginning. Pizarro and his friends came looking for gold. Oh, they found it, you can believe that. These Indians have more gold than I've ever seen in my life. Plenty for everybody. The Indians would have given us all we wanted. But no, that wasn't enough for Pizarro and the Conquerors. They started being greedy and quarrelsome—and plotting against each other. To make a long story short, there's not one of them left alive today.

"Now there's nothing but fighting." Don Diego went on sadly. "We fight the Indians; the Indians fight us. And then we fight among ourselves. The Viceroy, sent by His Majesty himself, doesn't know what to do. Well, I don't care. I have my cat; that's all that matters to me. They can keep the gold, much good it may do them. My cat," Don Diego repeated, dreamily.

"I'm glad you like cats," Jason said. "But there's something you don't understand. My cat and I, well, we're together. I mean . . ."

"Of course!" Don Diego cried. "How thoughtful of my family, on my mother's side. To send a cat—and a boy to help me look after it. Yes, that's it. You can be my orderly. Then I won't have to put up with that lazy, impudent Pedro. I try to shout at him, but he won't listen or else he talks back. He refuses to keep my quarters tidy—see for yourself." Don Diego flung out his arms in despair. "I can't seem to keep things straight alone. But now it's all going to be different. A cat! It feels homey already."

A trumpet blared outside. Don Diego clapped a hand to his head. "I'm late for close-order drill. I forgot. All the excitement . . ." He began rushing around the room, stumbling over the laundry, trying to buckle on his breastplate, while the helmet, much too big for his head, slipped down over his eyes.

Jason decided this was no time to mention Don Diego's mistake. He helped the Captain struggle into his armor. With half his buckles flying, the breathless Don Diego picked up his sword and tumbled headlong out the door.

Jason watched the Spaniard fumble his way across the barracks yard. A company of pike men stiffened to attention. From this distance Jason could not tell what orders Don Diego was shouting, but they must have been wrong, for the soldiers, all as stiff as their own pikes, kept marching off in different directions, wheeling and bumping into one another.

"Well," Jason said, "I've never seen a soldier like *that*."

"Wearing a uniform doesn't make someone a soldier," Gareth said. "I think he'd rather be home."

"He did seem awfully confused about things," Jason said. "I don't know what he'll do when his own cat arrives."

"We'll see about that later," Gareth said. "The only thing a cat worries about is what's happening right now. As we tell the kittens, you can only wash one paw at a time."

Jason did his best to put Don Diego's room in order, but it was hopeless. The Captain had so many odds and ends of things, bits of candles, belts with the buckles missing, rusted pistols, a couple of oil paintings (one portrait from his father's side of the family, one from his mother's) that Jason finally put it all in one heap in a corner of the room. Sheets of parchment covered the table, and when Jason tried to straighten them up he could not avoid noticing what Don Diego had been writing.

"It looks like he's trying to make a dictionary," Jason said to Gareth. "Here's all the Indian words on one side and here's where he explains what they mean.

"He's been writing a lot about the Indians, too," Jason went on. "He calls them Incas. There's pages and pages about how they live and what they wear—I wonder why he's doing that?"

"It might be that he's lonesome and homesick and doesn't have anything else to pass the time," said Gareth, who had curled up in Don Diego's spare helmet. "Or he may just be the kind of man who's very interested in what's happening, what he sees and does, and wants to make sure he'll remember."

Jason glanced through the papers. "I think he'd be better off writing history than trying to be a soldier."

"I'm sure he'd agree with you," Gareth said. "But, I suppose his family thought he belonged in the army."

"I guess they did," Jason said, "at least, on his father's side."

Toward the middle of the afternoon, Don Diego— flushed, smiling, his helmet all crooked—burst into the room. From the officers' mess he had brought food for dinner. Humming happily, he set it down on the table.

"Now," said Don Diego, rubbing his hands, "something to eat, then a nap, and after that—some tricks."

"You're going to do tricks?" Jason asked eagerly.

"Me? Goodness, no! The cat will."

"The cat?" Jason asked, perplexed. "But he doesn't do tricks."

"Perhaps he doesn't now," said Don Diego, raising a finger. "But we'll teach him. I've been looking forward to it all day. Time and patience, that's all it takes. And I have plenty of both."

"Did you ever teach a cat tricks before?" Jason asked.

"No, no, I can't say that I have," Don Diego answered. "But I've always wanted to."

"If you had," Jason went on, "you'd know that cats won't do tricks. Oh, they'll do them, but when *they* feel like it. And they'll make up their own, so it's no use trying to have them learn *your* tricks."

"But they're intelligent . . ."

"That doesn't have anything to do with it," Jason said. "With a cat, it's just not the same. If you wanted a pet to sit up and beg or play dead or give you his paw, you should have asked for a dog. If you wanted a pet to talk, you should have ordered a parrot.

"Some animals are good at some things," Jason explained, "and some are good at others. Cats are good at being cats, and that's enough."

Don Diego's mustache drooped in disappointment. For a moment Jason was afraid the Captain would cry. The Spaniard looked so terribly sad that Jason wished he hadn't said anything.

"I suppose I don't really know anything about cats," Don Diego said glumly. "I've never had one of my own. There was a cat in our family, on my mother's side, and I always admired it, and that's why I wanted one sent to me. I see now it was a mistake—another mistake." He sighed deeply. "I'm always making them."

"It wasn't a mistake at all," Jason said encouragingly. "Cats don't have to do tricks to be fun. Just watching them and playing with them is fun. You'll see what I mean."

Don Diego said he would try, although he still looked disappointed. After their nap, the Spaniard made no attempt to teach Gareth tricks. Instead, Don Diego sat down at his table and began working with his papers.

"I learned something new today," he said, brightening a little. "Did you know that Inca mothers stand their children up in holes in the ground so they won't run away? The children, that is? Isn't that amazing?" With his quill pen moving furiously, Don Diego made a long note of it.

Gareth had hopped up on Don Diego's table, where he sat watching the quill. Each time Don Diego came to the end of a line Gareth hooked out a padded paw and caught at the pen. The Captain looked up in surprise, then began to chuckle. "Now, that is a kind of trick, isn't it," he said. "It's a game he thought up by himself, so it's really better than a trick!"

Later, Gareth stretched out, purring, on the table. Don Diego leaned back and stroked the cat's ears. "You know," he said to Jason, "this cat makes me feel very pleasant. Isn't that strange? Just sitting here with him—I don't know—everything seems cozier. I don't think I'd like it if he sat up and begged. It wouldn't be . . . dignified, somehow. Maybe you're right, after all.

"Like me being a soldier," Don Diego added, sadly. "It's as silly as trying to teach a cat to do tricks."

꠶

In the days that followed, Don Diego was perfectly happy to have Gareth behave just like any cat; and he admitted, finally, that it was more fun that way. While Don Diego drilled his soldiers, Jason gradually put the room in order. After that, there was little for him and Gareth to do in the barracks. During the afternoons, they walked through the city and into the valley.

The name of the city was Cuzco, and the Incas had built it long before the Spaniards had arrived. The houses were mainly of stone; the streets very straight and well kept. In a way it reminded Jason of Egypt with its walls and palaces; there was even a great stone pyramid higher up on the mountain.

Of the Incas, Jason saw nothing. Since the Spaniards had captured Cuzco, the Inca warriors had withdrawn to the valley. There were a few Indians in the fields, but these were of the tribes the Incas themselves had conquered. As Don Diego explained it, the Incas were the rulers of all the other Indians in Peru. Now these rulers were fighting for their lives.

"I wish I could see a real Inca," Jason said one day, when he and Gareth had wandered a little beyond the city. To Jason's surprise, the cat did not answer. Then Jason understood why. In the field, as if they had risen from nowhere, stood four warriors in capes and striped leggings. Jason snatched Gareth up and tried to run.

One of the warriors whirled a three-stranded rope with heavy metal balls at the ends. An instant later, Jason and Gareth lay on the ground, tangled in the weighted cords. Lances leveled, the Incas moved forward.

SAYRI TUPAC ℘ The Incas had a small camp and
village at the edge of the valley. Still trussed up like flies in
a spiderweb, Jason and Gareth clung to each other while
the warriors carried them into the camp and dumped them
in front of Sayri Tupac, the Great Inca himself.

Jason had never seen a man so brilliantly dressed. Over a
long tunic the Inca wore a brightly decorated cape; around
his forehead were colored braids, with tassels and bits of
gold. From his ears hung enormous disks of pure gold. The
Inca turned a handsome, bronzed face toward Jason—a
face that was severe, commanding, and at the same time
filled with deep sadness.

"Our enemies lie at our feet," Sayri Tupac said. "Just as
my father and my brothers have lain at the feet of the
Conquerors. The Spaniards have asked for much gold to
ransom my brothers. Now the Inca shall demand the gold
back again as a ransom for you.

"We have paid," the Inca went on. "We shall see if the
Conquerors will do as much. If not . . . there shall be two
heads on our battle standards. A message has already been
sent to Cuzco," he said. "Your lives depend on the
answer."

Jason and Gareth were made to sit against the outside
wall of an earthen hut. The Great Inca had nothing further
to say to them, but a few of the warriors and some of
the women and children of the village gathered to peer

curiously not at Jason, but at Gareth. The Incas had seen boys before, in the Spanish garrison. Jason guessed there were no cats in Peru, for he heard one of the men explain that the animal must be some new kind of black puma.

Jason tried not to think of Sayri Tupac's words. If the Spaniards were busy fighting each other, Jason doubted they would take time to think about a boy and a cat. Certainly, they wouldn't give up any of the gold. Sayri Tupac's remarks about two heads on the battle standards did not make Jason feel very cheerful. But, as Gareth had said, you can only wash one paw at a time. To keep his mind off what might happen Jason tried to interest himself in the activity around him.

The more he watched them, the more the Incas reminded him of the Egyptians. Although their costumes were different, the Incas had the same dignity and graceful movements. In addition, the flashing gold of the Inca warriors' earrings, the feathered headdresses, the glittering lances gave the humble camp village the look of an imperial court. Jason could easily imagine how splendid the Incas had been in their great palaces at Cuzco. Like the Egyptians, the Incas had their own scribes—for the wool-robed men busy counting the stocks of provisions were surely scribes, Jason thought. Instead of clay tablets, the Incas seemed to keep their records on long cords made up of many strands of colored, knotted strings.

A few llamas, tended by a young herd boy, wandered past. These animals looked like very large sheep or very small, woolly camels, and they, too, had a quiet dignity about them. They gave Jason and Gareth a solemn glance, then ambled on.

The cords were putting Jason's legs to sleep. He tried to follow Gareth's example by relaxing and drowsing a little. He had just managed to close his eyes and rest when a great shout went up from the warriors. Jason twisted around as far as the cords allowed. At the far end of the village he saw the figure of a man on horseback. It was Don Diego.

The Spaniard reined up near the platform on which Sayri Tupac had his throne. Dismounting, the Spaniard caught his foot in the stirrup and nearly went flat on his face. Poor Don Diego looked terrified and uncomfortable. His helmet was crooked and, with no one to help him, his armor was on all wrong. Jason's heart sank. As much as he liked Don Diego, the awkward Spaniard hardly looked like the man to bargain with the glorious, stately Sayri Tupac.

Don Diego approached the throne. He began to speak, but his helmet slipped down over one ear. With a gesture of impatience, Don Diego pulled off his headpiece and threw it on the ground. He unbuckled his armor, too, and let it drop from his body like a shell.

"There," said Don Diego, "that's a lot better."

Jason could not believe his eyes. Without the heavy armor, dressed only in a simple doublet, Don Diego seemed taller and straighter. He held his head proudly and, when he spoke, his voice rang clearly and calmly.

"I do not wear the armor of the Conquerors," Don Diego said. "I greet you as one man to another. Your soldiers have taken two of my friends. I ask you to return them to me."

"Do the Spaniards talk of friendship?" Sayri Tupac asked scornfully. "We offered them friendship. They wanted only our gold."

"I understand your anger," Don Diego said. "But your quarrel is with men, not with a boy and an animal. If you are indeed a man and a warrior, you will understand that. You will let me take their place."

Sayri Tupac turned his eyes away, but he did not answer.

"There has been too much killing," Don Diego went on.
"The world has changed, for Spaniards and Incas both.
Neither of us can undo what has been done. We must learn
to live together, not die together."

Don Diego's voice rose over the camp. He spoke now of
the Incas themselves. He reminded them of the wise laws
they had made, of the mighty temples and palaces they had
built. War could do nothing but destroy them. He spoke of
their poetry and dances, the history of the ancient tribe. To
Jason, it seemed that Don Diego knew more about the
Incas than the Incas themselves.

When he finished, it was Sayri Tupac's turn to speak. "I
have listened with wonder," the Great Inca said. "No
Spaniard before has spoken in words we could understand.
If the Conquerors could only see that we want nothing but
to go in peace. If they could see us as men, with our own
ways . . ."

"I shall try to show them," Don Diego said. "One man
can promise nothing, but I shall do my best."

"That is ransom enough," said the Inca. "Understanding is
better than gold. Take the boy and the small black puma,"
he added. "You shall go from here unharmed."

In his barracks room in Cuzco Don Diego spent two days
writing at top speed. He hardly took time to eat or sleep,
never put on his armor, and paid no attention to the
trumpet calls from the square.

"I'm sending a memorandum to the Viceroy," he told
Jason. "I think half the trouble is that nobody knows what
the Incas are really like. It's time they found out."

Jason could not get over the change in Don Diego. The
Spaniard whistled gaily, walked about briskly; even his

69

mustache looked more cheerful. One afternoon, Don Diego burst into the room and brandished a sheet of parchment.

"A message from the Viceroy!" he cried. "He wants me to go to Lima and be his adviser! He says it would be a waste—a waste of time, mind you—to have someone like me drilling soldiers all day!"

The Spaniard did a little dance, fell over his own feet, hugged Jason and Gareth. "No more of this," he crowed, waving a hand at the helmets and breastplates. "No more bugles, no more 'Company, attention!' Now I can just be myself and do what I know how to do!

"There's another note, too," Don Diego said with a frown. "I don't understand. It says a cat has arrived from Spain at the request of Don Diego Francisco Hernández del Gato Herrera y Robles. Now, there's either two of me or my family, on my mother's side, has sent two cats. I must look into that. Meantime, you can start packing."

Don Diego hurried to the door. "I'll be right back," he called. "I want to show the General this letter. Somehow I think he'll be very happy about it."

After the Spaniard had gone, Jason and Gareth looked at each other. "Well," Jason said after a moment, "I never thought Don Diego would end up in the government."

"He'll be good at it," Gareth said. "Trying to make someone do what they aren't really good at is foolish. Don Diego realized that himself. We cats always knew it. How do you think I'd feel if I had to dress up in armor and drill soldiers all day?"

"That's silly," Jason said. "You wouldn't let anybody do that to you in the first place."

"Because I know I'm a cat," Gareth said. "Don Diego's just found out he's a man."

"By the way," Jason asked, "what is Don Diego going to do with *two* cats?"

"He'll only have one," Gareth said. "Because," the cat added with a wink, "we won't have time to wait for him."

Jason and Gareth's travels through time and space do not end in Peru. Where will Gareth's mysterious wink take the adventurers next? Will they ever return to the safety of the present?

Meet the Author: **Lloyd Alexander**

When he was fifteen, Lloyd Alexander, an avid reader of legends and hero tales, decided to become a writer. Many years passed before he achieved his goal. At first he wrote about the things he knew and loved: cats, musical instruments, family life. Years later he began to write fantasies, the form of fiction for which he is best known.

The mysterious comings and goings of his cat, Solomon, inspired Alexander to write *Time Cat*. As he began to imagine where Solomon would go if he could travel through time, Alexander suddenly realized he had the structure for a story.

Alexander has this to say about *Time Cat*: "*Time Cat*, of course, is a fantasy. Cats have only one life, as we all do. They can't really travel back through time, nor can we. But, except for that one fantastic element, the episodes are historically accurate. Cats were, in fact, worshipped in ancient Egypt, treated as toys in Japan, hunted as witches, shipwrecked, sold as living mousetraps. A fantasy—yes, certainly. But also a true one. Like all fantasies, it's about the real world and about us as real human beings."

Responding To Literature

1. You have read one of Jason and Gareth's adventures. Would you enjoy reading others? Where would you like the boy and his cat to travel next?

2. When Jason finally returns home, his mother is sure to wonder where he has been. What details will Jason include when he tells her about his journey to Peru?

3. In the wink of an eye, Jason leaves his familiar bedroom behind and arrives in Peru, a place he finds strange and mysterious. Why is the change of setting so important to this selection?

4. Gareth is a good friend to Jason and a very wise animal. What lesson does the cat help Jason learn about people and about himself from their experience with Don Diego?

5. Many Spaniards thought only of riches when they traveled to the land of the Incas. What is Don Diego's attitude toward the Incas?

Dinosaur Air

Claudia Lewis

Far and high
The atoms fly
While the breezes blow
And the wind sweeps by.

Atoms the dinosaurs
Breathed long ago,
Breath of kings
And of men I know,

Blown, blown,
Far over the sky
And around the world
As the wind sweeps by.

Breath of heroes
Aeons old,
Breath from the Aztec
Lands of gold,

Blown near and far,
Blown low and high,
Blown through time
In the ring of the sky.

Oh run with me
Through the captive air
Flowing around us
Everywhere—

Run with me,
The wind is high,
And time's in the wind,
Sweeping by.

Appreciating Author's Craft

Thinking About Multiple Settings

Setting, the time and place in which characters act, is a basic part of all fiction. Time travel fantasies, such as *Time Cat*, always include more than one setting. The characters move through time and space, their travels limited only by the author's imagination.

In *Time Cat*, Lloyd Alexander uses concrete details to make each setting seem real. To establish the first setting, he supplies the reader with details of Jason's life. Here are a few:

> Downstairs, in that space of time, he had accomplished the following:
> 1/ Spilled paint on the dining-room table.
> 2/ Dropped his model airplane and stepped on it.
> 3/ Coated the inside of one pocket of his jacket with glue, when the tube he had been saving for emergencies had come uncapped.

Alexander goes on to describe other settings in *Time Cat* as a wink whisks Jason, Gareth, and the reader to sixteenth-century Peru.

Writing About Multiple Settings

You can share the excitement Jason must have felt in his new environment. One way is to write a memorable description of one of the scenes. (For more ideas about writing, look at your Writer's Handbook.)

Setting	Details of Setting
Don Diego's room	musket, helmets, breastplate, laundry, boots, sword, table
Cuzco	
Inca village	

Prewriting The list includes details about Don Diego's room. Add details from the story that describe Cuzco and the Inca village.

Writing If you could visit Peru with Jason and Gareth, which scene would you prefer to see: Don Diego's room, Cuzco, or the Inca village? Write a description of that scene based on details from the chart. Before you begin writing, refer to the selection for additional details if you need to. Try to make your description so precise that a reader could imagine the sights, sounds, smells, and textures of the scene.

Revising Read your draft to a partner and discuss the words you used to describe the scene. Are any words unclear? Then revise your draft, taking your partner's suggestions into consideration. Proofread for errors. Then write your final copy.

Presenting Read your description to the class. As you read, ask your classmates to sketch the scene. If your classmates have enough information to make a detailed drawing, you will know that your description was a success.

Extending Your Reading

Expressing Yourself

Choose one or more of the following activities:

Find Out About Cats What were Gareth's ancestors like? Read books and magazine articles to learn about the different ways people have treated cats throughout history. Report your findings to the class.

Write a Poem About Gareth Work with several classmates to write a poem about Jason's cat. To begin, make a list of words that describe what Gareth looks like and how he acts. Use the list to write your group poem. Take turns reading the lines of your poem to the rest of the class.

Listen to the Music of Peru The traditional music of present-day Peru is not very different from Peruvian music at the time of the Incas. Listen to some Peruvian music. You may find recordings or tapes in a library or music store. If possible, play the records or tapes for your classmates.

Make a Collage Make a collage that expresses your feelings about the poem "Dinosaur Air." Choose materials which have colors and textures that match the mood of the poem.

More Books About Time Travel

A Game of Catch by Helen Cresswell. Macmillan Publishing Co. Have you ever been lucky enough to explore a castle? Kate and her brother Hugh explore an English castle-turned-museum. There they discover not only objects from the past, but people from the past.

A Girl Called Boy by Belinda Hurmence. Houghton Mifflin Co. A pampered eleven-year-old girl from North Carolina is scornful of her family's slave origins until she slips back in time to the 1850s and finds herself fleeing from slave patrols. As she struggles to return to her own time, she makes some startling discoveries.

A String in the Harp by Nancy Bond. Macmillan Publishing Co. Peter feels hostile and lonely when he moves to northern Wales with his father. Peter's relationship with his family and surroundings begins to improve after he discovers a harp tuning key and is introduced to the life of a sixth-century bard, or storyteller.

Thimbles by David Wiseman. Houghton Mifflin Co. Something amazing happens when Catherine Aiken puts on an old, dented thimble. Whisked back in time to the England of 1819, she becomes the daughter of mill workers about to participate in an event that will change history.

To Nowhere and Back by Margaret J. Anderson. Alfred A. Knopf. Elizabeth, a practical American girl who is visiting England for a year, discovers a creepy, abandoned cottage and finds that she can move in and out of the mind and body of a girl born one hundred years earlier.

Zeely

by Virginia Hamilton

illustrated by Symeon Shimin

Introducing

Zeely

Elizabeth Perry and her little brother John are traveling by train to Uncle Ross's farm for the summer. Elizabeth has a feeling that the visit, beginning with their first train ride, is going to be extraordinary. To mark the occasion, she temporarily renames herself Geeder and her brother Toeboy. As she watches the passing scenery, she muses on the significance of her father's last words to her, "And now I leave it all to you."

Family Histories

If you imagine the history of human beings as a novel without end, you might think of people of different ethnic and racial backgrounds as belonging to different chapters. A family's history could be traced through the chapter in which it appears. When Geeder looks at the family photographs in Uncle Ross's parlor, she begins to understand more about her family and wonders what contribution she will make to her family's history.

Thinking About Theme

Authors have reasons for writing that reach beyond informing or entertaining. They try to lead readers to discover some new ways of looking at the world. These underlying meanings are the themes of a work. In *Zeely*, author Virginia Hamilton expresses an important theme through a mystery that Geeder attempts to solve.

As you're reading this excerpt on your own, look for the mystery that Geeder discovers.

Zeely

There was an awful racket and swoosh as the books John Perry carried slipped out of his arms and scattered over the floor.

"Wouldn't you know he'd do it? Wouldn't you just *know* it!" The voice of his sister, Elizabeth, echoed through the huge waiting room. Her mother shushed her.

"After all," said Mrs. Perry, "it's not so terrible to drop an armload of books. It could happen to anyone."

"But why does it happen to us?" Elizabeth cried. "And always when we're in a hurry to go somewhere!"

John Perry stood close to his father. He wanted to pick up his books, but the effort of running after them and bending down where they lay was more than he could make. He could not get his legs to move. Never had he been in a train-station waiting room. It was full of quiet people quietly going places. Now all of them stared at him. He lowered his head, trying to hide his face.

"No harm done, John," Mr. Perry said. "Next time, you needn't carry so many books." In a moment, he had gathered them up, giving half to Elizabeth to carry and half to John.

"No harm done!" Elizabeth whispered. "Goodness sakes, everyone in the whole place will think we're just little babies!"

"Elizabeth, stop that whispering," her mother said.

Elizabeth clapped her hand over her mouth. She didn't know she had spoken out loud to herself. She hadn't meant to. But she often talked to herself when she was nervous or upset. Like John, she'd never been in a train station. Before, her father and mother had driven them to the country. This time would be different.

"Aren't train stations just grand?" she said. "Look at those pillars—I bet they're all of three feet around. And the windows! Did you ever see anything so very high up?"

The windows were enormously wide and high. John Perry fought his fear and lifted his head. He smiled up at the windows. Sunlight streaming down exposed sparkles of dust in a shaft to where they stood. Mr. and Mrs. Perry looked up, too. They all stood there, separated from the busy waiting room by the peaceful light and shadow.

It was Mrs. Perry who remembered there was a train to catch. "Oh, my! Hurry, you two!" she said to John and Elizabeth.

Elizabeth fell in step beside her father, who had started toward the train platform. Mr. Perry carried both John's and Elizabeth's suitcases. He urged them along more quickly, for the gate to the train had opened. Most of the people had gotten aboard.

"Elizabeth, I want you to sit and act like a lady," said Elizabeth's mother.

Elizabeth did not look back to where Mrs. Perry walked with John. "Goodness," she said to herself, "do you think

I don't know what's what? Leave me alone and I'll do what I'm supposed to do!"

Elizabeth heard her mother talking to John. "Remember to comb your hair," she was saying, "and don't bother people with questions."

"You can tell him not to open his mouth for the whole trip."

"Elizabeth," her father said, "calm down."

"Just tell him not to bother *me!*"

"Elizabeth!" her father said.

"Mind that you do whatever Elizabeth says . . ." It was Mrs. Perry talking to John.

Elizabeth heard her. She smiled and held her head up like a proper lady.

When Elizabeth first saw the train, she stopped. Mr. Perry shifted the luggage to one hand so he could take Elizabeth by the arm and lead her along. "I'm about to drop a suitcase," he said to her, "so you'd better hurry."

"Is that it?" Elizabeth said. "Is that the train? How do we find our seats?" The train was quite long. Billows of steam rose from beneath the engine.

"I bet it weighs a ton!" said John, coming up behind Elizabeth. He walked around, looking at the engine. "I bet I could climb it," he said. "I bet I could make it go fast!"

Mrs. Perry hurried them aboard. Mr. Perry found their seats for them without any trouble. He put their suitcases in a rack overhead. When John and Elizabeth were seated, Mr. Perry stood a moment, looking down at them.

"Now remember," he said to Elizabeth, "after the midnight stop, the train will not stop again until morning. And the first stop of the morning, you and John gather your belongings and get off."

"Where do we get off?" Elizabeth asked. "Which is front and which is back?"

"Where's the bathroom?" asked John.

"Is there a water fountain?" asked Elizabeth.

"You can get off at either end," Mr. Perry said. "Where you find a door open and the conductor waiting, get off." Then, he showed them where the bathrooms and water fountain were.

Seated again in her seat, Elizabeth made her fingers dance on the window. "Do I have to tell anyone when I'm getting off?" she asked her father.

"Just get off at the first stop of the morning," Mr. Perry repeated. "You'll find Uncle Ross waiting for you there on the train platform."

There was little else to say. Mrs. Perry leaned down and kissed Elizabeth and John. She told them to be good and to have a good time. They were to remember to obey Uncle Ross and not to play too hard. Mr. Perry kissed them and then looked carefully at Elizabeth.

"And now," he said to her, "I leave it all to you."

Elizabeth smiled at her father, tossed her head and looked as though she could take care of anything.

Mr. and Mrs. Perry hurried off the train. They had only a few seconds to wave at Elizabeth and John before the train pulled out of the station.

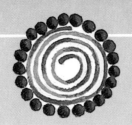

Elizabeth forgot all about sitting like a lady. She sat on her knees with her head pressed against the window. The glass cooled her hot face and hands and she was able to put her thoughts together.

"Well, the school term's over," she said. Her lips moved against the window but her voice made barely a sound. "We'll spend the whole summer on the farm with Uncle Ross. I ought to make up something special just because we've never ever gone alone like this!" She began figuring out what she might do that would be as important as travelling to the country without her father and mother.

John Perry leaned around Elizabeth to see out the window. He was terribly excited about making the trip but his manner was not as sure as his sister's. He was smaller than Elizabeth, but otherwise he was enough like her to be her twin. His eyes were black, like hers, and his skin, brown, with a faint red hue. He had a shock of dark, curly hair that tumbled over his forehead just as Elizabeth's did.

"You know what I'm going to do?" he said to Elizabeth. "I'm going to take off my shoes and socks. I don't see why I have to wait until we get to Uncle Ross' before I go barefoot."

"You'd better not," Elizabeth said. "I'll tell mother and you'll be sorry."

"You're the meanest girl I know!" John said. He sat back glumly in his seat.

Elizabeth wore short pants and a shirt for the train ride. There were seven strands of bright beads looped around her neck. She would have loved making the trip without John. She liked being by herself. Alone, she could *be* anybody at all and she would have only herself to take care of.

The train swept through a long tunnel. Elizabeth sat very still. She could feel John, rigid, beside her. "Are you scared, John?" she giggled. "Don't be afraid. It's just a mean, black, spooky tunnel!"

John held on tightly to the armrests of his seat. "I don't care for tunnels," he said. He had never been in a tunnel on a train and he did not like it at all.

By the time the train entered the open air again, Elizabeth had figured out what special thing would be as important as travelling alone to the country.

"I want you to listen," she told John. "From now on, you are to call yourself Toeboy—understand? No more John Perry, and not just for the train trip but for the whole summer." He was Toeboy, she told him, because at the farm he could go around without shoes all the time if he wanted to.

"I'm going to be Geeder," she said. "I am Miss Geeder Perry from this second on. Horses answer to 'Gee,' don't they? I bet I can call a mare to me even better than Uncle Ross!"

Toeboy whinnied and began to prance up and down, knocking into the pile of books stacked on the seat beside him. They clattered into the aisle. It took Geeder ten minutes to quiet her brother without raising her voice or hitting him.

"I could just give you a good smack, Toeboy!" she said. She was furious but didn't dare touch him. In the last few weeks, Toeboy had become fond of letter writing. He would whip out his note pad and scribble off something to her father if she so much as looked at him.

"Now, I'm not going to yell at you," she said, "because then people might stare. They'll think I'm not old enough to take care of you."

"You're not," Toeboy said. "I can take care of myself, thank you."

Geeder ignored him. She made a neat pile of the books on the floor in the space between the seats. The train rushed on as the last sunlight of the day slanted into rows of tall apartment buildings.

"Why do you get the window seat?" Toeboy asked, after a while. He was tired of leaning around Geeder to see.

"Because I've *got* it," Geeder said, "and I'm going to *keep* it."

Toeboy could tell by the tone of her voice that she meant what she said. He decided to read his books.

Geeder pressed her face against the window. She knew Toeboy was beside her and that their coach was fairly full of people. But she felt cut off from him, from the train, as if she were outside with the scenery.

"I never thought there could be so many buildings, with so many windows and people." Geeder's lips moved, making the slightest sound.

The train moved along an elevated track and she could see building after building for what seemed miles. The train went so fast she felt lonely for all the people left behind. Long streets looked like spokes of a wheel connected to nothing and going nowhere.

"What things happen to all these people?" Geeder whispered. "I don't suppose they all have farms to go to in the summer, like me and Toeboy."

That made her smile. Oh, it was nice that school was over so that she and Toeboy could leave. . . . It wasn't that she didn't like her home. She liked it well enough. You could go to the park or to a show. You could go for a drive in the car and have hamburgers and ice cream or you could play along the river. There was lots to do. But lately she'd grown tired doing things she had done time after time. It wasn't that she liked going to Uncle Ross' any better. The truth was that she didn't remember what it was like there.

"Let's see, there's the farm and the town, and there's Uncle Ross," she said to herself. But try as she might, she couldn't recall what she did at the farm three years ago. "Maybe I didn't do anything. Maybe I was just too young to do much."

This time, she promised herself, she would do everything and see everything and remember everything she saw.

"I won't be silly, either. I won't play silly games with silly girls."

Suddenly, her father's last words came back to her. At the same time, she saw that the tall buildings had given way to open country. There were houses and a few farms and fields. The train had gone beyond the river and she hadn't seen any of it. From then on, she set her mind on seeing everything. The waning day she saw as clear as morning in the country; her father's words, bright as sunlight in the fields.

And now, I leave it all to you," her father had said.

"Why, he means something will happen and I'm to take care of it!" she said.

Toeboy thought Geeder spoke to him. He'd been waiting for her to say something above a whisper so he would know she wasn't still angry with him.

"Geeder," he said, softly, "just look at this."

She ignored him.

"Geeder, it's something you'll never believe."

"Toeboy, you read your books and don't bother me."

"It says here," he began, "there are these people living way in the middle of Australia where there isn't any water. When they want a drink, they pick a big, fat frog

90

and squeeze all the water out of it into their mouths."

Geeder gasped and spun around in her seat. "That's just awful!" she said, taking the book away from him to look it over.

"It doesn't hurt the frogs," Toeboy said. "They just go along until they fill up with water. Then, they get drunk up again."

Geeder tossed him the book. "Please don't bother me, Toeboy. I've too much to think about without worrying about you."

"What do you have to think about?" he asked.

"Oh, things," Geeder said, "things that happen."

"What things?" he asked.

"Never you mind, Toeboy," she said. "Be quiet and read your books."

Toeboy reached in his pocket for his note pad. Geeder saw him. She at once smiled pleasantly at her brother.

"Pretty soon, we'll go eat," she said, "and you can have ice cream and cake after you have dinner. Oh, we'll eat everything and then we'll come back here. They'll turn out the lights and you can sit by the window. You'll be able to see everything in the night—won't that be fun? Then, we'll go to sleep and before you know it, we'll be there and Uncle Ross will take us to the farm."

Toeboy forgot about writing to his father. The mention of food made his mouth water.

"Will the dining car be scary?" he asked.

"Not like the tunnel," she said. "Don't you worry. I'll take care of it."

The night ride passed quickly, as Geeder said it would. The trip had seemed almost too short. In the morning, Uncle Ross was there at the station to meet them. Geeder had nearly forgotten what he looked like. She had a picture of Uncle Ross in her wallet and a picture of him in her mind. The one in her mind was closer to what she saw waiting on the train platform: a big, powerful man, like her father, whose smile was broad and gentle.

Uncle Ross' eyes shone as he caught sight of them and he tipped his hat eagerly with a friendly swoop of his arm. As Geeder ran up to him, laughing, the suitcase banging against her leg, he held out an arm for her to hold on to.

"Well, look here!" he said. "Look what's come to stay!"

"I'm Toeboy!" Toeboy shouted, running up and catching hold of Uncle Ross' free arm. "The train wasn't scary at all."

"And I'm Geeder," said Geeder. "You must remember because we'll be Geeder and Toeboy for the whole summer on the farm."

"Geeder is it?" Uncle Ross said, "and Toeboy. New names for a new summer. I like that! Give me a chance to catch my breath and I won't forget those names, ever!"

Uncle Ross hurried them into his battered old truck. Geeder recalled that it smelled always of leather and cigars.

At the farm, Geeder saw everything for what seemed the first time. She went in and out of the rooms, looking over all the antique furniture and fixtures Uncle Ross had collected at auctions over many years.

Uncle Ross and Toeboy walked behind her. "I'd hate to think you'd forgotten what my house looked like inside," Uncle Ross said, teasing her.

Geeder stood fingering a faded piece of silk folded neatly on an old end table. "It's not that I don't remember," she said. "I guess it never mattered before whether I remembered or not."

"But it matters now?" Uncle Ross asked.

"Oh, yes," Geeder said. She felt a sudden, sweet surge of joy inside. "Everything matters now!"

"Why?" asked Toeboy.

"Just never you mind," she said to him. "But I'll tell you this much. I'm three years older than the last time I was here. That means I know ten times as much as I did then."

Uncle Ross smiled, noting the great change in the children. He said nothing about it, however. He left them so they could roam the house on their own. "Well, call me if you find anything you don't know about," he said to them as he left.

There was a pantry in Uncle Ross' house. Toeboy and Geeder hung on to the door and looked inside carefully.

"I don't remember this at all," Toeboy said.

"Well, I do," Geeder said. "I don't remember it being so large, though, with so much food."

They couldn't decide if the pantry had been there the last time they visited the farm, so they called Uncle Ross. When he came, he told them the pantry had been just where they found it since the house was built.

"There's not another house in these parts with a pantry this size," he told them. He stood rocking on his heels in the center of the room, smiling proudly. "Each year, I put up beans, tomatoes, applesauce and jelly, among other things. Oh, I don't use half of it in a year," he said, "but I like giving it to folks in the village. These days, not many people put up food the way I was taught to."

The pantry was a large square. On every side were cupboards full of canned goods up to the ceiling. Geeder walked to the center of the room and slowly turned around until she had every cupboard fixed in her mind.

"Isn't it just the nicest place?" she said. "I love it, with all the jars and big cupboards."

Uncle Ross laughed. "Well, then, you can come in every day and pick out all of the food we'll need for each meal. That way, you'll get to know this pantry as well as I do and it will get to know you."

Toeboy wasn't much interested in the canned goods or the cupboards, even if they did reach clear up to the ceiling. But he did want to stand in his bare feet on the cement floor. He took off his shoes and socks hastily, and stood there. The coolness curled his toes.

"I think I'll just sit on the floor," Geeder said. She sat down with her back against the wall. She felt comfortable and decided she would sit on the floor for five or ten minutes each day.

Off the pantry there was a pump room.

"What in the world kind of place is this?" asked Toeboy.

"Uncle Ross—Uncle Ross!" Geeder called. He had left so that they could explore again. "Look, come and see this place!"

Uncle Ross came in a hurry, wondering what discovery the children had made in his old, familiar house. Then he saw it was the pump room. It was his favorite place of all.

"Now, you've come to something!" Uncle Ross said. "It's been thirty years since a house was built with one of these rooms."

"What in the world do you use it for?" Toeboy asked.

"Maybe you won't want to use it for anything," Uncle

Ross said, "but I come in here when I need a drink of water that's finer than any other."

The pump room was quite a small place with just a hand pump attached to a square tub.

"Before there was running water in houses," Uncle Ross said, "people had pump rooms. There, they filled buckets with ice-cold well water for drinking and for heating on the top of wood-burning stoves."

Toeboy went up to the pump and cautiously pumped the handle a few times. There wasn't even a trickle of water.

"The pump has to be primed," Uncle Ross said to Toeboy. "Go get a pitcher from the dining room and fill it with water from the tap in the kitchen."

When Toeboy came back with the full pitcher, Uncle Ross showed him how to pour it slowly into the opening around the plunger.

"Now. You pump the handle," he said to Geeder.

Geeder pumped. Soon, they heard a dry, harsh sound. A minute later, water came gushing out.

"Have a drink," Uncle Ross said. He took a tin cup from a hook by the door and filled it, first offering it to Geeder and then to Toeboy.

"Oh!" Geeder said. "That's just the sweetest water!"

From that moment on, they refused to drink the perfectly good water from the sink in the kitchen and feasted in the pump room on well water cold as ice.

The rest of the house was large and spread out. Geeder supposed all farmhouses were like that. Her favorite place was the parlor; it was silent, with blinds and curtains drawn to keep out the heat.

Standing in the room, she didn't know she had begun to talk to herself. "Look at all those old pictures," she said. Photographs, yellow with age, lined the walls and the tops of tables. "I'll bet that one is Uncle Ross when he was a boy. And that one is him for sure as a young man. I don't even have a memory of those other people. Probably Uncle Ross doesn't either, the pictures are so old."

There was a large photograph of a woman she knew to be Uncle Ross' wife, Aunt Leah. She was no longer living.

"She's awfully pretty," Geeder whispered. "I wish I could have known her."

The parlor had comfortable chairs, a sofa with many soft pillows and tables with drawers full of candy. Some of the candy tasted as though it had lain in the drawers for years, but Geeder ate it anyway. There was an upright piano against the far wall, away from the windows.

"I think I'll just play it once," Geeder said. She sat down on the piano bench and touched the keys gently. The sound came forth muted, as if it has waited a long time. The soft tone thrilled her.

"I can play a few songs a little bit." She spoke more to the piano than to herself. "I wish I could play well. I wish I knew a lot of pretty songs that would just fill up this room!"

A breeze pulled the blinds in and out against the window screens. The lace curtains were sucked up and down along the blinds, making a queer sound all of a sudden. Geeder felt a chill creep up her neck. The photographs seemed to look through her, as though she were a stranger.

She got up and, not looking back, flounced out of the room. "There's nothing you can *do* with an old piano," she said.

She wandered into the hall, where there was a cherrywood staircase. She had noticed it when she first came into the house. Uncle Ross had said it was new, that the old one had fallen down in a heap a long time ago. It led, curving gently around, to the bedrooms above. The stairs had been in the back of her mind ever since she sat down at the piano. And the banister was the kind of thing she could touch and know.

"Better than old, yellowed photographs anytime," she said. She tried sniffing the banister. "It smells just like the tallest tree in the woods!"

Upstairs, she and Toeboy had separate bedrooms on opposite sides of a long corridor. Her room had a large, soft bed, a bureau with a mirror that she could turn any way she wished and two antique cherry-wood chairs with silk cushions. She opened her suitcase and put all her clothes away in the closet and bureau. At the bottom of the suitcase was a box full of the rest of her necklaces. These she hung from the bedposts and the backs of the chairs. When she lay on the bed, the necklaces made her feel that she rested among stars.

Across the room from the bed were windows that looked out on the rear yard, a big, empty barn and a smaller shed.

Since he no longer farmed, Uncle Ross kept no live-stock about. There was just a fenced-in yard at the side of the house for the chickens.

Soon, Geeder got up from the bed and left her room. Slowly, she went over the whole house. Uncle Ross was somewhere outside, and she supposed Toeboy was with him. She had no one to bother her and could take her time. She went to Toeboy's room. His bed was large like hers and his windows looked out over the front yard and the high hedge that shielded the house from the road. She put all Toeboy's clothes away and stacked his books neatly on the floor by the bed.

"We'll have to get a bookcase for all these books," she said, "or he'll have them scattered from one end of the house to the other."

She went to Uncle Ross' room. "I don't suppose he'd

mind if I just look in," she said. "I won't touch anything."
She crept inside, careful not to make a sound, nor to
bump against any furniture. Uncle Ross' room was much
larger than hers and Toeboy's. He had a long, wide desk
by the windows. There were many photographs on it,
too. Geeder was pleased to find a picture of herself and
Toeboy. "Now when was that taken—and who took it?"
She couldn't recall posing for the picture. But she noticed
at once that she and Toeboy were no bigger than babies.
"Oh, the last time we were here," she whispered, "when
we played silly games!"

Geeder walked around Uncle Ross' room several times,
taking in everything she saw. All around her was a faint
scent of sachet. It smelled the same as the photographs
on Uncle Ross' desk looked—old, dry, clouded and dusty.

"I smell cigars, too," she whispered, "and soap and—my
goodness—hay!"

Geeder stood still in the room, then slowly backed out
of it. A chill crept up her neck.

"Oh," she said. "Old things. Waiting for something new
to happen."

She walked slowly down the winding staircase, gently
holding on to the cherry-wood banister. Downstairs, she
stopped in the pump room for a drink of water. When
she had finished, she sighed with satisfaction and went
quickly outside.

Sunlight hit her full in the face. Heat, with the scent of
grass, blew in her nostrils. "Toeboy! Where are you? It's
hot as blazes!"

She found Toeboy digging in the rich, black soil by the
barn. He had found a squirming colony of earthworms.
"Here, let me attach them," Geeder said. She tied the
worms together, carefully, so as not to harm them. The
worms wiggled. She and Toeboy laughed.

"They'll make a nice octopus for Uncle Ross's pond," Toeboy said.

"The pond!" Geeder had not remembered it. "Toeboy, let's get going!"

The pond was far back on Uncle Ross' land, in a pie-shaped section behind his west field. The section had never been much good for farming. Sycamore trees grew at random in it, and in the middle of these was the pond. It was not a deep pond, but it was good for wading up to the waist. They took off their clothes and waded in, heedless of the cold. When they had had enough, they put on their clothes again and sat dangling their feet in the water.

Geeder looked out through the trees, listening to sounds of trucks on the road which passed the house. She could even hear people talking a long way off. She imagined she heard what went on in town—people shopping and saying hello. It was then that she thought to rename the town.

"I'll call it Crystal," she said to Toeboy. "If you stand on the road, you can probably see the beginning, the middle and the end of it, just the way you can see through a piece of glass."

Geeder thought about the road. It curved for a mile through Crystal and then wound away from the town around a forest of catalpa trees to Uncle Ross' farm.

"Leadback Road! That's what I'll call it," she said. "Because where does it lead to?"

"Here!" Toeboy said.

"That's right!" Geeder said. "Crystal has a crack in it, Toeboy, and the crack is Leadback Road!"

The first day at the farm, Geeder and Toeboy looked
over the hogs in Uncle Ross' west field. These were no
ordinary animals, but prize razorback hogs owned by a
Mr. Nat Tayber and his daughter, who rented land from
Uncle Ross.

"Look at the size of those hogs!" Toeboy said.

"They're big, all right," Geeder said, "and they're mean. I
wouldn't get too close to them even if I had to."

They leaned on the fence, looking in at the hogs. The
hogs wallowed around, eating and rooting in the earth
with their snouts. Often they came close to the fence but
veered away as they caught the scent of Geeder and
Toeboy.

"Let's go," said Geeder. "I don't believe they like us
here."

They fed a bit of corn to Uncle Ross' two hundred
leghorn chickens. They could feed them as much corn as
they liked, Uncle Ross had said. And they could gather up
eggs whenever they had a mind to.

"Well, it's the truth. I can do whatever I want," Geeder
said to herself. Still, not one thing had taken place that
fit with her father's words *"And now, I leave it all to
you."*

That was why, when evening came, Geeder decided to
spread sheets and blankets out on the front lawn. She
and Toeboy would sleep outside and maybe they would
see a comet.

Toeboy liked looking up into the sky, as long as Geeder
was talking. The sound of her voice made the night less
strange and he felt safe. He had made his bed partly

beneath a sprawling lilac bush close to the house. Geeder had made hers near the high hedge that shielded the house from the road. Toeboy felt so good that he decided to get up and make his bed next to Geeder's.

"I think I'll come over there," he called to her.

"Better not," she said. "Just better stay where you are."

"But I want to sleep by the hedge, too," he said.

"I know one thing," Geeder said. "Late at night in the country, night travellers walk along dark roads."

"What?"

"Night travellers," Geeder said again, "and they usually come up when you're just about asleep."

"What kind of things are they?" asked Toeboy. He dug his legs deeper among the branches of the lilac bush.

"I'll tell you this," Geeder said. "If you see one, you'd better close your eyes fast and dive as far under the covers as you can go. They don't like kids watching them. In fact, they don't like anybody watching them!"

Toeboy stayed uneasily beneath the lilac bush. He was glad to be so near the house, for if he heard any sound, he could race inside. He did not mind at all seeing half stars and half-moon through the lilac leaves.

Geeder turned around to see what Toeboy was doing and saw that he had pulled most of his bedding all the way under the lilac shrub. That nearly made her laugh out loud. She had made up the whole thing about the night travellers. She was only trying to frighten Toeboy—not for any really mean reason, but just because he was little and was easy to scare. As far as she knew, nobody walked late at night along this dark road.

But maybe ghosts do, she thought. A chill passed up her spine and she closed her eyes tight for an instant to make it go away.

"Toeboy," she called, "are you still awake?"

"I'm awake," he said. "I don't want to sleep yet." He lay fingering the cool leaves of the lilac.

"Then I'll tell you all about stars," said Geeder, "since you're so wide awake."

Geeder talked about the stars and the night. She knew Toeboy had gone to sleep when he no longer asked her anything or chuckled about what she said.

A long time passed. Geeder dozed and awoke with a start. The grass beyond the tip of her toes was wet with dew. She pulled the blankets more tightly around her, tucking her feet safely inside. She had closed her eyes again when she heard a rustling sound on Leadback Road.

Some old animal, she thought. The sound grew louder and she could not think what it was. Suddenly, what she had told Toeboy flashed through her mind.

Night travellers! She dove under the covers.

But something's happening! she told herself, poking her head out again.

It took all her courage to crawl out of the covers and the few feet over the wet grass up to the hedge. She trembled with fear but peeked through the hedge in spite of it. What she saw made her bend low, hugging the ground for protection. Truthfully, she wasn't sure what she saw. The branches of the hedge didn't allow much of a view.

Something tall and white was moving down the road. It didn't quite touch the ground. Geeder could hear no sound of footsteps. She couldn't see its head or arms. Beside it and moving with it was something that squeaked ominously. The white, very long figure made a rustling sound when she held her breath. It passed by toward town.

Geeder watched, moving her head ever so slowly until she could no longer see it. After waiting for what seemed hours, quaking at each sound and murmur of the night, she crept back to bed, pulling the covers over her eyes. She lay, cold and scared, unable to think and afraid even to clear her dry throat. This way, she fell asleep. She awoke in the morning, refreshed but stiff in every muscle.

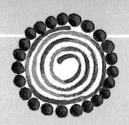

Geeder lay for a moment, watching mist rise from the pink, sweet clover that sprinkled the lawn. The air smelled clean and fresh and was not yet hot from the sun.

"I've got to decide," she whispered. In the stillness, the sound of her own voice startled her. She turned carefully around to see if Toeboy had stirred. The tangled bedding deep in the lilac bush did not move.

"If I tell Toeboy about the night traveller," she whispered, "he might not want to sleep outside any more. Just think of it! Not more than a few hours ago, an awful, spooky thing walked by here!"

Geeder wasn't at all sure she wanted to sleep outside again, herself.

"Goodness knows what a night traveller will do if it sees you watching! Maybe I'd better tell Uncle Ross. . . . Maybe I shouldn't."

Geeder knew it would take her a while to figure out what course to take. Almost any minute now, the people Uncle Ross rented land to would come down the road. Uncle Ross had said they came every morning as soon as the sun was well up in the sky. It was just about time, and watching them would be something to do.

When her dew-soaked blankets grew warm from the sun, Geeder whistled for Toeboy as softly as she could. Turning around, she saw one eye peek out from the lilac bush.

"Wake up, Toeboy!" she whispered loudly. "I think I hear them coming!"

Toeboy leaped up before he looked where he was going and hit his head against a branch. Leaves spilled dew all over him. He was wet and still half asleep when Geeder yanked him to the ground before they could be seen.

They knelt low by the hedge. Trying not to move or blink an eye, they watched Mr. Tayber and his daughter come into view along Leadback Road. What they saw was no ordinary sight. They watched, spellbound, for nothing in the world could have prepared them for the sight of Miss Zeely Tayber.

Zeely Tayber was more than six and a half feet tall, thin and deeply dark as a pole of Ceylon ebony. She wore a long smock that reached to her ankles. Her arms, hands and feet were bare, and her thin, oblong head didn't seem to fit quite right on her shoulders.

She had very high cheekbones and her eyes seemed to turn inward on themselves. Geeder couldn't say what expression she saw on Zeely's face. She knew only that it was calm, that it had pride in it, and that the face was the most beautiful she had ever seen.

Zeely's long fingers looked exactly like bean pods left a long time in the sun.

Geeder wanted to make sure Toeboy noticed Zeely's hands but the Taybers were too close, and she was afraid they would hear her.

Mr. Tayber and Zeely carried feed pails, which made a grating sound. It was the only sound on the road besides that of Mr. Tayber's heavy footsteps. Zeely made no sound at all.

You could think she would, thought Geeder, she was so long and tall.

Geeder and Toeboy stayed quiet as the Taybers passed, and the Taybers gave no sign that they saw them hiding there. Uncle Ross had said that they were not known to speak much, even to one another. They had not lived in Crystal always, as Uncle Ross had.

Geeder and Toeboy watched the Taybers until they went out of sight. It was then that Toeboy said, "Let's go watch them in the field."

"No," said Geeder quietly, "no, Toeboy." She could not

possibly have made him understand how stunned she had been at seeing Miss Zeely Tayber for the first time. Never in her life had she seen anyone quite like her.

Later on, as they fed the chickens, Geeder talked to Toeboy about the arrival of the Taybers in Crystal.

"They must have come early one morning," she told him. "They might have come from the west but I suspect they came from Tallahassee. They brought all their wild animals with them in a wagon train and they bought that house they live in from Mr. Crawley."

"How could they come in a wagon train?" Toeboy wanted to know. Geeder was thinking and didn't answer him.

"Mr. Tayber came down the road to see about using some of the west field," Geeder said. "Uncle Ross was to get a third of the profit from the sale of the best razor-back hogs."

"But why would Uncle Ross rent land to strangers?" Toeboy asked. "And what is 'a third of the profit'?"

"Oh, goodness, Toeboy!" Geeder said. "I don't know what 'a third of the profit' would be. And if Uncle Ross waited until he got to know the Taybers the way you know ordinary people, he'd wait forever. Listen." She stood very close to Toeboy, as though all the chickens might hear and she didn't want them to. "All of Crystal knows only a few things about the Taybers."

"What things?" Toeboy asked.

"Well, they know that Zeely Tayber is awfully tall for a girl. Even Nat Tayber is very tall," Geeder said, "but not too tall for a grown man."

"What else do they know?" asked Toeboy.

"The Taybers like to be left alone," Geeder said, counting off on her fingers. "Zeely's mother is dead. Both Nat and Zeely have thin noses and very high cheekbones."

"Maybe the Taybers are Indians," Toeboy said.

Geeder had to laugh. "The Taybers are colored people," she said, "just like you and me and Uncle Ross. But they are different from any people I've ever seen. We don't know what kind of person Zeely is." Geeder's voice was full of the awe she felt for her. "But you know what I think? I think we've found a new people that nobody's ever heard of!"

All that morning, Geeder talked to Toeboy about Zeely. When they sat down for lunch with Uncle Ross, Toeboy was surprised by the off-handed way Geeder asked, "How long have those Tayber people been around this town?"

"Oh, it's been about a year and a half now," Uncle Ross said.

"That's a long time," Geeder said. "I guess you've gotten to know Mr. Tayber and his girl real well in all that time."

Uncle Ross smiled. "No," he said, "I wouldn't say that. The Taybers aren't easy to know, although they are speaking-polite to most folks."

"What would you say then?" asked Toeboy.

"What would I say when?" Uncle Ross replied.

Geeder wished Toeboy would just keep quiet. "He means to say that if you don't know them well, then what way *do* you know them?" she asked. "And why don't you know them well when they're in the west field every day working over the animals?"

Uncle Ross took a careful look at Toeboy and a much longer look at Geeder.

"Toeboy means to say all that?" he said to Geeder. "Well, I mean to say just what I did say. Mr. Tayber and his daughter live to themselves. They stay aloof from the whole town." He paused. "One day, the town had no thought of them. The next day, there they were, hammering and putting storm windows in that old house once owned by Jacob Crawley."

"Just like that?" Geeder said, snapping her fingers.

"No, not exactly like that," Uncle Ross said. "Now that I think about it, there had been time . . . room . . . for people like them among us. It's like it took them a long time to get here. The first time we see them, they are taking care to fix up that house. Strangers. And they stay on taking their time, still strangers. That's all right, the way I see it."

"Strangers," Geeder said. But that was all she said. She asked no more questions.

But by nightfall, Geeder was ready to talk about Zeely Tayber once more. As she and Toeboy lay in their beds on the lawn, she began.

"You would think a lady like Zeely would have all kinds of friends," Geeder said. "I mean, being so tall and being so pretty. But there she goes with just old Mr. Tayber. She hardly even talks to *him*."

"He doesn't talk much to her, either," Toeboy said.

"That's because both Zeely and Mr. Tayber are different," Geeder said, "with ways about them none of us can understand."

Toeboy lay beneath the lilac bush, hugging the covers around himself. He listened to the rise and fall of Geeder's voice and was lulled into a deep sleep.

Geeder stopped talking. She was watching the stars when there grew in her mind a lovely picture. . . . It was daytime, with sunlight spilling over Uncle Ross' farm. She sat in shade on a grassy slope beside Leadback Road. Miss Zeely Tayber came gliding down the road. Her face and arms were shiny from heat and walking so long in the sun. She came right up to Geeder. She had been looking for her.

"Geeder, have you waited long?" Miss Zeely said, "I would dearly love a drink of water from the pump room."

Geeder brought Miss Zeely a drink of water in a tall glass, and a silk handkerchief. Miss Zeely sat beside Geeder, sipping the water. She wiped her face with the handkerchief and then dried her hands. When she had finished, she folded the hanky and placed it in Geeder's palm.

"Geeder Perry," said Miss Zeely, "I don't know what I would do without you."

Geeder pretended she hadn't done anything at all. . . .

"Miss Zeely Tayber," she whispered to the stars, "oh, Miss Zeely!"

Her hand touched something cool and heavy beside her. Uncle Ross' flashlight! She had taken it from his workroom. She meant to shine the light on the night traveller just as it passed by the house.

Suddenly alert and watchful, she listened to the silence around her.

"If the night traveller tries to bother me, I'll throw the flashlight at it," she muttered. "And if that doesn't stop it, I'll scream and wake up the whole town!"

But Geeder was tricked by the fresh night air into falling asleep. Many times she roused herself but did not awaken. Once she said in her sleep, "Is that you? Is that you coming?" It seemed that a voice came through the hedge, murmuring, "Yes, child, now sleep." It was her mother's voice. She slept more calmly then. She dreamed of home and people she knew there. In the morning, she was mad as a bull at having fallen asleep and had no recollection of the dream.

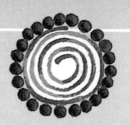

As the weeks passed, fine and sluggish, Geeder and
Toeboy fell into a lazy routine. Each morning, they arose
early to watch the Taybers come down Leadback Road.
Each night, they talked of Zeely Tayber under the stars.
Yet, try as she might, Geeder couldn't learn anything
new about Miss Zeely. She feared all that was to happen
had already taken place.

Some of the village children got into the habit of stopping by the farm to see if Geeder and Toeboy wanted to
play. Toeboy either went off with them or invited them to
wade in Uncle Ross' pond. When the children stayed at
the farm, Geeder hid in the sycamores.

"I can't think straight about Zeely with them around,"
she said to herself. She didn't want anyone other than
Toeboy to know about Zeely until she, herself, knew
more. Many times she had to take Toeboy aside to warn
him never to mention Zeely to the others.

"I don't see why," Toeboy said.

"Toeboy, if you do, I'll never ever talk to you again!"

When Toeboy ran off to town with the children, Geeder
waded and floated in the pond. She tried to outdistance
the water striders, but the long legs of the striders fairly
skimmed over the pond. Often she dug in the earth,
looking for insects. She found a host of maggots feasting
on an apple core. She didn't know they were the larvae of
flies until Uncle Ross told her.

"All life changes," Uncle Ross said. "Some eggs change
into chickens, some worms into butterflies."

The way Uncle Ross said what he did made Geeder feel
strange inside.

"It's too hot here," she said. "I think I'll just get away for a while." She slipped off to a nearby farm where there were fields of wheat and corn.

Geeder sat down in the middle of a long corn row. She pulled weeds to chew on. Purple morning glories twined up the cornstalks. Their scent mixed with that of the cornsilk and the black soil.

"It's awfully quiet here," she said. She didn't know why, but she felt kind of lonely.

"Everything is just dull. Nothing's any fun any more."

She stayed hidden in the corn until the odor of the morning glories brought yellow jackets on the back of the heat.

Geeder went to the wheat fields. The wheat closed in behind her as she crept through it. The slightest breeze caused the wheat to whisper and bow.

"It talks to itself," she said, "just the way I do." She made a nest by bending the wheat to the ground. She lay on it, listening. She was cooler here. The wheat was still green, keeping its moisture.

"I bet Miss Zeely Tayber is lying down somewhere, resting like I am. I bet she doesn't have a soul to talk to, either."

Geeder closed her eyes and folded her arms beneath her head. In no time at all, Miss Zeely Tayber came walking out from the dark of her thoughts. . . . She and Miss Zeely locked arms and ran to the other side of the wheat field, where Miss Zeely lived in a great stone house. There was a swimming pond hidden by plots of corn cockles and bluebells. She and Miss Zeely stayed forever just swimming and taking their ease of the sun. No one could find them. . . .

Geeder slept through the hottest part of the day, waking only when the sun slid off westward. Her mouth was dry; she was chilled from the damp earth. She did not feel at all rested.

"What's the matter with me?" she asked herself. "What's wrong with everything?"

When she returned to Uncle Ross' farm, she found that supper was ready. She ate little and talked hardly at all. Uncle Ross glanced at her often but said nothing about the odd way she was acting. Instead, he told her and Toeboy something that took them by surprise.

"Nat Tayber plans to move forty of his prize razorback hogs tomorrow morning," he said.

"Move them where?" asked Toeboy.

"All the way down the road," Uncle Ross said, "through town and then out to Red Barn."

"What's Red Barn?" asked Geeder, her voice barely above a whisper.

"Why, I know you've seen it," Uncle Ross said. "You must have passed it coming in on the train. It used to be a farm but now it's a clearing house for livestock. It's about a mile and a half from here, a big place."

"And Mr. Tayber is going to move hogs all that way?" asked Toeboy.

"Yes, to have them weighed and sold," Uncle Ross said.

"I bet Miss Zeely is going to help him!" Geeder said.

"I expect she will," Uncle Ross said.

Geeder kept her eyes on her plate, and forced herself to eat.

I want to be sure and see Miss Zeely, she thought. Maybe she'll ask Uncle Ross if I can help her with the sows. If she'll ask him, I'll be able to walk right beside her all the way into town—maybe clear to Red Barn!

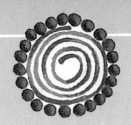

When the morning came, Geeder and Toeboy had the long, boring task of feeding Uncle Ross' two hundred leghorns.

"Any other day, I wouldn't mind," Geeder grumbled, "but if we're to see old Nat move his hogs, we'll have to hurry." At seven o'clock, she sent Toeboy off to fib to Uncle Ross.

"Geeder and I don't want any breakfast," Toeboy said. "We're not hungry at all." He was starving but he tried not to show it as Uncle Ross stared at him hard. Toeboy promised himself that later he would tell Uncle Ross the truth.

"You and Geeder be early for lunch then," Uncle Ross said.

Toeboy said they would and ran back to the chicken yard in search of Geeder.

Geeder was busily throwing great arcs of chipped corn in every direction. She loved the way it glinted golden bright in the sun. It was Toeboy's job to empty the water pans and troughs and refill them with fresh water.

"Why don't you watch where you throw the feed?" he yelled at Geeder. He had to stop his work to brush corn from his hair. A lot of feed fell on top of the chicken coop, where the roosters would find it eventually.

"Just stay out of my way," Geeder said. "I've got to feed these chickens, don't I?"

They weren't half through with the chickens when a terrible, throbbing squeal pierced the air. Birds in the Chinese elm trees, bobwhites and bluejays, set up a furious chatter, then flew away. Geeder dropped her feed

pail and started running. She had reached the gate of the
hen yard when her good sense told her to stop. She
rushed back to the chickens, stumbling and groping for
the feed pail.

"Something awful has happened," she said. "Hurry up,
chickens, I've got to go help Miss Zeely!"

By the time she and Toeboy reached the west field, Nat
Tayber and Uncle Ross stood over a young sow.

"She's caught her hindquarter in the fence," Uncle Ross
said. The lower shank of the sow's left leg was torn and
bleeding through mud-matted hair. She quivered over her
whole body and snapped and squealed as Nat Tayber ran
his fingers over the wound.

Zeely Tayber was there, standing at a distance, shuck-
ing corn into pails. She stood tall and straight, with a
long shadow of herself thrown by the sun toward the
animals.

"She acts like nothing has happened," Geeder whispered
to herself.

Zeely stood absolutely still except for the movement of
her hands.

Geeder tried whistling, but if Zeely Tayber heard her,
she gave no sign. Once, Zeely paused to look in the
direction of the injured sow. Then, as before, she went on
with her work and was silent.

Nat Tayber and Uncle Ross stared at the bleeding sow.

"We'd better get her to your barn," Nat Tayber said.

"We'll have to lift her," Uncle Ross said, "and that's not
going to be easy."

Nat Tayber found some twine and tied the sow's legs
together. That done, he and Uncle Ross lifted the sow
gently and, struggling, carried her to the barn.

Geeder and Toeboy stayed by the hog pen.

"Geeder, let's go," Toeboy said. "This place smells awful!"

"I don't care if it does," Geeder said. "I want to see what Zeely's going to do. You can go if you want to."

They stood watching Zeely but kept their distance from her. Razorbacks and great brute hogs, some weighing as much as four hundred pounds, milled around her like so many little children.

"She doesn't seem to mind them at all," Geeder said.

The hogs made angry snorts at Geeder and Toeboy, however, sensing that the two didn't belong there.

All at once, there was a flurry of movement among the animals. Zeely moved about in her graceful, aloof way. She collected all the empty pails as though she meant to leave.

"Zeely!" Geeder shouted. "Aren't you going to move the animals today?" Her voice surprised her. It was quite loud in the quiet field.

Geeder never found out what Zeely answered. Zeely had turned toward her when an unearthly squeal came from Uncle Ross' barn. Zeely walked over to the broken fence and weighted it down with heavy rocks so that the smaller pigs couldn't root under it. Then she made her way from the field, swinging the gate closed behind her. She headed down Leadback Road, passed Uncle Ross' house and did not look to the left or to the right. Geeder watched her go out of sight, wondering about her, hoping she would turn around. Zeely didn't do anything more than walk away down the road.

When Toeboy and Geeder reached the barn, they found Uncle Ross filling in a hole he had dug.

"What's that hole for?" Toeboy asked.

"Entrails of the sow," Uncle Ross said. Seeing Geeder's questioning face, he motioned her and Toeboy toward the barn door. "You'll find her in there," he said.

Inside the barn, they found the sow. "Why, they've

butchered her!" Geeder said. The sow was already
skinned and hanging high overhead on an oak
crossbeam. The carcass was bloody red. Geeder had to
turn her face away.

"I hope I don't have to eat any of that," Toeboy said. He
gulped hard, for the sight of the raw meat made him sick.

"Oh, I couldn't eat it, I just couldn't!" Geeder said.

"You two get away, now," Uncle Ross said, coming up
behind them. "Go to the shed where there's something
for you to do."

"But I want to see Mr. Tayber move his hogs," Geeder said.

"Well, he won't be moving them today," said Uncle Ross.
"Too much time lost because of the sow. He'll have to
move them tomorrow. You go on to the shed. There's
plenty for you to do there."

The day before, Uncle Ross had told them what he
wanted them to do in the shed. They were to stack magazines and catalogs in neat bundles and tie them so they
could be carted away. Geeder and Toeboy were more than
glad to leave the barn. They rushed out into the sunlight,
leaving the sad carcass of the sow and the memory of it
behind.

Geeder had an odd feeling whenever she entered the
shed. It was cool and shadowy, always. Both she and
Toeboy were barefoot and the earthen floor of the shed
felt clean and fresh. The whole place made whispering
seem quite natural. The roof was louvered boards, over
which a large tarpaulin was fastened in bad weather.
Today, the tarpaulin was folded away and long stripes of
sunlight slanted to the floor. The sun got tangled in dust
and cobwebs and glowed in dark corners. All was still.
What little noise Geeder and Toeboy made was muffled,
fading quickly. They took a good look around before
settling down to work.

They sat close together. Toeboy stacked the catalogs, and Geeder had the magazines.

"I love going through old pictures," Geeder said. "It's the best fun of anything."

"It's not fair," Toeboy said. "You could let me have some of the magazines."

"Well, you can't have any," Geeder said. "Just do what you're supposed to and be quiet about it."

Toeboy was mad enough at Geeder to hit her. But he knew she would start a fight if he did and she would probably win, too. He contented himself with the catalogs. He had two bundles of fifty stacked and tied before Geeder had stacked any magazines.

"You're not supposed to read them," he told her. "That's not fair at all."

"I'm just looking at the pictures before I stack them," she said.

"You'd better not let Uncle Ross catch you."

"You worry so much about nothing!" Geeder said.

"I believe I'll just go tell Uncle Ross," Toeboy said. He got up, heading for the door. Geeder smiled after him and continued turning the glossy pages of a magazine.

Toeboy stood at the corner of the shed. He waited for Geeder to come after him but she didn't. He stood, fidgeting and trying hard to be quiet. Finally, he came back inside. He knew instantly that something was wrong.

Geeder bent low over a magazine. On her lap were two more magazines that slowly slid to the floor. She pressed her hand against the page, as if to hold on to what she saw there. Then, she sat very still and her breath came in a long, low sigh.

"Geeder?" Toeboy whispered. "I'm not going to tell. I was only teasing you."

She didn't hear him. He crept up beside her and tried taking the magazine from her, but she wouldn't let it go.

He looked over her shoulder. What he saw caused him to leap away, as though he had seen a ghost.

"I knew it all the time! I knew it!" Geeder said to him.

Geeder had found something extraordinary, a photograph of an African woman of royal birth. She was a Mututsi. She belonged to the Batutsi tribe. The magazine Geeder held said that the Batutsis were so tall they were almost giants. They were known all over the world as Watutsis, the word for them in the Swahili language. Except for the tribal gown the girl wore and the royal headband wound tightly around her head, she could have been Zeely Tayber standing tall and serene in Uncle Ross' west field.

Toeboy carefully read what was written under the photograph of the African girl. "Maybe Zeely Tayber is a queen," he said at last.

Geeder stared at Toeboy. It took her a few seconds to compose herself enough to say, "Well, of course, Toeboy—what do you think? I never doubted for a minute that Miss Zeely Tayber was anything else!"

She was quiet a long while then, staring at the photograph. It was as if her mind had left her. She simply sat with her mouth open, holding the picture; not one whisper passed her lips.

Uncle Ross happened by the shed. He didn't see Geeder and Toeboy at first, they sat so still in the shadows. But soon, his eyes grew accustomed to the darkness of the shed as he peeked in and he smiled and entered. Geeder aroused herself, getting up to meet Uncle Ross. She handed him the magazine without a word. Uncle Ross carried it to the doorway; there, in the light, he stood gazing at the photograph. His face grew puzzled. Geeder was to remember all day and all night what he said at that moment.

"The same nose," he muttered, "those slanted

eyes . . . black, too, black as night." He looked from the
photograph to Geeder, then to Toeboy and back to Geeder
again. "So you believe Zeely Tayber to be some kind of
royalty," he said, finally.

"There isn't any doubt that Zeely's a queen," Geeder
said. Her voice was calm. "The picture is proof."

"You may have discovered the people Zeely is descended
from," Uncle Ross said, "but I can't see that that's going
to make her a queen." He was about to say more when
he noticed Geeder's stubborn expression. He knew then
that anything he might say would make no difference.
He left the shed without saying anything else. And when
he had gone, Geeder danced around with the photograph
clutched in her arms. Toeboy hopped on one foot the
length of the shed.

"Oh, it's just grand," Geeder said. "Everything was left
to me and I took care of it all by myself!"

*As you might suspect, Geeder's involvement with the
mysterious Zeely Tayber does not end with the discovery
of a photograph in a magazine. Where does Geeder's
fascination with Zeely lead her? What does she discover
along the way?*

Meet the Author: **Virginia Hamilton**

The source and strength, the "staff of life," of Virginia Hamilton's writing is her life and roots in Yellow Springs, Ohio, a village that was a station on the Underground Railroad (a system that helped escaped slaves before the Civil War). She was a bright, spoiled youngest child who started to write at an early age, inspired by tales about her ancestors.

After more than a decade in New York City, where her books were first published, Hamilton returned to Yellow Springs "knowing who and what I am," an experienced writer and winner of many literary awards, including the Newbery Medal and the National Book Award for *M. C. Higgins the Great*.

In describing her work, Hamilton says, "I attempt in each book to take hold of one single theme of the black experience and present it as clearly as I can. . . . You might well ask, what is it I'm getting at? Not actually knowing, I sense that finding out is far less important than the quest and the pleasure of writing along the way. . . Like Zeely, I test my strength against darkness."

Responding to Literature

1. Author Virginia Hamilton describes Geeder so thoroughly that Geeder seems more like a real person than a character in a book. If Geeder were real, would she be someone you would like to know? Give reasons for your answer.

2. Geeder and Toeboy spend an eventful summer on the farm. Suppose each one wrote a letter to their parents about their vacation. What details would each include? How would the letters differ?

3. What mystery does Geeder discover during her visit? What happens that convinces her she's solved the mystery?

4. Geeder spends many long hours speculating about Zeely Tayber. Why do you think Zeely has such a strong effect on Geeder?

5. Author Hamilton contributes to the mood of her story by letting the reader experience events through Geeder's eyes. Review the excerpt to find three or more examples of Geeder's imagination at work.

Unfolding Bud

One is amazed
By a water-lily bud
Unfolding
With each passing day,
Taking on a richer color
And new dimensions.

One is not amazed,
At a first glance,
By a poem,
Which is as tight-closed
As a tiny bud.

Yet one is surprised
To see the poem
Gradually unfolding,
Revealing its rich inner self,
As one reads it
Again
And over again.

Naoshi Koriyama

Appreciating Author's Craft

Thinking About Theme

Readers may find their understanding of events in their own lives increases after they read a certain book because the author has used the book to comment on human beings and the world. These comments form the underlying meaning, or theme, of a literary work and are expressed through plot, character, and other literary elements. Most works, including *Zeely*, have a main theme and several minor ones.

In *Zeely*, author Virginia Hamilton has Uncle Ross state the main theme in a conversation with Geeder. "'All life changes,' Uncle Ross said. 'Some eggs change into chickens, some worms into butterflies.'" Even if a reader does not recognize Uncle Ross's statement as the theme of *Zeely*, this idea will influence the reader's understanding of the book and, possibly, of life.

Writing About Theme

Zeely Tayber has entered Geeder's life and changed it forever. You can write an ending to the story in which Zeely plays a part in expressing the theme of change. (For more ideas about writing, look at your Writer's Handbook.)

Prewriting   To get started, add to the list below two or three examples from the selection that express the theme.

Theme	Examples
all life changes	Geeder and Toeboy take a train alone.
	Geeder grows tired of the things she can do at home.
	Geeder finds a photograph of an African queen who looks like Zeely.

Writing Reread the examples that express the theme "all life changes" that you added to the list. What story ending do these examples suggest to you? Now write an ending for *Zeely* based on the examples.

Revising Read your draft to a friend. Discuss how well the story ending expresses the theme of change. Revise any parts that do not seem to fit. Proofread for errors. Then write your final copy.

Presenting Read your story ending to a group. Ask if the ending seems logical and if it expresses the theme based on the excerpt from *Zeely*. When you have read the entire book, compare Virginia Hamilton's ending for *Zeely* with the one you wrote.

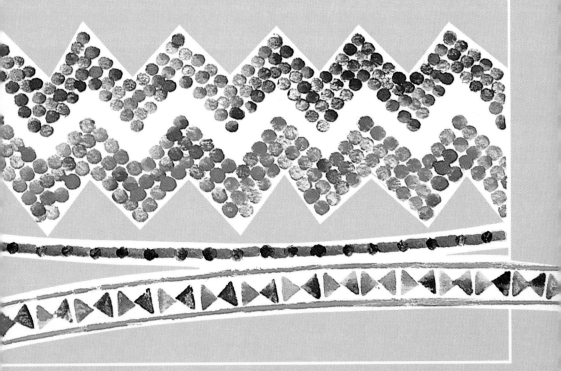

Extending Your Reading

Expressing Yourself
Choose one or more of these activities:

Research the Watutsi Gather as much information as you can from the library about the Watutsi, the African tribe from which Zeely may have been descended. Show photographs to your classmates and tell them what you have learned about the tribe.

Make a Portrait of Zeely Based upon photographs of the Watutsi, as well as the description of Zeely in the story, draw a picture of the proud and beautiful black woman.

Draw a Floor Plan What did Uncle Ross's house look like? Refer to the story to draw a floor plan, such as one an architect might make.

Read Aloud Choose a passage from *Zeely* and read it aloud, with different people reading the dialogue of the various characters. Pick a narrator to read the words that are not in quotes.

Design a Title Reread "Unfolding Bud" on page 125. Then draw a title that expresses the mood of the poem.

Collect African Folk tales Find some collections of African folk tales at the library. Read one or several of your favorite stories to your classmates.

More Books About Discoveries

Switcharound by Lois Lowry. Dell Publishing Co. When Caroline and her brother J.P. arrive in Des Moines to visit their father and his new family, Caroline discovers that she has to watch the six-month-old twins and J.P. is assigned to coach a baseball team. Since Caroline hates babies and J.P. hates sports, they decide to take revenge.

Arthur For the Very First Time by Patricia Maclachlan. Harper & Row, Publishers. When Arthur is sent to the country for the summer, his world expands suddenly to include a wacky new friend, a pregnant pig, and a chicken who likes to hear people speak French. Along the way, Arthur discovers some important things about his family and his place in it.

The Indian in the Cupboard by Lynne Reid Banks. Doubleday and Company. At first Omri is not particularly excited by the plastic Indian, a birthday gift from his best friend. The Indian fits nicely into an old cupboard that his brother gives him, though. He locks the cupboard with a key from his mother and so begins the most incredible adventure of his life.

The Mystery of Drear House by Virginia Hamilton. Greenwillow Books. In this sequel to *The House of Dies Drear*, unsolved mysteries and strange happenings surround the former home of abolitionist Drear. Once a station on the Underground Railroad, the house, with its connecting caves and tunnels, contains a treasure that the current residents are determined to preserve. Some other people's plans differ ominously.

SCOTT JOPLIN
and the Ragtime Years
Mark Evans

Introducing

SCOTT JOPLIN

and the Ragtime Years

Scott Joplin saw a piano for the first time when he was seven years old. He was fascinated. Before long, all his neighbors in Texarkana, Texas, had heard of young Scott's remarkable talent as a piano player. With the help of a music teacher trained in Europe, Scott studied classical music and composition. As he grew older, Scott drew inspiration from his own black musical tradition, with its roots in African music. He spent hours listening to spiritual music, work songs, and traveling musical shows. Blending classical and folk traditions, he created a style of piano music called ragtime and made a unique contribution to American music.

Ragtime Music

Author Mark Evans's book, *Scott Joplin and the Ragtime Years* describes the life of an important musician. At the same time, it traces the development of ragtime music.

Ragtime is an energetic style of music played on a piano in "ragged time." A ragtime piano player uses the left hand to play regular, stomping, bass rhythms. The right hand plays complicated melodies using a technique called syncopation, in which the notes fall on the unaccented beats; in this case, between the regular beats played by the left hand. The effect is jagged, lilting, and danceable. Syncopated rhythms sound very different from the regular rhythms found in the classical music of Scott Joplin's time.

Ragtime was very popular in the late nineteenth and early twentieth centuries. Scott Joplin's "Maple Leaf Rag" was the first hit in American music history. More than 100,000 copies of the sheet music for the tune were sold in 1899. The same song was a hit again seventy-four years later as the theme song for the movie *The Sting*.

Thinking About Biography

A biography is the history of a person's life. The biographer's first task is to collect as much information as possible about the person. Then the biographer must decide which aspects of the person's life to emphasize and which points about the person's character to stress. The biographer tries to present his subject in a way that will help the reader understand not just *what* the subject did, but *why* the person did those things. (For more information about *Biography*, look in your Handbook of Literary Terms.)

As you're reading this excerpt from a biography on your own, discover how Scott Joplin's music was different from any that came before it.

SCOTT JOPLIN

and the Ragtime Years

Young Scott Joplin

Scott Joplin had always been a curious boy, but in all his seven years, he had never seen anything as fascinating or as interesting. He stood very still for a moment, then slowly and silently walked over to the unusual object in the corner of the room. He thrust his right hand forward to touch it, and he jumped when it made a sound. For young Scott Joplin, it was a moment he would never forget. He had seen his first piano.

The instrument, a deep brown upright, was covered with black and white keys. In front of it was an old, cloth-covered chair. Gently, Scott touched the keys again, one after another. Each one sounded different. Then he got down on his knees and, using both hands, tried pressing the pedals up and down. One did not go up and down at all. The other made a squeaking sound. Scott had never wandered into the room with the piano before, but he had been to this house in Texarkana several times, since he lived only a few doors away.

Scott Joplin was born in Marshall, Texas, on November 24, 1868. His father, Giles Joplin, was from North

Carolina, and his mother, Florence Givens Joplin, was from Kentucky. They were poor and they were black. It was the period after the Civil War known as the Reconstruction, when people were still trying to adjust to different ways of life than they had known before the war.

Florence Joplin worked long hours. Every day, she would toil from morning to night, cleaning houses and washing and drying thick sacks of laundry. Scott's father worked for the Iron Mountain and Southern Railroad. He, too, worked very hard, and for little money. But even though the Joplins were not rich, they loved each other, and cared very much for their six children.

Most important for young Scott, there was music all the time. Giles Joplin played the violin, and Florence liked to sing. She did not enjoy washing other people's laundry or cleaning their houses, but by singing, she could think of other things.

Scott's brother, Willie, was learning to play the guitar, and Robert, who had a full, robust voice, had started to sing. Soon, Willie began to play his father's violin, and, when Giles Joplin came home after working all day for the railroad, he would occasionally give him a lesson.

Scott was only a small boy, but he was just as eager as his older brothers to learn something about music. After he saw the neighbor's piano for the first time, he no longer dreamed of playing the banjo or the violin. He didn't want to play the guitar or sing. He wanted to learn to play the piano.

For the next few weeks, Scott kept rushing over to see the Joplins' neighbor—and the piano. He listened to her play many notes at the same time. Before long, he had managed to climb into the chair in front of the keyboard and was trying to play the piano himself.

In a few months, Scott attempted to pick out some simple melodies. He tried to discover how to find the patterns of notes on the piano that sounded like the songs his mother would sing. By the autumn of 1875, he was having more fun at the piano than doing anything else. He would rather play music than read or write, or even run up and down the streets of Texarkana with his friends. And, when his mother cleaned the houses of people who owned pianos, she would often take Scott with her and arrange for him to practice while she worked.

On Scott's birthday, a month before Christmas Eve, his father gave him a present. He told him it was a present for his birthday, for Christmas, and for many birthdays to come. Even though the Joplins had barely enough money to pay for their food and clothes, Giles Joplin had managed to set a little aside to purchase a square piano.

It wasn't a new piano, of course, and the people who had owned it hadn't taken very good care of it. Not only did the pedals squeak, but several of the keys stuck when they were pressed. Also, some of the notes sounded rather strange. Scott did not yet realize that the piano was flat and should be tuned so that the notes would all sound at the appropriate pitch. To him, it was the most wonderful piano in the world.

Scott loved to play. He would experiment and discover relationships between the various black and white keys. Before long, he was improvising his own melodies. He would make up a melody and play it with his right hand. Then he would try to figure out combinations of notes that could be played with his left hand, underneath the melody.

Scott began to play the piano for his friends. Most of the boys and girls in the neighborhood liked music, and, except for one friend who seemed a little jealous at the attention Scott was receiving, they liked to hear him play.

One of the teachers at Scott's school in Texarkana, Mag Washington, gave music lessons to some of the students. She helped Scott and answered his questions about the piano. He also had some lessons with J. C. Johnson, a local music teacher who taught several of Scott's friends.

Neighbors began to talk about Scott, and before long, he was playing well enough to impress many of the people of Texarkana. Some of his mother's friends were maids or servants in the homes of wealthy people across town. Scott's father told the men at the railroad about his son. Word began to spread that Giles Joplin's little boy was remarkably talented as a musician.

Since Scott had not really had many lessons, he played what came naturally to him. The rhythms and sounds of the Negro music he heard around him were part of his background. He began to translate these sounds at the keyboard.

One day, an elderly stranger knocked on the Joplins' door. Scott's mother answered the door, and she was surprised to find a man looking for Scott.

"What did my son do?" said Scott's mother, for she immediately thought that Scott had broken someone's window or accidentally trampled across someone's garden.

"I am told he plays the piano," said the man, speaking slowly with a German accent. "I am a music teacher, and I would like to meet your little boy." He went on to explain to Scott's mother that he was very interested in the possibility of giving her son music lessons. He invited her to bring Scott to his home for a meeting.

So, one Saturday morning, Scott's mother woke him early. Scott always liked to get up early on Saturdays, but he sensed that this was for something special.

"Wash your face," she said. "And don't play outside. I don't want you to get dirty."

Scott thought that this was all very curious, but he washed his face, and his hands, and stayed inside. Then his mother told him to put on a clean shirt.

"Be sure that it stays clean," she said. "We're going to see someone."

Then Florence Joplin explained about the visit from the music teacher and told her son how interested the man was in Scott's musical talent.

Scott listened wide-eyed, as his mother explained that a real professor of music wanted to meet him. In fact, that very morning they would walk all the way across town to the small frame house where the teacher lived.

So Scott was careful and did not get his hands or face dirty. He made sure that he did not soil his shirt. When the time came, Scott and his mother went across town, and Scott knocked timidly on the door.

The man who greeted him was small and soft-spoken. He had white hair, and he seemed older than any of the

This was the world Scott Joplin knew as a youngster.

adults Scott had seen. He shook Scott's hand, and Scott noticed his long, tapering fingers. He wore a rumpled gray suit, and in his pocket was a small gold chain attached to a stopwatch.

"You must play for me," said the teacher. "I have heard a lot about you."

Scott's mother was proud of him, for he played very well. The professor smiled and nodded his head several times. Scott played some of the little pieces he had made up by himself. He also improvised for the professor.

"Can you play scales?" said the teacher, smiling at Scott. Scott hesitated. He had never practiced scales.

"Perhaps you don't know what a scale is," said the teacher. "I will show you." He sat down at the piano, and his long fingers seemed to race across the keys.

Scott tried to play one of the passages the teacher called a scale. His fingers slipped, and he seemed to play all the wrong notes at once.

The teacher laughed gently. "No matter," he said. "We will learn to play scales together."

The "professor," as he called himself, asked Scott if he would like to take lessons every week, and learn something about music that he had never learned before. Scott, of course, could hardly restrain himself. There was nothing he would like more than that.

Scott's mother, however, knew what Giles Joplin would say. Scott's father was poor, but proud. He would want to pay for the lessons, and the Joplins could not really afford to pay for Scott's musical instruction.

The old German music teacher understood what was going through Florence Joplin's mind.

"Naturally," he said, "I must insist that your son study with me on a scholarship."

Scott did not know what a scholarship was, but if it meant he could take lessons from the professor, he thought it was a splendid idea.

"When I was a little boy in Germany," said the teacher, "my parents were very poor too. I wanted to study music in Berlin, which is a very big city. Berlin is a thousand million times bigger than Texarkana. I was given a scholarship to take lessons from an old professor who was even older than I am today."

The teacher told Mrs. Joplin she would be doing him a favor if she let Scott take lessons from him. "You see, I have many pupils," he said. "But none of them has talent. They do not practice. They do not play well. Your little boy will practice, and he will play well. And someday, he will learn to write music that everyone will want to hear."

Scott smiled. He liked the professor, and he wanted to start his lessons right away.

Scott Grows Up

Young Scott was supposed to visit his teacher's home once a week for an hour. But the old professor would often keep his favorite pupil for several hours, and, before long, Scott was tripping across the unpaved streets of Texarkana several times a week, humming and singing to himself.

Although Scott had a wonderful time with his music lessons, all the time was not spent on having fun. Scott's teacher was a fine musician, and he was determined to see that Scott learned as much about music as he possibly could. He began correcting Scott's mistakes on the piano and insisted that Scott spend at least part of the time practicing scales.

The elderly German music teacher and the little black boy became good friends quickly. Although Scott enjoyed practicing the piano, he wanted more than anything to make up his own musical ideas. Another teacher might have discouraged him from using his imagination so soon. But the professor realized that Scott was an unusually talented little boy, and he wasn't surprised when Scott asked him if he would learn to write down the symbols for musical sounds.

On one very special afternoon, Scott's teacher listened to him play his scales, and when he finished, the professor smiled. "Today we are going to begin studying something new," he said. "We are going to start studying harmony and counterpoint."

Scott was terribly excited when he heard this news, because he realized that studying these subjects was the beginning of musical composition.

"You already have some ideas for compositions," said the professor in his German accent, "but you don't know the rules of harmony."

"Isn't it easier just to make up songs?" Scott asked.

The professor shook his head, "It may be fun, but if you want to write great music someday, you will have to study these rules."

Scott could hardly contain his excitement when he returned home. His mother was very pleased upon hearing that the professor was going to help Scott write music as well as play it. His father didn't really understand what the words "harmony" and "counterpoint" meant, but if they pleased his son, he was happy too.

Before he was thirteen, Scott was already playing sonatas by Mozart and Beethoven, and analyzing some chorales by Bach. On one occasion, he decided to have some fun. He took a nocturne by Chopin and began to change the rhythms. Scott often liked to sing to himself, and he managed to invent melodies which had an unusual rhythmic lilt. Instead of playing the left-hand part the way it was originally written, he began to play some notes faster than others. He remembered that the professor had told him about a special type of rhythmic feeling known as syncopation. With syncopation, the accent falls on the weak beat, adding a "snap" or lilt to the melody. Since the accent is expected on the strong beat, syncopation comes as a surprise. Chopin had not included syncopation in his nocturne, but Scott was supplying some of it himself.

"What are you doing?" demanded his teacher.

Scott tried to explain that he was having fun, but his teacher was not amused.

"When you play Chopin," he said, "you must play the music Chopin's way, not your way!"

Scott felt embarrassed. His teacher was seldom angry at him. "I thought it would be so much fun to have some pieces to play that make people feel like dancing."

"If you want pieces to express that feeling," said the professor, "you must write your own."

Scott played the nocturne correctly, and his teacher was satisfied. But Scott decided right then and there that someday he would write pieces for the piano that would be as popular as those written by the great Frederick Chopin. Scott would daydream by the hour of a time when he would hear other people playing his melodies, just as he heard the professor play Chopin.

After each lesson, Scott's teacher would tell him a story. The stories were always plots of famous operas. After finishing, the professor would sit down and play the piano, performing the various themes and explaining the whole idea of an opera to Scott. Although his pupil had never seen an opera, he could not imagine anything more wonderful. The professor thought the finest operas of all had been written by Mozart, and he would quickly dash from his chair to the keyboard, singing the themes in his deep voice. Scott thought the professor was a wonderful pianist, but that he was almost unmusical in his manner of singing. The teacher, of course, sang as if he were a great baritone performing in the opera house at Salzburg.

Scott was also interested in the newer operas, and asked his teacher to explain the music of Giuseppe Verdi. The professor agreed, but somehow he could not be as enthusiastic about more modern works as he could regarding those of the old masters.

One afternoon, Scott asked his teacher why the operas were always written in German, Italian, or French.

"That is a silly question," said the professor. "The composers who write operas expect them to be performed in their own countries."

"Aren't there any operas in English?" demanded Scott, pouting as he thought about the fact that operas never seemed to be performed in a language he understood.

"I have never heard of an opera in English," said the professor. "Perhaps you will write one someday."

Scott thought about the teacher's remarks all the way home. He was still thinking about the idea of writing an opera when he walked through the door. His father asked him what he was thinking about.

Scott did not answer.

His father asked him again.

Once more there was no reply.

Now Scott's father raised his voice. This time Scott stopped daydreaming and answered quickly.

"You can write an opera tomorrow," said Giles Joplin. "Today we have work to be done."

As the weeks went by, Scott made up his mind that he would write an opera when he grew up. He thought it would be wonderful if he could be the first American to write an opera. Scott soon realized that a number of Americans had already tried their hand at writing operas. But he decided that if he could not be the first American to write an opera, he would be the best!

The small black boy who bounded around Texarkana thinking about his music lessons was growing up. Scott was usually quiet and gentle, and he thought more about his music than anything else. He thrilled to the stories the professor told him, about elegant lords and ladies in the European courts. He dreamed of the day when he could walk out on a stage and play for an audience.

But as time went on, life became more and more difficult around the Joplin house. Giles Joplin worked very hard for the railroad, and Florence Joplin spent more time than ever trying to help meet the family's expenses. Scott's older brothers and sisters were growing up. Willie Joplin had his own job at the McCarthy Hotel, and Monroe was working for the railroad. Scott always thought he would be able to help the family too, through his music.

But Scott's father could not see his son living the life of a musician. He knew that musicians wandered from town to town, and that they never had a steady source of income. Giles Joplin felt that Scott should think about going to work instead of studying music.

The foreman at the local railroad seemed interested in helping the family, and if Scott wanted to go to work with a pick and ax, the railroad might be willing to employ him. Scott hated the idea of working for the railroad. The family's poverty was always a problem, and because he

Giles Joplin worked around trains similar to this one.

147

loved his father, he found it hard to insist that music was the only career for him. If his parents had been wealthy, they might have sent him to a famous music school, or even to Europe to master his craft. But to a poor black family in Texarkana, these were just daydreams.

On occasion Scott heard his parents arguing, and although he did not understand why they argued, these conversations made him unhappy. One day Giles Joplin decided to leave home. He explained to Scott that sometimes even mothers and fathers find it difficult to stay together. It was a sad time for Scott.

Finally, he turned to the professor for advice about his future as a musician. The elderly man was devoted to Scott, and he wished that the same opportunities would be open to talented young musicians, regardless of whether they were rich or poor. He wished young Scott could go to a big city in the East to pursue his music.

When Scott told him he was thinking of leaving home, the professor asked quietly, "What are you going to do?"

"I'll play the piano," Scott replied. "Anywhere and everywhere I can."

The professor smiled. "It was never easy for Mozart or Schubert or even Beethoven," he said. "It may not be easy for you. But if you really want to become a great musician, you can."

Scott stood by the door, and his teacher placed his wrinkled hands on Scott's shoulders.

"Remember your old teacher," said the professor. "And remember the day I told you to play Chopin only in

Chopin's way. Someday, if you are true to yourself, all America will be playing Scott Joplin in his way."

Scott felt like crying, but he thought he was too old to do that. He wasn't sure where he was going. He didn't have any friends outside Texarkana. But he knew he would continue his music, and he knew that one way or another he would find a way to write a special type of music all his own. He managed a smile and shook his teacher's hand.

The Wandering Minstrel

When Scott began his travels, he was only a teenager, but he knew that the time had come for him to assume the responsibilities of a man. Inside, he felt unsure and hesitant to face the world. Texarkana had not provided him with wealth or fame, but the little town had been easy to understand.

Scott stood on the bank of the Mississippi River. The area was teeming with excitement. Men were busily loading large crates and boxes of fine clothing. There were tall, strong men with broad shoulders and deep voices, ordering their employees about.

Scott had applied for work on a small riverboat. As the whistle announced its arrival, Scott glanced down at his hands. He knew what his fingers could do when placed upon a piano keyboard. Now he had to show the rest of the world.

Scott resolved to listen and learn from every kind of music in the Mississippi Valley.

As the boat began moving, Scott found himself seated at

an old upright piano. He started playing familiar tunes. He was used to playing in front of people, but never an audience like this. The rough men who worked on the loading docks, the gamblers, the itinerant adventurers were a different group of listeners.

For the next few months, Scott wandered around the Mississippi Valley. He did odd jobs, looking for the opportunity to work as a musician wherever he could. He played in bars, pool halls, clubs, and even in outdoor camps of settlers who lived in tents. Wherever he could find a piano and a willing employer, he worked hard. Always, he kept his ears wide open. Until now, Scott's musical horizons had been limited by Texarkana. Now, as he traveled from one new place to another, meeting new people and listening to all kinds of music, his ideas for melodies, harmonies, and rhythms changed.

In the years following the Civil War, America had a rich musical heritage. While men and women interested in culture devoted their thoughts to the music of Europe, the nation was gradually developing an exciting folk heritage of its own.

Music had always played an important role in the lives of black people. Scott had been exposed to some of the music of black people in Texarkana. But he had far more opportunities after he began his travels. Not only did he begin discovering other forms of music created by his own people, but he became acquainted with dance tunes, marches, ballads, songs from the Civil War, spirituals, and a whole variety of popular music which appealed to men of all races.

Most of the performers who introduced this music were self-taught. Many of them could not even read music. But when an idea for a melody found its proper expression, even an untutored musician could perform with great power and expression. Up until now, Scott had been accustomed to thinking of music that was written down, in which each note is carefully put on paper. But he had tried improvisation, making up new melodies or harmonies as he went along.

Scott was exposed to hundreds of singers and musicians who traveled as he did, earning their living in the Mississippi Valley. Scott absorbed their music. Some of it appealed to him, and some did not. But he began hearing new rhythms and began developing a personal style of music that would stay with him forever.

Scott was too young to remember the Civil War or the tempestuous years that preceded it. Now he heard the work songs sung by black men and women in the antebellum[1] years. Different songs were sung for different types of work. Scott heard the roustabout songs casually sung in deep, booming voices by the waterfront workers. A different repertory of songs might be found on every plantation. "Corn songs" were sung during the cornshucking frolics.

Scott's travels took him from Texas to Louisiana. New Orleans had its own special music, with influences of French, Spanish, and African cultures blended together. He

1. before the Civil War

Scott Joplin

found out about the dances that had been performed by the slaves in Louisiana. The music and the steps for these dances still existed in the memories of the people he met. There was the calinda, a dance in which two lines of dancers faced each other, moving back and forth in time to the music. He discovered the bamboula, in which couples danced together to the beat of a drum. The slaves had called their dance songs "fiddle songs" or "devil songs."

Scott had already heard spirituals in Texarkana, but in Arkansas, Missouri, and Kansas he heard new spirituals with gently moving melodies. Many of the black men he met had served as soldiers during the Civil War. He heard the songs they loved, and listened to their stories of triumphs and tragedies in their military campaigns. Scott heard a man sing "John Brown's Body." The words had been composed by an anonymous soldier; the music had been written by a white song leader, William Steffe. His camp-meeting song had already been adapted once before. Julia Ward Howe wrote her lyric, "The Battle Hymn of the Republic" to this music.

Scott began hearing stories about the lives of black ex-slaves in contraband camps in the Confederate Army. He learned about their music, and thought to himself that the music he played should move audiences with the same vigor and enthusiasm as the melodies he was hearing.

One day, Scott was wandering from saloon to pool hall. He did not especially enjoy playing in these places, because the men who frequented them seemed more interested in money than in music. But he felt that he needed the experience, and sometimes jobs were hard to find.

"If you want to hear some real music and see some real dancing," said a man who happened to be standing near the piano, "why don't you go out and play in a variety show?"

Scott began asking the man questions about the variety show.

"You can find every type of act you would imagine," said the man. "They could use a boy that played the piano as well as you do."

Scott's first introduction to variety shows was abrupt. In later years, these itinerant tent shows would be regarded as vaudeville. In the Mississippi Valley, he discovered medicine shows, complete with traveling salesmen who used the entertainment as a means of promoting their wares.

He also visited the forty-niner camps. These "camps" were gatherings which watched nomadic tent shows, supposedly depicting the life that had existed in the time of the California Gold Rush of 1849.

The highlight of the forty-niner camps was the can-can, a wild French dance performed by a chorus of girls who moved about the stage with reckless abandon. Scott also discovered the world of gamblers. Card sharps from New Orleans wore elegant clothing, and their silk hats were not as smooth as their fingers when they manipulated a deck of cards. The roulette wheel was always available to a musician who thought he could make a fortune and would end up losing his night's wages.

Scott met black men who worked on the steamboats, in the mines, on railroads, or in the lumber camps. These men all made up their own songs, many of which were never written down. Scott tried to remember the best ones, and, if he could, play them on the piano. He would make up his own harmonies to go along with the melodies.

Scott still remembered to write letters home, and always wrote to his old music teacher about his continued interest in serious music. Scott heard stories about serious musicians in the East and great performers of concert music in Europe. One of his most exciting adventures came when he had an opportunity to discover the Fisk Jubilee Singers. Shortly before Scott was born, Fisk University, a black college, had been opened in Nashville, Tennessee. A white teacher, George L. White, organized a chorus of singers. Although he encouraged them to sing vocal compositions of the great masters, White also let the young men and women perform Negro folk melodies and spirituals. Eventually, this chorus became known as the Fisk Jubilee Singers.

White took them on many tours. They began performing in Nashville, and then went to small towns in Tennessee. The American public, particularly white men and women in the North, had their first opportunity to discover the religious music of the former slaves.

Eventually, the Fisk Jubilee Singers performed at the World Peace Jubilee in 1872. This Boston concert made them famous, and they were invited to tour Europe. They performed before kings, queens and noblemen, and before rich and poor people in Europe as well.

John Wesley Work, Sr., became the musical director of the group, and when he died in 1925, his son, John

Riverboats were an important form of transportation during Scott Joplin's time.

Wesley Work, Jr., took over. Scott Joplin was overwhelmed when he first heard about the Fisk Jubilee Singers. He had never realized that Negro spirituals could have such meaning on the concert stage. In later years, Scott himself would discover new ways in which the rhythms and melodies of black men and women could be adapted for concert performance.

Scott also heard remarkable stories about Thomas Greene Bethune, an ex-slave from Columbus, Georgia. Known as "Blind Tom," the blind youth had demonstrated an incredible facility for playing the piano. Even though he could not see, he could duplicate, playing by ear, complicated selections of classical music. He could copy excerpts from Beethoven sonatas, Chopin nocturnes, and operatic fantasies. He improvised, made up his own melodies and themes as he went along, and maintained a huge repertoire.[2] The man who had owned Blind Tom as a slave was Colonel Bethune. The colonel and his family remained as Tom's guardians after the war. They became his managers and earned a great deal of money by scheduling Tom's concerts.

Scott began hearing about small ensembles[3] of black singers who were touring. Several Negro musical societies had been organized in various large cities. Scott also heard performances by new Negro brass bands that had been organized by black people after the war.

Scott also discovered minstrel music. The most famous minstrel company was Callendar's Consolidated Spectacular Colored Minstrels. Many black musicians began their practical training in the minstrel companies, which usually

2. list of pieces that a musician is prepared to perform

3. group of musicians

consisted of only men. Ballads, comic songs, and specialty numbers were all performed. A few musicians who played the banjo or guitar would accompany the performance. They would go to the factories or mines and entertain the workers, promising an exciting time for the evening show. Since blacks were not welcome in town, they might be compelled after the show to sleep in the railroad station, waiting for another train to take them somewhere else. But the big minstrel companies traveled by trains in special Pullman cars and stayed at hotels. The full brass bands that entered a city for a large minstrel company would play military marches, and the bandsmen, clad in brightly colored coats, would parade down the town's main street. The indoor show would open with music played by the band and introduced by a flamboyant master of ceremonies. After the first act, the company would present an olio, a variety show. For a finale, the entire company would appear on stage. Minstrel shows would be regarded as an exploitation of black people; many performers were white men in blackface. But for Scott Joplin, they were one of many influences he absorbed during his wandering years.

Scott discovered the music of James Bland, who was regarded by many as the successor to Stephen Foster. Bland learned about the music of former slaves while studying at Howard University in Washington, D.C. He became famous as an entertainer in Washington, and joined a minstrel troupe.

Scott discovered black cowboys who had their own

stories and songs. On the riverboats, he found singing waiters who could dance across the deck before serving someone's dinner. There were barbershop quartets in the small towns and hamlets along the river.

For Scott Joplin, these years were an important time of discovery. In the world of post-Civil War America, the musical styles of black and white cultures were beginning to merge. And Scott himself began thinking about ways in which the intoxicating rhythms of black folk music could be combined with the harmony and scales of European concert music.

He had heard the simple black folk melodies known as "rags." These were derived from antebellum times when slaves had played banjos and fiddles while stomping their feet for rhythm. The term "rag" itself came from the

Marching band

technique of "picking" the piano, or playing it in a banjo style—and from the expression, "ragpicker."

Scott began making up his own ideas at the piano, exploring this world of rag tunes on his own. The result, in which the left hand played the stomping rhythms and the right hand played the syncopated melodies, was the astonishing music that is known today, throughout the world, as "ragtime."

The story of Scott Joplin's life takes many twists and turns, as does the story of ragtime music. What difficulties does the brilliant young musician and composer face in the society of his day? What are his triumphs?

Meet the Author: **Mark Evans**

From early childhood, Mark Evans has been interested in both words and music. When he was very young, Evans began composing music and writing verses to fit. Now he has twin careers as a writer and musician. He writes lyrics, plays, and books. He also composes, conducts, and plays the piano and organ.

Evans gets ideas for writing from people he meets or by asking himself the question "What if?" He plans his books carefully, so that when he sits down to write, the work goes quickly.

He has expressed his feeling about writing in this poem.

"Why do I write?" I am asking myself.
Not just to place one more book on my shelf.
If I am honest, outspoken, and frank,
It's really quite easy to leave the page blank.

Then I imagine my dreams taking flight.
Think of the things I can do when I write.
I may make a trip or fly to the moon.
I may sail a ship or ride a balloon.
Or go back in time before there were cars.
Or try leaping forward and end up on Mars.
I may meet a pirate, or dragon, or king.
Or even a basset hound trying to sing.
I may go to London, Vienna, or Rome,
by writing and still I need never leave home.
I like to imagine the lives we can lead.
By writing a story you might choose to read.

RESPONDING TO LITERATURE

1. Jean Fritz, a well-known author of children's books, once said, "I think of history and biography as stories and am convinced that the best stories are the true ones." Based on the excerpt from *Scott Joplin and the Ragtime Years*, do you agree or disagree with this statement? Give reasons for your answer.

2. Pretend you have been asked to write a short biography of Scott Joplin for an album of his ragtime piano music. What would you tell readers of the album cover about Joplin?

3. How was Scott Joplin's music different from any that came before it?

4. Once, when Joplin was having fun playing the music of Chopin in a more modern way, his teacher became upset. "When you play Chopin," he said, "you must play the music Chopin's way, not your way!" What effect did this experience have on Joplin's development as a musician?

5. A successful biography persuades the reader that the subject of the biography was worth writing about. Do you think Evans wrote a successful biography? Tell why.

The Piper

Piping down the valleys wild,
   Piping songs of pleasant glee,
On a cloud I saw a child,
   And he laughing said to me:

"Pipe a song about a lamb!"
   So I piped with merry cheer.
"Piper, pipe that song again";
   So I piped: he wept to hear.

"Drop thy pipe, thy happy pipe;
   Sing thy songs of happy cheer!"
So I sang the same again,
   While he wept with joy to hear.

"Piper, sit thee down and write
   In a book that all may read."
So he vanished from my sight;
   And I plucked a hollow reed,

And I made a rural pen,
   And I stained the water clear,
And I wrote my happy songs
   Every child may joy to hear.

—William Blake

Appreciating Author's Craft

Thinking About Style in Biography

A biography is the history of a person's life. (The history of a person's life, *written by that person*, is an autobiography.) People enjoy reading biographies because they are curious about other people's lives. They may gain insight into their own feelings and ideas by reading about the feelings, ideas, and actions of other people.

The first task of a person who sets out to write a biography is to gather information about the subject from newspapers, letters, diaries, interviews, and other sources. The biographer decides which aspects of the subject's life to stress. This helps the biographer determine which facts to include in the biography and which facts to leave out.

Once the biographer has gathered the information, a question arises. How can the biographer make the facts interesting? Biographer Mark Evans discovered that Scott Joplin took lessons from a music professor. Evans probably did not have a record of Joplin's conversations with the professor. Evans used his imagination to re-create conversations they might have had based on the facts he had collected. Information about a subject's thoughts and feelings is also scarce. So the biographer uses facts to imagine those thoughts and feelings and tries to present an accurate picture of the subject.

Writing Biography

Suppose you were a feature writer for a newspaper in Texarkana, Texas, and had been assigned to write a feature story about musical genius Scott Joplin. What points would you stress in your story? (For more ideas about writing, look at your Writer's Handbook.)

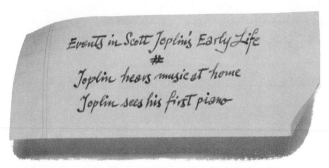

Events in Scott Joplin's Early Life
#
Joplin hears music at home
Joplin sees his first piano

Prewriting The list includes two incidents from Scott Joplin's early life that should be mentioned in a feature story. Copy the list and add three more incidents.

Writing Read your completed list of events from Joplin's early years. Then write a two-paragraph feature story based on the information you gathered. Remember to include not only facts but the feelings Joplin had about his life and music.

Revising Read your draft to a partner. Ask if any of the facts you included do not support the points you are making about Scott Joplin. Make changes based on your partner's suggestions. Then revise your draft. Be sure that each paragraph has one main idea. Proofread for errors in spelling and punctuation. Write your final copy.

Presenting Read your feature story to the class. Ask classmates who have read the excerpt if your story seems accurate.

Extending Your Reading

Expressing Yourself

Choose one or more of these activities:

Research Scott Joplin's Operas What were Scott Joplin's operas like? Find out as much as you can about the operas Joplin composed. If possible, bring in a tape or record of a Scott Joplin opera to share with your class.

Hold a Scott Joplin Music Festival Gather sheet music, tapes, and records of Scott Joplin's music. Display the collection in your classroom.

Design an Album Cover Design a cover for an album of Scott Joplin's piano rags. Try to make your illustration fit the mood of Joplin's music.

Interview Scott Joplin Stage a mock television interview program for your class. Choose a friend to play Scott Joplin. Interview Joplin about his travels and music.

Read the Poem with a Partner Read "The Piper" aloud to your classmates. Have a partner read with you. One of you should read the piper's words and one the child's. If you like, have live or recorded music playing softly in the background.

More Books About Sound

The Ear and Hearing by Brian R. Ward. Franklin Watts. Hearing is a fascinating and complicated process. In this clear, colorful book, the author explains how your ears work, how hearing problems develop, how your brain controls hearing, and how your ears help you do many other things besides hear.

Music Lessons For Alex by Caroline Arnold. Clarion Books. Alex knew she wanted to play the violin the first time she heard an orchestra perform. In words and photographs, this book tells the true story of Alex's first year as a violinist.

Songs and Stories of Uganda by Moses Serwadda. Thomas Y. Crowell Company. You will read clever tales, funny tales, and warning tales in this book of traditional songs and stories from Uganda. The music and chants which are part of the African storytelling tradition are included so you can recreate the stories accurately.

The Optimists of Nine Elms by Anthony Simmons. Pantheon Books. In their travels around the neighborhood, two English children meet Old Sam, who plays a pump organ on street corners, and his dog. The lives of all the characters take a surprising turn after their first meeting.

Sizzle and Splat by Ronald Kidd. E. P. Dutton and Company. Sizzle is a trumpet player in her local youth orchestra; Splat plays the tuba. Sizzle and Splat don't get along very well, but when they find themselves mixed up in the kidnapping of the orchestra's sponsor, they join forces to solve the mystery.

Our Nation's Capital

Three Glimpses of Washington, D.C.

Introducing

Our Nation's Capital
Three Glimpses of Washington, D.C.

One of the most beautiful capitals in the world, Washington, D.C., is the center of government of the United States and the site of monuments and museums of national importance. From the White House to the Smithsonian Institution to the Washington Monument, our capital city is an architectural and cultural treasure.

Three National Institutions

Washington, D.C., is rich in history. Its major institutions have fascinating stories that are intertwined with the history of our nation. In this section, you will read the stories of three of Washington's best-known landmarks.

The Supreme Court in America's Story will help you understand the role of this third branch of the federal government. You will see Washington the way it was in the first years of the Republic and you will meet John Marshall, a man whose vision helped define the role of the Supreme Court.

"A Fight to the Finish: The Washington Monument," a chapter from *Incredible Constructions and the People Who Built Them*, tells the surprising, 100-

year story behind the construction of the Washington Monument.

The final selection of this section, *Auks, Rocks, and the Odd Dinosaur: Inside Stories from the Smithsonian's Museum of Natural History*, introduces a famous museum and some of the objects it houses. You will discover how the museum came to be and you will learn about the man responsible for its collections.

Thinking About Tone in Nonfiction

Books of information, magazine articles, and newspaper reports are all based on facts. They are nonfiction. Nonfictional writing is one important way we receive information about the world. What makes a nonfictional work come alive for the reader is the way the author organizes information to make a point, the writing style the author uses, and the tone, or the author's attitude toward the subject and the readers.

As you're reading these nonfictional selections on your own, decide why the landmarks mentioned are important to the history and culture of the United States.

The Supreme Court today

The first home
of the Supreme Court,
in New York City

The
Supreme Court
in America's Story

Helen Stone Peterson

In the Beginning

On a day in mid-January 1801, John Marshall walked down a dirt road in Washington, D.C. The smile on his good-natured face matched the twinkle in his dark eyes.

The tall, slender man picked his way around mud holes and tree stumps. The government had moved to its new capital about six months before. Trees had been chopped down to make room for the city. In years to come, Washington would be one of the most beautiful capitals in the world, but in 1801 only a few buildings were up and they were not finished.

Forty-five-year-old John Marshall was headed for the new President's House. A lawyer, Mr. Marshall was the nation's secretary of state. One of his duties was to help President John Adams with his mail.

Now he was taking the president a letter from John Jay of New York. Mr. Jay had been the first chief justice of the Supreme Court. Like all members of the Court, he had been given his job for life but after six years, he had left the post. Since then, there had been two more chief justices. Now, with the government only twelve years old, the post was open again. President Adams had written Mr. Jay and asked him to return to it.

John Marshall passed some shacks where carpenters lived and then entered the big, white, unfinished President's House. There he was warmly welcomed by President Adams, a plump little man. Opening John Jay's letter, the president learned that the ex-chief justice would not return to the office.

The position lacks "weight and dignity," wrote Mr. Jay.

Whom would he name now? Suddenly President Adams looked straight at John Marshall. Then he said:

"I believe I must nominate you."

Mr. Marshall felt a shock of surprise. The two men had never talked about this possibility.

"I was pleased as well as surprised," John Marshall wrote later.

President Adams was also pleased. Long afterward he said, "My gift of John Marshall to the people of the United States was the proudest act of my life."

Now the president sent Mr. Marshall's name to the United States Senate. The Senate must approve each person the president chooses to be a justice, or judge, of the Supreme Court.

The Supreme Court is the highest law court in the land. It was created by the Constitution, the nation's written plan of government. The Constitution says that only two kinds of lawsuits may begin in the Supreme Court. They are lawsuits between states, and those to do with foreign ambassadors. All others come to the Supreme Court after being first argued in lower courts.

The Constitution left it to Congress to set up lower national, or federal, courts. The First Congress did that in 1789. It set up district courts, one or more in each state. In addition Congress divided the country into a number of circuits, or sections, and provided for circuit courts. This is the middle level of the national court system today. Alone at the top is the Supreme Court.

The national courts may take cases between citizens of different states and they may take cases growing out of laws that Congress makes for the whole nation. Some important cases work their way up to the Supreme Court. It decides whether lower courts have settled them correctly. It has the final say in this.

However, not many cases came before the Supreme Court in its beginning years. By 1801 the Court still had little business. The members met together only a few weeks every year.

John Marshall in the robes of his office

The Supreme Court was head of one of the three great branches of the new national government. Yet the judicial branch, or courts, did not play nearly so important a role as the other two branches—Congress and the president. For the Supreme Court lacked power.

This had to be changed, John Marshall felt, as he waited to learn if the Senate would accept him as chief justice. He believed that the Court must grow more powerful. Only then could it take an important part in running the country.

John Marshall was born in a log cabin in Virginia. He had little classroom schooling of any kind but he had a fine mind and liked to read. During the Revolution he fought to free his beloved country from England. Later he served in Congress. By 1801 he was known as one of the country's leaders.

The last week in January that year, John Marshall

received good news. The Senate had voted to confirm him as the fourth chief justice of the Supreme Court.

Soon, in early February, the Court opened. That was the first time it had met in Washington, D.C. The Court then was made up of five justices plus Chief Justice Marshall. They had no courtroom of their own. Although grand plans had been made to house Congress and the president, the Supreme Court had been forgotten. A clerk's room in the beautiful, unfinished capitol building was loaned to the justices.

Before the end of February, Chief Justice Marshall closed the term. There had been no cases for the Supreme Court to decide.

Some days later, on March 4, the chief justice took part in the inauguration of Thomas Jefferson of Virginia as the nation's third president. The ceremony was held in the Senate chamber, which was crowded with Mr. Jefferson's joyful followers. John Adams, bitter over losing the presidential election, was not there. He was rattling along in his carriage toward his home in Massachusetts.

John Marshall faced Thomas Jefferson, who stood straight and tall. As chief justice, one of Mr. Marshall's duties was to have the president repeat the oath of office. This is the promise to support the Constitution.

The two men were distant cousins, yet their ideas about government were very different. With all his heart John Marshall believed there must be a strong national, or central, government to build the new nation.

On the other hand, Thomas Jefferson favored leaving a great deal of power in the state governments. This included the states' own courts. He feared that John Marshall would try to seize too much power for the Supreme Court.

In Washington, the Supreme Court met in a clerk's room in the still unfinished capitol building.

Before very long Chief Justice Marshall found himself in the middle of a quarrel between President Jefferson and a man named William Marbury. Mr. Marbury was one of forty-two men appointed as justices of the peace by President Adams just before leaving office. However, in the last minute rush, the commissions, or signed papers, were not sent to all the men.

President Jefferson believed the new, thinly settled capital area didn't need so many law officials. He had some of the papers held back, including the one for Mr. Marbury.

William Marbury went straight to the Supreme Court and started a lawsuit there, called *Marbury* v. *Madison*. He asked that the Court order the new secretary of state, James Madison, to hand over his paper. Under a law passed by the First Congress, the Supreme Court had the right to take this case.

The case was heard in 1803. William Marbury's

lawyer brought witnesses into the small courtroom to be questioned and he talked a long time, telling the black-robed justices Mr. Marbury's side of things. A lawyer for the other side was present, but he didn't bother to make any argument and Secretary Madison did not even appear. It seemed as if the case would prove to be an unimportant one.

But Chief Justice Marshall had thought the case over most carefully. He saw it could be decided in a way that would add great power to the Court, so he was eager to reach out and seize the opportunity. When the justices talked the case over among themselves, he won all of them to his point of view.

Then the chief justice wrote the Court's opinion. This is the statement that tells what the Court has decided, and why.

Two weeks after the hearing had been held, the justices were back in their small courtroom and Chief Justice Marshall announced their decision. As a result of that decision, the case was to be one of the most important in American history.

This Court cannot order the secretary of state to give William Marbury his commission, the chief justice declared, for the Constitution allows only two kinds of lawsuits to begin in the Supreme Court and this lawsuit is not one of them. Then what about the law that let Mr. Marbury start his case here?

The answer by Chief Justice Marshall was clear: That law is not in keeping with the Constitution. Therefore it is unconstitutional and can no longer be a law.

Now the Constitution does not state, in exact words, that the Supreme Court can rule that a national law is unconstitutional but the Court had the duty of guarding the Constitution, Chief Justice Marshall claimed. Therefore, if the law of the

Constitution and a law passed by Congress did not agree, the Court had to decide in favor of the Constitution.

"It is emphatically the province and duty of the judicial department to say what the law is," wrote John Marshall in this famous opinion.

For the first time, the Court found a law passed by Congress and signed by the president to be unconstitutional. From that day on, this special power of the Supreme Court has been part of our system of government. The court interprets the Constitution. That is, the justices decide what its broad language and general provisions mean. The Court strikes down a law when the justices rule it violates the Constitution. It is this great power that has made the court a mighty force in American life.

With masterly skill Chief Justice John Marshall used the little lawsuit started by William Marbury to win an enormous victory for the Supreme Court.

Read The Supreme Court in America's Story *to find out how the Court has grown and changed in the years following* Marbury v. Madison.

Responding to Literature

1. The Supreme Court is the highest court in the land. Our country has federal, state, and local courts as well. Why does a country need courts?

2. The first sentences of a newspaper article should tell the reader the "who," "what," "where," and "when" of a story. Suppose you were a newspaper reporter in Washington, D.C., when the Supreme Court decided the *Marbury* versus *Madison* case. Make a list of the "who," "what," "where," and "when" of the decision.

3. The United States Constitution created three equal branches of government, the presidency, the Congress, and the Supreme Court. However, the Supreme Court did not have much power until *Marbury* versus *Madison*. Why was the case so important to the role of the Supreme Court?

4. In nonfictional writing, accurate and thorough research is vital. To what sources might the author of *The Supreme Court in America's Story* have turned for information about the history of the Court?

A Fight
to the Finish

The Washington Monument

Mel Boring

Building a monument to George Washington does not seem so incredible; more than two hundred memorials have been named after him. Those in the United States include 1 state, 7 mountains, 8 streams, 9 colleges, 10 lakes, 33 counties, 121 towns and the capital city. Countless statues of Washington stand all over our country, as well as in London, Paris, Rio de Janeiro, Caracas, Tokyo and Budapest. The portrait on the American dollar bill may be the most famous face in the world.

George Washington was said to be first in war, first in peace and first in the hearts of his countrymen. Yet in the building of the Washington Monument, he proved to be last in their pocketbooks. It took a hundred years for Americans to dedicate a national monument to him.

In 1783 the Continental Congress made a unanimous decision to build a monument to Washington. Nothing further was done, however, until Washington died in 1799. United States Congressman John Marshall interrupted Washington's

funeral to remind the American people of this sixteen-year-old unkept promise. He suggested a memorial grave for the first president beneath the Capitol Rotunda. But no one acted on Marshall's—or anyone else's—proposal for the next thirty years.

Meanwhile Washington's relatives could not agree on a place to bury him. His wife, Martha, agreed at first to bury him in Washington, D.C., but Washington's brother, John Augustine Washington, insisted he be buried at Mount Vernon, Virginia, Washington's home. So did Washington's adopted son, George Washington Parke Custis. Martha finally gave in to them, and that is where America's first president is buried.

By 1833 Americans who were weary of Congress's delay on a monument to Washington formed the Washington National Monument Society. John Marshall, who was by then Chief Justice of the United States Supreme Court, was elected president of the society. The society would do what the government could not, or so they thought. As it turned out, they quarreled more than Congress had.

Three years later the society had raised $28,000; not enough to build the monument, but enough for a contest to choose the best design. Architect Robert Mills won with his model of a six-hundred-foot, four-sided tower that tapered to a pyramidal top. The base of this obelisk was a huge temple of Roman design. The society ignored the temple but began raising money for the tower. They estimated its cost at one million dollars.

Three well-known women were appointed to raise the money. They were Dolley Madison and Louisa Quincy Adams, former presidents' wives, and Mrs. Alexander Hamilton, wife of the former treasury secretary. They found their job impossible. In 1837 the country was in a financial slump; people had very little money to give. Congress was not willing to give money, either. At that time one million dollars was over a hundred times what a person could earn in a lifetime.

Ten years later the society had succeeded in collecting $87,000, which was enough to start construction. On the Fourth of July, 1848, the monument's cornerstone was laid. The stone was over thirty-six feet high and weighed 24,500 pounds. It had been hollowed out so that tokens of Washington's times could be placed inside. These included a 1783 penny, a United States flag, a Bible and newspaper clippings covering Washington's death.

Fifteen thousand people attended the cornerstone ceremony. Guests included Washington's son, President James K. Polk and other government officials—among them little-known Congressman Abraham Lincoln—state representatives and many Native Americans. There were speeches, prayers and fireworks—even some unexpected "fireworks" when people fought over chips of the marble cornerstone that were given away as souvenirs.

The society hoped the cornerstone celebration would find enthusiasm for the monument, helping them raise more money. Most Americans had seen drawings of the memorial and liked it. Again, however, the fund raisers were left empty-handed. Why? Probably because the country was still in an economic depression and remained so throughout the 1840s. Another reason might be that though the new generation wanted the monument, they did not want to be the ones to pay for it. It is not uncommon for people to feel this way.

From 1848 to 1854 the Washington National Monument Society managed to collect $300,000 and the first 152 feet of the 600-foot tower were built.

Pure white marble covered an inside wall of granite. The marble blocks were about 2 feet high, 1½ feet thick, and varied in width from 1 to 3 feet. The marble and granite walls were 15 feet thick at the base. In 1855 Congress pledged $200,000 toward the monument so that the building could continue. Construction was going smoothly. Then that same year there was a strange turn of events.

A secret society had formed whose members were prejudiced against "foreigners" as well as Catholics and the Catholic Church. These people, who called themselves the American Party, set out to destroy the monument because foreign countries and the Catholic Church had donated to it.

Through lying and trickery, the Know-Nothings, as other people called them, took control of the monument society in 1855. Over the next three years they raised a mere $285.09 and added four feet of construction to the tower. They used a poorer grade of marble, spoiling the appearance of the monument. The American people were outraged; and Congress withdrew its $200,000.

When the Know-Nothings were ousted and some of the original members of the monument society regained control in 1858, the cheap stone had to be removed. One fifty-foot pole-and-rope hoist was missing and another was broken. With inadequate equipment and no money, construction stopped. It had been seventy-five years since the idea of the monument was born, and only one-fourth of it was finished. For the next twenty-one years, no further work was done.

Part of the reason for this new delay was the Civil War. In those dark years cows, sheep and pigs—raised to feed the Union Army troops—grazed at the foot of the monument. Author Mark Twain saw the jagged obelisk and called it "a factory chimney with

The foundation was enlarged in the 1870s.

Stones are raised by chain-and-pulley crane.

the top broken off." After the war ended in 1865, the monument society had even greater difficulty collecting money.

In 1876, during the nation's hundredth anniversary, the society gave the job of building the monument back to the United States government. Congress, in a patriotic mood, again voted $200,000 to finish the construction. A completion date was set for October 19, 1881, one hundred years after General Cornwallis surrendered to George Washington in the Revolutionary War.

The squabbling was far from over, however. People now argued that the monument should be modernized. They claimed the old foundation wouldn't hold up the six-hundred-foot tower. So the Army Corps of Engineers widened and deepened the foundation. It now runs fifty-seven feet below the tower floor and is solid enough to enable the tower to withstand 145-mile-an-hour winds.

Other people fought to make the tower shorter so that it would be more stable. This argument ended when the United States ambassador to Italy learned that the proper dimensions of an obelisk called for its height to be ten times its width. Since it was 55 feet wide, the height was cut from 600 to 555 feet.

monument
ed, as Mark
ain once said, like
actory chimney
the top broken
during the Civil

THE CITY OF WASHINGTON.

View from the Potomac River looking north

One final construction problem left its mark on the monument itself. When construction resumed in 1879, engineers had trouble matching new marble with the old on the outside. They found and used marble that looked the same shade as the older marble. Years later the upper marble began to darken. That's why there's a ring around the Washington Monument, 152 feet up, to this day.

The 1881 deadline was long past when in December, 1884, the capstone was finally placed on the monument. It had a notch five inches wide at the top. This was to hold in place the nine-inch-high aluminum tip of the tower. It was the largest piece of aluminum ever cast, weighing one hundred ounces. On December 6, 1884, six officials climbed to the top to set the aluminum point in place.

With flags flapping in high winds, guns saluting and the crowd's shouts blown away on the wind, the monument was completed. Dedicated on Washington's birthday in 1885, the monument did not open to the public until 1888 because of unfinished interior work. The government had paid three-fourths of the total $1,187,710.31 it had cost.

Some twenty-three thousand stones were cemented together to make the monument. Weighing

187

about 150 million pounds, it sways ever so slightly in a strong wind. At noon in summer, when the sun heats the south face, the stone expands and bends the tip of the monument northward a few hundredths of an inch.

From windows at the top of the tower, visitors—one and a half million every year—can see the White House, the Capitol Building, the Potomac River and Arlington Cemetery. On the granite blocks that line the inside, they can read the inscriptions of those who donated stones. The state of Virginia's stone, given around 1850, says: "Virginia Who Gave Washington to America Gives this Granite." For more than half a century after it was built, the Washington Monument was the tallest stone structure in the world. Today it ranks second. (The tallest is the tower commemorating the battle of San Jacinto, near Houston, Texas, at 570 feet.)

At the cornerstone-laying ceremony on July 4, 1848, Robert C. Winthrop, Speaker of the United States House of Representatives, prolonged the ceremony in the hot summer sun. Winthrop ended his ninety-minute speech by saying that in the future people everywhere would prolong the fame of George Washington. Ironically, people had certainly prolonged the building of a monument to him.

The Washington Monument capstone was set in place in 1884, as shown in this engraving.

Responding to Literature

1. "A Fight to the Finish: The Washington Monument" has dozens of facts and figures. Do you think these facts and figures make the selection more interesting than it would be without them? Tell why.

2. If you were trying to convince your fellow representatives to Congress to budget money for a monument to George Washington, what arguments would you use?

3. Suppose you were writing a short brochure for tourists who visit the Washington Monument. What information would you include about the monument and its history?

4. What were some reasons the Washington National Monument Society had so much trouble raising funds to build the memorial?

5. Why do you think the Washington Monument is one of the most visited memorials in Washington, D.C.?

Lincoln Monument: Washington

Let's go see old Abe
Sitting in the marble and the moonlight,
Sitting lonely in the marble and the moonlight,
Quiet for ten thousand centuries, old Abe.
Quiet for a million, million years.

Quiet—

And yet a voice forever
Against the
Timeless walls
Of time—
Old Abe.

Langston Hughes

Meet the Poet: **Langston Hughes**

Langston Hughes had a varied, adventurous, and productive life. He wrote poems, short stories, books for children, plays, newspaper columns, biographies and autobiographies, and radio and television scripts. He compiled anthologies, translated the works of other poets, organized theater groups, and traveled to many countries. Hughes is, however, best known as a poet, and his influence remains strong today, more than twenty years after his death.

Hughes's career as a poet began when his classmates chose him to write a poem for graduation.

"The day I was elected, I went home and wondered what I should write . . . In the first half of the poem, I said that our school had the finest teachers there ever were. And in the latter half, I said our class was the greatest class ever graduated. So at graduation, when I read the poem, naturally everybody applauded loudly.

"That was the way I began to write poetry."

Auks, Rocks and the Odd Dinosaur

*Inside Stories from the
Smithsonian's Museum of Natural History*

Peggy Thomson

The great auk is scruffy of feather. The bull
mummy from Egypt has something not quite right
about its interior. So does the pickled rift worm. The
Hope diamond has a cops-and-robbers past. It's not
perfect either. And the tail of the flesh-eating
dinosaur *Antrodemus* does not match the body, for
good reason.

Bird, bull, worm, gem, dinosaur—they are treasures
of the National Museum of Natural History. The
diamond is worth a fortune, but then so are the
others, though they are rag and skin and bone. While
some are very plain to look at, they become special as
their inside stories are known.

You may meet them all face to face in Washington,
D.C., where Natural History, as part of the Smithsonian Institution, stands next door to American
History and catty-cornered to Air and Space. Or you
may meet them, along with other special objects, in
the pages of this book.

In the museum you'll find the great auk and the
rest scattered through the exhibit halls upstairs and
down. Most are behind glass. Some, like the Indian
tiger, stand free where they need vacuum cleaning
and an eyeballs wash.

A few, like the buffalo hair balls, are on view where
they can be handled. "Stumpers" such as these are

intended to puzzle, which is why they appear with question marks and invitations to touch. At least one stumper also stumped the scientists, who thought a lumpy rock was a fossilized dinosaur dropping. Then they learned it was not.

If you seek out each of these objects on foot, you will meet guards and guard dogs on patrol, and you will walk more than two miles.

Guards, ever on the lookout, say they see three types of visitors. They see Commuters, who rush in one door and out another, using the museum for a shortcut; Cruisers, who dip in and out of halls, drifting; and Very much Interested People, who head straight for Dinosaurs or the Insect Zoo or Gems. The VIPs, though they become sidetracked like anyone else, seem to have a plan, and some of them cover exhibits inch by inch.

The museum serves everyone. But mostly it serves science. It does so by collecting and by scrutinizing all that it collects—birds, beasts, rocks, bugs, plants, fish and not only these, but the tools and clothes of primitive peoples, their vocabularies, their dreams and myths. The museum gathers them, studies them, saves them, shows them. For the history of the planet and its inhabitants is read from these bones and tools just as information is read from books.

One man—Spencer Fullerton Baird—began the museum's collecting. When he was hired in 1850 as the Smithsonian's assistant head (there wasn't then, or for many years to come, a separate natural history museum), he brought along his own natural history collection. It was the best in the country, containing birds of 500 species, mammals, reptiles, fishes in great numbers and fossil bones. It filled two railroad boxcars. Some of it Baird had gathered as a boy on country bird walks with an older brother. He'd gathered more as a youth, by this time walking alone, whistling tunes and reciting poetry to entertain himself. In the year he was 19, he'd covered 2,100 miles sometimes 40 or 50 in a day, and he wore out three sets of soles to his boots.

There wasn't then a formal training program in natural history, so Baird studied medicine for a year. Mostly he learned by observation and reading and teaching. (He taught his pupils outdoors, on field trips.) He also learned by corresponding with experienced naturalists. A letter he wrote about a flycatcher to bird painter James Audubon won him a lifetime tutor and friend, who replied that Baird had an "old head" on a boy's shoulders. When Baird later wanted a letter of "flaming recommendation" to get a museum job in Washington, Audubon was glad to write it.

S. F. Baird

Even heartily recommended, Baird did not get the job for four more years, not until he was 27. When he did (and brought along his boxcars of skins and bones), he proved himself a demon worker. He made order out of the mountains of crates and bales and barrels inherited from the United States Exploring Expedition, and he said he was ready for more. At that time the U.S. Government was sending numbers of exploring parties to patrol borders, and to survey, to plot railroad routes across the Rocky Mountains and to build wagon roads. Baird, seeing the great possibilities, trained many of the travelers—army doctors and soldiers—to collect for him along with their other duties. They carried collecting equipment in their packs. They pressed plants and skinned specimens by campfires, shipping things back when they could.

In addition, Baird sent out his own people, who enlisted still others—trappers and traders and missionaries, even lighthouse keepers, who provided him with whales. He had a whole network. One of his

part of vast study collections
not seen by the public

men said there was not a schoolboy with a talent for fishing or finding nests whom Baird didn't know and encourage.

Baird equipped his collectors from Washington. He sent them kegs of alcohol and ammunition, fish-collecting trunks, sieves, insect pins and advice: how to stitch extra pockets to jackets, how to pickle a skin and how to pack eggs in twists of paper, not in moss. "Try hard for salamanders," he urged in a letter, "some in water, some on land, under logs." He added, "I won't give much for a live ostrich, but will give a bottle of first rate Scuppernong wine . . . for his skeleton."

To all, without a typewriter, without a secretary, he wrote long, cheering, newsy letters. One young collector replied that Baird's letters made him "feel strong in the backbone." Baird also never forgot to describe his excitement on opening the packets from the field. He named new species after their faraway finders. And the finders named new species—some 40—for him, among them a Baird's tapir, a Baird's octopus, a Baird's dolphin and a Baird's sandpiper.

Audubon gave the name to a Baird's sparrow.

Some of the young collectors Baird put to work in Washington. They had a club called the Megatherium Club, which held oyster roasts and had special yells. They gathered at Baird's house, invited by Mrs. Baird, who won her husband's affection with the fine labels she wrote for his specimens. In snatches of time from other museum duties Baird wrote huge volumes on the birds, fishes, snakes and mammals of North America. When he wrote at home, he kept a small barrel of reptiles by his desk for his little daughter Lucy to play with.

In the Baird years the collections began their rapid growth—to 2 million things at the time of his death, to 68 million now. Collections grow as natural history collections have to grow. For one single animal does not tell the story of its species. Whether it's a rhinoceros or a shellfish the size of a speck of dust, examples are needed of male, female and young; from times past and present; from this locality, from that; collected in winter, in spring, in sickness, in health.

Collections also grow because scientists, who are everywhere, diving, digging, chipping, scanning, keep finding new and different things. Beyond the 26 million insects at hand, they net new and different insects in the canopies of trees. They scoop them from the dew in tire treads, pick them off snowfields and cactuses.

In similar ways vast numbers of new things are gathered up, not out of greediness, but from a need to fill in gaps and chinks. In Baird's day the rush was on to collect everything. Now there's still a rush, for species go extinct. But there's a lid on collecting. Restraint comes from the danger of depleting supplies in nature and from the awful problems of storage and care. Scientists admit they still *want* everything, but they are agonizingly selective about what they take.

The objects on exhibit are a tiny fraction of the collections. Even the visitors who look at everything and think they've seen the museum haven't really seen it. They've seen the *exhibits*. Some things are too fragile to go out on view, and some are needed for study.

Visitors don't see the scientists at work. That part of the museum is out of sight, where people are decoding the patterns in minerals and photographing ticks' tongues and where one person is recording frog jumps while another is testing the breaks in mastodon bones. Were the bones broken by the trampling of other animals or by ancient peoples, getting at marrow for food? It makes a difference for dating when human beings first came to North America.

Except for the coral reef, which has windows into its lab, the labs are closed to the public. So is the huge new $50-million "closet," a storage complex out beyond the city limits where totem poles and bamboos get just the temperature and humidity they need.

Visitors see a sample of the whole, just as the items in this book are a sampling of the exhibits. Meet these scraps and pieces close up—the great auk, precious rocks, *Antrodemus* and the rest. Learn their inside stories and some information and gossip you will not find on their labels.

Responding to Literature

1. Though all three selections in this section are nonfiction, each is about a different topic and each author writes differently. Which of the selections did you enjoy reading most? Why?

2. Why are the Supreme Court, Washington Monument, and Natural History Museum important to the history and culture of the United States?

3. If you were giving a short speech about the early years of the Natural History Museum, what information would you include?

4. There were no college programs in natural science in Spencer Baird's day, but Baird became a famous naturalist. How did he learn his field?

5. Is the Natural History Museum intended primarily to entertain and educate visitors or to advance scientific research? Give reasons for your answer.

Appreciating Author's Craft

Thinking About Tone in Nonfiction

The purpose of nonfiction, whether it be a newspaper article, a how-to book, or an essay, is to present facts and show how these facts lead to ideas, or concepts. A writer of nonfiction first researches the subject. Helen Stone Peterson, the author of *The Supreme Court in America's Story*, probably read court records, newspaper accounts, and letters, among other sources, to get the facts she needed for her book.

The author then organizes the material to present key facts in a way that is easy to follow, supports the author's ideas about the subject, and expresses the tone the author chooses. In this excerpt author Peterson gives facts and draws a conclusion from them using a matter-of-fact, respectful tone.

> The Supreme Court was head of one of the three great branches of the new national government. Yet the judicial branch, or courts, did not play nearly so important a role as the other two branches—Congress and the president. For the Supreme Court lacked power.

Writing Nonfiction

You have read about three fascinating landmarks located in our nation's capital. How could you persuade someone to visit Washington, D.C., to see these landmarks? You could write a kind of nonfiction—a persuasive paragraph. (For more ideas about writing, look at your Writer's Handbook.)

Prewriting Add a fact about the Supreme Court, the Washington Monument, and the Natural History Museum and tell why that fact might persuade someone to visit the landmark.

Fact	*Reason to Visit*
The Supreme Court was located in the unfinished Capitol.	Find out where the Supreme Court is now located.
The Know-Nothings added a poor grade of marble to the Washington Monument.	Find out if all the marble in the Washington Monument matches.
"Stumpers" at the Museum of Natural History are intended to puzzle visitors.	Figure out what the "stumpers" are.

Writing Before you begin writing a paragraph persuading people to visit Washington, D.C., review the facts and reasons to visit on the chart. Begin with a topic sentence that states the opinion that people should visit Washington, D.C. Then tell why you have this opinion. Use the facts and reasons from the chart to back up your opinion.

Revising Read your draft to a partner. Ask your partner if the facts and reasons in your paragraph back up your opinion. Eliminate any facts that do not support your opinion expressed in the topic sentence. Then revise your draft so that all the facts support your opinion. Proofread for errors. Finally, write your final copy.

Presenting Ask a group of people how many would like to visit or revisit Washington, D.C. Then read your persuasive paragraph. See if any people changed their minds about visiting Washington based on the facts in your paragraph.

Extending Your Reading

Expressing Yourself
Choose one or more of these activities:

Locate the Landmarks Find the Supreme Court, the Washington Monument, and the Natural History Museum on a map of Washington, D.C. Gather post cards and photographs of these landmarks and display them with the map.

Collect Stamps Find postage stamps that show the Supreme Court, the Washington Monument, the Smithsonian Institution, and people who were important to their development such as Spencer Baird and John Marshall. Label and display the stamps.

Try a Case Create a court in your school or classroom. Decide upon a school issue. Choose "judges" to hear the case and "lawyers" to argue both sides.

Build a Model of the Washington Monument Following the formula used to build the Washington Monument (the height is ten times the width at the bottom), build a model of the memorial.

Design Your Own Monument Choose a famous person you would like to honor. Draw plans for a suitable memorial to the person.

Start a Natural History Museum Encourage classmates to bring in items they have collected such as rocks, shells, or insects. Label the items and display them attractively. Invite another classroom to visit your museum.

More Books About Our Nation's Capital

White House Sportsmen by Edmund Lindop and Joseph Jares. Houghton, Mifflin Company. If you've ever wondered what presidents do during their less serious moments, this book will help satisfy your curiosity. Each chapter is filled with tidbits about sportsmen presidents from Abraham Lincoln, a renowned wrestler, to John F. Kennedy, a great all-round sportsman.

The Burning of Washington August 1814 by Mary Kay Phelan. Crowell Junior Books. The author takes us back as "eye witnesses" to a sorrowful and dramatic time in the history of our nation's capital—the destruction of Washington, D.C., by the British in 1814.

Me and Willie and Pa: The Story of Abraham Lincoln and His Son Tad by F. N. Monjo. Simon and Shuster. Tad Lincoln, the president's favorite son, tells stories about his brother Willie, his father's election, the Civil War, and many other subjects as if he were talking to close friends.

The Enormous Egg by Oliver Butterworth. Atlantic Monthly Press. What would you do if you owned an egg that hatched into a triceratops? Nate Twitchell finds himself in precisely that predicament. Nate visits Washington, D.C., so scientists can examine his pet, and he and the baby dinosaur become involved in some hilarious events.

Women in the White House: Four First Ladies by Bennett Wayne. Garrard Publishing Company. If you read this book, you will have a clear picture of the lines of four interesting and colorful first ladies, Martha Washington, Abigail Adams, Dolley Madison, and Mary Todd Lincoln.

The Wise and Clever Maiden

by Helen A. Murphy
Illustrated by David Small

Introducing

The Wise and Clever Maiden

A young king, though heralded by his lords and ladies as wise and good, relies on advisers to make decisions for him. When a witty and beautiful peasant maiden storms into his court with a problem, however, her dispute prompts the king to make a decision by himself. The maiden's response to his judgment is courageous and clever. Who will win the war of wits between the maiden and the king?

Plays as Literature

Helen A. Murphy's *The Wise and Clever Maiden* is a play, one of the oldest and most popular kinds of literature. Plays may have first developed from religious celebrations, rites, or storytelling traditions. Murphy's play includes a folk tale. (For more information, look up *Folk tale* in your Handbook.)

Plays are different from other kinds of literature such as novels. Novels rely on dialogue and narrative and are complete in printed form. The reader's imagination pictures the characters and fills in the details not included in the text. Plays, unlike novels, are not complete until they are

performed, when the audience sees the actors and hears their voices. Dialogue (what the characters say) and action, not description, tell the story.

Thinking About Character Conflict and Plot

The plot of a play unfolds through dialogue. Usually a conflict develops between characters and creates some sort of problem. The audience wonders how the conflict, the struggle between the characters, will be settled. The more the audience cares about the characters, the more it cares how the conflict is settled. A good playwright uses the first part of a play to create a believable and interesting conflict. The rest of the play provides an entertaining and instructive ending to that conflict.

As you're reading the play on your own, find out how the agreement the maiden strikes with the king changes the fate of both characters.

The Wise and Clever Maiden

Characters

THE YOUNG KING	INNKEEPER
THE PRIME MINISTER	APPRENTICE
THE CHIEF MAGISTRATE	FARMER
THE MAIDEN	LORDS AND LADIES

2 GUARDS

Before Rise: *Two* GUARDS *enter in front of curtain.*

1ST GUARD *(Chanting in the manner of a herald)*: The King holds court! Silence, all. The King holds court!

2ND GUARD *(Also chanting)*: The King holds court! Silence, all. The King holds court.

1ST GUARD: The wise and good young King gives justice to all.

2ND GUARD *(In confidential manner)*: He does it very well, too, for such a young king.

1ST GUARD: Very well indeed, with the help of the Prime Minister and the fussy Magistrate. Do you think the trials are going to last much longer?

2ND GUARD: They've been going for hours and hours and hours. Let's go into the courtroom. They must have come almost to the end by now. *(They exit.)*

Scene 1

SETTING: *A room in a palace.*

AT RISE: *The* INNKEEPER *and his* APPRENTICE *are standing before the* YOUNG KING, *the* PRIME MINISTER *and the* MAGISTRATE.

The COURTIERS *stand about.* GUARDS *stand by the door. At one side of room stands a group of peasants. The* INNKEEPER *is almost worn out with arguing and he is very angry.*

INNKEEPER: That's all I have to say about it, Young King, so there.

APPRENTICE: It's not all I have to say about it. I've slaved at the Inn for seven long years—that's the length of my apprenticeship. Now I want to go home to my own village and open my own little inn, and I'm refused my wages. He won't give me my apprentice wages.

INNKEEPER: He never earned apprentice wages. He hardly stirred his stumps these last seven years. He slept under the chestnut trees all summer, and beside the fire all winter, and when travellers came to the inn they had to stable their horses themselves! And eat! Why he would eat more in one hour than my guests would in a day! I had to lock my stores away to keep anything safe at all.

APPRENTICE: He had to lock his stores away! Why, your Majesty, there never were any stores to lock away. He would wait for travellers and then send me to the farmers' yards to steal anything I could find to make a meal of.

MAGISTRATE: Silence! This is the court. You are in the presence of the Young King! *(The* INNKEEPER *and the* APPRENTICE *glare at each other as the guards hold them at either end of the table. The* PRIME MINISTER *and* MAGISTRATE *whisper to the* YOUNG KING, *who rises to give the verdict. He thinks he looks more important standing up. The court must rise with him.)*

YOUNG KING: Hear my verdict, and obey to the letter. You, lazy Apprentice, leave with us a reckoning of how much you think the Innkeeper owes you for your work. You, Innkeeper, make a reckoning of how much the Apprentice owes you for food above and over his just due. They'll be about the same, I should judge. Then, in six months, come back for my final decision. In the meantime—*(He seems to forget what he should say and the advisors whisper to him again.)* Oh, yes, in the meantime carry out these orders. Apprentice, see to it that you work well doing all the chores you promised to do: carry water, keep the fires burning and the wood cut, wait upon the travellers, and sleep only at night, as we all should. You, Innkeeper, see that this growing lad gets three meals a day. Real meals. He cannot work well if he isn't fed well. Now keep a strict account of your days, and my soldiers will call every week or so to see how things fare with you both. Any complaints, and there'll be regrets when we meet here again, six months from now. *(The **PRIME MINISTER** and the **MAGISTRATE** have been very nervous, but now that the verdict has been given according to their instructions they sigh with relief and turn to the next case. The **INNKEEPER** and the **APPRENTICE** either leave the room or wait by the door to hear the coming case. The **YOUNG KING** turns to receive the expected congratulations from the **LORDS** and **LADIES**. He struts* *up and down in a cocky manner.)* Now how was that for wisdom and justice, my lovely lords and ladies?

COURTIERS: Wonderful, your Majesty, more wonderful every minute.

LORD: You are so wise for one so young.

LADY: Your brain must be marvelous to judge like that.

YOUNG KING: I'm exhausted with the effort. Are there many more cases today?

MAGISTRATE: There's one about two peasants.

YOUNG KING: Oh, my head, my poor head.

COURTIERS: His poor head. The poor Young King! *(There is much confusion and noise off-stage.)*

PRIME MINISTER: Silence! Court is closed!

GUARDS: The court is closed! The court is closed! *(The* **YOUNG KING** *comes downstage to talk with* **COURTIERS.** *The* **GUARDS** *begin to usher out the peasants. The* **PRIME MINISTER** *and* **MAGISTRATE** *argue over details and pick up various documents.)*

YOUNG KING: So you really *do* think me wise and wonderful, my friends?

ALL *(Bowing)*: Yes, your Majesty.

YOUNG KING: And just? You do think me very just?

ALL *(Bowing)*: Yes, indeed, your Majesty.

YOUNG KING: And good? I am a good king, am I not? Do say I am a good king to you all.

LADY *(Bowing)*: Good and good as good can be, your Majesty. *(During this the noise outside grows to a*

disturbance, and the GUARDS *are heard roaring above the din.)*

GUARDS: Stop that noise! There's no more court! *(A stolid* FARMER, *none too bright, pushes past the* GUARDS. *An enchanting, merry and altogether lovely* MAIDEN *pushes him into the room and enters herself, panting, excited and victorious.)*

1ST GUARD: They simply won't get out, your Majesty. They will not go!

PRIME MINISTER: Have you told them court is closed?

2ND GUARD: We've told them all and everything, but still they will not go.

MAIDEN *(Oblivious of the court, pushing through the* COURTIERS *and seeking the* KING*)*: Where is this young king who thinks he can settle everything?

I'm going to see him this very day. Ah, there you are. *(She looks at him, becomes slightly respectful, bows hastily as if the curtsey were a necessary evil, and then continues.)* We've been outside there for hours. I've walked too far this hot dusty day to be sent off without a hearing. You have to hear my case. *(The* **YOUNG KING** *seems interested enough to climb back to his chair, and the court resumes its place.)* Thank you. I'm sorry to trouble you, but you are the King, the servant of the people. Well, I'm sick and tired of my bargains with this lout, this dunce, this—this—well, this! *(She indicates the poor* **FARMER,** *who stands dumbfounded before the court.)*

MAGISTRATE: This is no way to enter the palace. Where is your proper respect? You have heard that the court is closed. You will have to come again on court day next month.

YOUNG KING *(Seeing her disappointment)*: Since we are all in place, let her at least state her case and make her claim. She is right. I am the servant of my people. *(All seem amazed at the* **YOUNG KING***'s sudden independent action.)*

MAGISTRATE: You have heard the Young King. Present your case.

PRIME MINISTER: Stand respectfully before us. Let the man speak first.

FARMER: She won't marry me because she gets the best of the bargain. *(All seem puzzled but the* **MAIDEN,** *who is amused at the blunt speech. She is quite poised and self-possessed.)*

YOUNG KING: Well, that's a funny statement. Explain yourself.

FARMER: You see, it's this way. Our grandfathers left us a little plot of land. We both own it. My farm is on one side of it, and her farm is on the other. But our grandfathers thought it would be nice for only one of us to own it, seeing as how all our people are dead, and there are just the two of us left. So I asked her to marry me, and she said the day the bargain's fair, all right, she'll marry me. But the bargain never is fair.

MAGISTRATE *(To* **KING** *and* **PRIME MINISTER***)*: Really, can you make head or tail out of this?

PRIME MINISTER: There isn't any case in all this rigamarole.

YOUNG KING: I think there is—and a very nice case, too. Let the maiden speak. *(To the girl)* Come, you state the case so that all may understand it.

MAIDEN: It's as he says about us inheriting the strip of land, sirs, but after I was left alone in this world I just thought I'd take my time before I married. The bargain I made with him is very fair. I plant. It's easier for a girl to sow the seed than to pull up heavy loads of vegetables. So I do the planting and he does the harvesting. Then we divide it. That's all. Yet he isn't satisfied.

FARMER: We divide, but listen to how we divide. Go on, tell them.

MAIDEN: The first year I said he could have all that came up above the ground and I'd keep all that came under. That's just what we did.

FARMER: Just what we did! She planted turnips and got them all, and I got the wormy tops. Even my pigs couldn't eat them! *(The court is becoming interested, even slightly amused.)*

MAIDEN: Listen to him fussing! What did I do last year? Planted again. Told him to take all below the ground if it would make him happy.

YOUNG KING *(To FARMER)*: Did it make you happy? *(FARMER shakes his head and seems very miserable.)* Just what did she plant, Farmer?

FARMER: Cabbages. They don't even have roots worth anything. *(The court is now highly amused, to the discomfort of the poor FARMER who doesn't seem to have sense enough to hold his own.)*

PRIME MINISTER *(Thundering at MAIDEN)*: I daresay that this year he takes what is below ground. Answer me!

MAIDEN *(Hardly intimidated, but not too bold)*: Yes, he takes what is below the ground, and again I take what grows on the top. And is he satisfied? No, and no, and no.

MAGISTRATE: And this year you planted?

MAIDEN: Lima beans. *(The court can't help but laugh. Even the advisors join in.)*

FARMER: Laugh if you want to, but it's no joke to me! She'll keep right on planting her own way. It will be potatoes and tomatoes; beets and beans; parsnips and lentils. It will always be her crop, and we'll never be married.

YOUNG KING: If she doesn't want to marry him she is very, very clever. You really don't want to marry him, do you?

MAIDEN: I've thought about it now and then, your Majesty, but I've no mind to settle down with the very first one who knocks at my door. I might take a fancy to apples that grow higher on the tree.

PRIME MINISTER *(Rather upset by the friendly manner of the* **MAIDEN** *and the* **KING***)*: Come, the verdict!

MAGISTRATE: This will bear a bit of thinking over. Come, your Majesty. We must put our heads together.

YOUNG KING: My ancient and good old friends, you may put your own heads together and consult with each other all you please, but I will give this verdict quite unaided. *(All gasp.)* My poor young man, you must go home and forget about this bargain. Marry some other girl, and forget about this trickster. Also I decree that all of the plot of land, and all in it and on it, shall be yours, now and forever. *(All seem amazed.)* No go before she finds some other way to get the better of you.

*(***FARMER***, relieved that the question is settled, goes.)*

PRIME MINISTER: This is terribly out of order. The maiden should have something. You should have consulted us.

YOUNG KING: The maiden is going to have the highest apple on the tree. Lords, look upon the ladies. Beautiful creatures, aren't they?

LORDS: Beautiful beyond description. Works of art. Creations. Noble, beautiful and good, your Majesty.

YOUNG KING: Ladies, you hear? You try to please the Lords?

LADIES: We spend hours before our mirrors. We want to look lovely for them and for you, and for the kingdom.

We wear our brains out thinking of new colors and clothes to please you all. We wash in milk and dress in silk, for we are the ladies of the court.

YOUNG KING: Quite so. Now look upon this maiden. She has bare feet. She has a gay striped country dress of coarse cloth. She probably washes in rain water, and her hair is combed by the wind itself. She has a loveliness such as is never seen in the court.

LADY (Slightly sarcastic): My, my! What a poet the Young King is!

YOUNG KING: Above all, she has brains. She is a wise and clever maiden, and a brave one, too. So, lords and ladies of the court, keep right on looking at each other. You are suited to each other. As for me, I've made up my mind to marry at last, and it shall be none other than this girl who has a mind of her own. Listen, all of you. I proclaim to you that I shall marry this peasant maid. (In the excitement that follows this speech, the MAIDEN moves to center stage and waits for silence. All look at her.)

MAIDEN: So says the Young King, and I thank him for the honor, but listen to this, my lords and ladies of the court. I haven't said I'll marry the King. I haven't said that I'll live here with the milk and silk and the mirrors and all. I like my own ways, and I'm not one to be ordered about by anyone, even the King. You know, and he knows, that I can't be ordered to marry him.
(To KING) You should have asked me first.

YOUNG KING: Again you are wise and clever! But you must stay here. It's been very dull here. I'll not say a word about your marrying, only do stay. Let me ask you to be my Queen at the end of the month. Please stay.

PRIME MINISTER: *(To MAGISTRATE)*: I've never seen him like this before. The girl mustn't stay. We can't have a peasant for a Queen.

MAGISTRATE: It would be better to keep her. He'll soon become annoyed with her country manners and ways. *(To court)* I call this court to attention. I am the Magistrate. I shall pass the verdict myself. The maiden stays in court one month. She will give her answer to the King one month from today in this room before this company.

MAIDEN: Since there's nothing I can do now but stay, I will promise that I'll give my answer after living here in the palace one month. But I want a paper—a written paper with a seal of the court on it—

PRIME MINISTER *(Impatiently)*: For pity's sake, what for?

MAIDEN: I want an agreement—otherwise, I'll just sit glum and dumb for the whole month and say no in the end.

YOUNG KING: Write her the agreement. *(MAGISTRATE takes quill and parchment and writes.)*

MAIDEN: Write this down for all to read. We, the King and the court, do promise that the Maiden may leave the palace if she so chooses at the end of the month. She may stay if she chooses at the end of the month, even if the King changes his mind about her. But if she goes she may take with her anything she wishes.

PRIME MINISTER: We can't set the seal to this. She may take anything or everything.

LORDS AND LADIES *(All speaking together)*: She may take all of our beautiful clothes. She may take the tapestries and silver. She may take our jewels and gold and treasures. The royal liveries and the spears—the horses—there's no telling what she wouldn't take!

MAIDEN: That's my agreement. If it doesn't suit, farewell to my conversation. I'll be speechless for the whole month. Then it will be "Farewell, your Majesty, and do try to forget me!"

YOUNG KING: Sign that paper, and let me put on the seal! *(The paper is signed. The **KING** puts on the seal and gives it to the **MAIDEN**.)*

LADIES: Well, of all the vixens! Put away the curling tongs and get out the dictionaries. Do you see who is going to rule this court?

GUARDS: A wise and clever maiden—*(All stare at **MAIDEN**.)*

CURTAIN

Scene 2

SETTING: *Same as first scene.*

AT RISE: *The **LORDS** and **LADIES** with the **PRIME MINISTER** and **MAGISTRATE** are all standing about talking and laughing and listening to some joke that the **MAIDEN** is telling them. She is now dressed as a princess but yet has retained the merry manner of the peasant that she is. The **YOUNG KING** is absent.*

PRIME MINISTER: What was the answer to the riddle, Maiden?

MAIDEN: Now you don't mean to tell me that you can't guess!

LORD: Oh, do tell us. We never are clever enough to answer your riddles. (*The* **YOUNG KING** *enters. None pay heed to him. He seems unhappy.*)

LADY: Tell us the riddle once more—please do!

MAIDEN: This is the last time, so listen carefully. It seems that a cuckoo-bird stole into a robin's nest, and laid her eggs there for the robin to take care of. When the eggs were hatched, the cuckoo-bird came back and said—

YOUNG KING (*In a rage*): We are not interested in birds and nests. This is the court! (*All look up but pay little heed to the dignity of the court as they take their places.*)

MAGISTRATE: Call the court to order!

GUARDS: The King holds court! Silence. The King holds court!

PRIME MINISTER: Now then, Lords and Ladies of the court, we are here to listen to the Maiden's decision. She has spent a month with us.

LORD: Such a month! Such fun!

LADY: The whole palace is changed. It's so much merrier.

PRIME MINISTER: That is true. I have been looking up the lineage of our Maiden, and I find that she is really of a very noble family, so I see no reason to object to her accepting our Young King's hand. So come, your Majesty, ask your question quickly. Merely a matter of form, you understand, because of our agreement.

YOUNG KING: Look how they crowd about her, smile at her. They want her to stay whether I do or not. Well, Maiden, today we are about to ask you whether or not you would stay here, and—(*He hesitates.*)

LADY: Of course she'll stay. Won't you, Maiden? Tell her to stay.

MAIDEN: You forget. You do not tell me to stay. I make up my own mind about that. Remember the bargain? I come and go as I please. Remember the bargain? I accept you or not as I please. Remember the bargain? Then, I have made up my mind. I am going to stay, and I am going to marry the Young King— maybe— *(All crowd about her again. The* YOUNG KING *is sulky.)*

YOUNG KING *(To himself)*: Look how they hang upon every word. I might as well be a slave or a statue for all they ever see me or listen to me. Well, I'm going into the garden. *(He leaves the room quietly and seen by none save the* MAIDEN. *She has been watching him while talking to others.)*

MAIDEN: Go with your King. It will be cooler in the garden. *(All exit but the* PRIME MINISTER.*)*

PRIME MINISTER: What do you suppose is the matter with the King?

MAIDEN: That's a simple riddle to answer. He's unhappy because people have stopped calling him clever and wonderful. He wants to be praised for the things you think of for him. He wants to order us all about and he wants us to like being ordered.

PRIME MINISTER: He *is* the King, you know.

MAIDEN: Yes, I know. *(She sighs.)* I know. Poor, spoiled King, who can't answer his own questions without making a fuss about it! Now look at him out there in the garden, moving away from the poor little court ladies just because they aren't all bowing and scraping to him any more! *(*YOUNG KING *enters.)*

YOUNG KING: Why are you here? Why don't you go into the garden with the others?

MAIDEN: I find it warm outside.

YOUNG KING: Warm! Do you forget how warm it used to be on your hillside where you planted cabbages and carrots? Aren't you forgetting a great deal these last few days? You are even forgetting who I am. You think I'm just nothing at all. The whole court will soon forget I am their King. When you speak, they gasp. When you smile, they laugh. When you sigh, they weep. They are like waves that come and go with the moon—and you are the moon! You might as well know the truth. I'm tired of the whole thing.

MAIDEN: I thought you would be tired of it, long before this. But a bargain is a bargain, and the day isn't over until sunset, so let's keep it until—

YOUNG KING: You and your bargains! Your everlasting bargains! *(He exits and the* **MAIDEN** *watches, truly sad and troubled.)*

MAIDEN: Poor Young King! Will he never understand? He can't bear to have others admired. He is sick and miserable because the stupid court no longer flatters him. Sir, I think I'll go back to my hillside. It's much fairer and lovelier there. Then things can be as they were before I came. I didn't mean to upset everything.

PRIME MINISTER: *(Trying to comfort her as she sinks into the* **KING'S** *chair and begins to cry)*: You are a very fortunate maiden to have that sunny hillside. Remember that the King has to be here, whether he likes it or not. I know he is going to find it very dull after you have gone. The whole court will keep asking for you, you know. They have all grown very fond of you, my clever little maiden.

MAIDEN: I'll leave this court before sunset, and I'll go as I came too—in my own clothes—and I'll take what I want when I go, too.

PRIME MINISTER: What will that be?

MAIDEN: Arrange to have the carriage and the horses outside as soon as possible. Meet me by the throne room and I'll tell you what to prepare for me to take. *(PRIME MINISTER exits. MAIDEN sings.)*

Oh, who will ever my true friend be,
Whether I will or no?
And who will travel the roads with me,
And go wherever I go?

(YOUNG KING and MAGISTRATE enter.)

YOUNG KING: I don't know who he will be, but I wish him luck when he follows you, poor thing.

MAIDEN: Yes, sir. Of course, sir, quite right. *(She bows out in mock respect, leaving* **YOUNG KING** *furious.* **MAGISTRATE** *listens to her as she passes him and whispers to him. Then he signals* **GUARDS** *to follow her.)*

YOUNG KING: What did she say to you? What does she want?

MAGISTRATE: She asked me to help her to get ready the things she wants to take. I sent the guards to help her.

YOUNG KING: For once in my life I gave my own verdict myself. Look at the trouble I've caused. I'll listen to you and the Prime Minister at all times from now on, sir, for I never want another mistake like this one! Conceited thing with her witty mind!

MAGISTRATE: I was wrong about your verdict. It really was a very good one. I think it high time you made more decisions yourself, my King. *(Enter* **GUARDS** *who are carrying a tray of food which they place upon the table.)* What's the meaning of this? Since when have we eaten in this room and at this hour?

1ST GUARD: The Maiden, sir.

2ND GUARD: She ordered it, sir.

MAGISTRATE: She is going too far indeed! I'll speak to her about this. *(He leaves by one door as* **MAIDEN** *enters the other. She is dressed as she was in the first scene. The* **PRIME MINISTER** *is with her.)*

MAIDEN: My things are all ready, you see. I'm going as I came, old dress and all. Don't be sad any more. I'm going even before sunset.

YOUNG KING *(Lamely)*: I'm sorry that it didn't all come out right. Of course, it's going to be quite quiet about the court, but I must say you were very clever to ask me to wait this month before making a decision.

PRIME MINISTER: It will seem very quiet and dull indeed.

MAIDEN: But, oh, so peaceful. I'll be peaceful, too, up on the hillside in my little cottage. It's very nice there. The sounds of birds, and the brook, and the wind in the grove will be restful after the chatter of the court. And there'll be no stuffy dresses, either—and no silly shoes!

YOUNG KING: I guess it's best to say farewell and have done with it.

MAIDEN: Quite the best. I can't say I'm altogether happy about having done with it, as you say, but we'll part friends anyway. And on that, let's have this small supper together. I would like something to eat before taking the long climb up the hill. Come and break bread with me, as we peasants say among ourselves.

PRIME MINISTER: Yes, come, your Majesty, and part company at a feast. The Maiden wishes to go before the Lords and Ladies return.

YOUNG KING: I'll take a little wine, then, and a cake.

MAIDEN: Not cake and wine, your Majesty, but a goblet of fine goats' milk and a piece of cheese, and a slice of country brown bread, for I've a longer walk than cake and wine will carry me on. *(In silence the* **GUARDS** *wait upon them and the three eat, evidently absorbed in the parting. The* **GUARDS** *alone seem restless, as though waiting for some kind of signal.)*

YOUNG KING: This really tastes wonderful, Maiden. You know, you might come and visit me sometimes.

MAIDEN: Better to have you come up the hillside and see my kingdom from my doorsill. Better come up for more milk and cheese, and honey, too. I'll say a little charm so you'll have to come! You must close your eyes and drink this milk whilst I say it. It's a way the peasants have when they want their guests to come to them. *(The* **KING** *closes his eyes. The* **PRIME MINISTER** *hands the* **MAIDEN** *a paper of powder which she drops into the milk and then she hands the goblet to the* **KING.***)*
You must ever my true friend be,
Whether you will or no,
With a hearty welcome when you come
And a Godspeed when you go.

YOUNG KING: I like that. Say it again. You must my true friend be. What comes next? *(As* **MAIDEN** *speaks, the* **YOUNG KING** *falls over on table in sleep. The* **GUARDS** *and* **PRIME MINISTER** *watch closely.)*

MAIDEN: You must ever my true friend be
Whether you will or no,
With a hearty welcome—quick, the ropes! When you come—tie him up and get him out of here. And a Godspeed—there, fine. Now get him to the carriage before anyone sees us. Come on, Prime Minister. You can bring the legal papers and things. *(The* **GUARDS** *start to lift the* **KING** *who is tied up. As they lift him, one of them bumps against him. The milk upsets and some of it splashes on the* **KING***'s face. He stirs and the motion seems to wake him up.)* Oh, he's waking up! He didn't drink much of the milk after all. Whatever will we do now?

PRIME MINISTER *(To **GUARD**)*: You clumsy creature! Now we are in a queer fix. Get those ropes off him. Too late! Let them alone.

YOUNG KING: What's this trouble? Oh, my head! What's this all about? *(Now fully conscious)* I say, what's the meaning of this? Get these ropes off! I'll have you all in dungeons. *(Now aware of the **PRIME MINISTER** and turns to him)* Even you! Call the Magistrate! Call the soldiers!

PRIME MINISTER: No, your Majesty, we'll not call the Magistrate. And you'll not throw us in dungeons. You'll listen to me once more, and then you may pass your own verdicts

forever. Maiden, show him your evidence, clearing you of any crime.

MAIDEN *(Showing parchment)*: See—our written agreement. By your own hand and seal it was promised that I could take with me whatever I wished from the palace.

YOUNG KING: So you tricked me. You would have left me here and then the pack of you would have walked off with the treasures of the palace. Well, go on and take what you have chosen. *(MAIDEN is crying.)* Don't stand there whimpering and sniffling. And all that talk about you must ever my true friend be.

PRIME MINISTER: I must admit that you really *are* quite stupid. Why, the maiden is taking neither treasures nor riches. She is even refusing herself the fun of taking her fine new clothes, and the beautiful horse you gave her. She is taking the only worth-while thing in the palace. She wants only one thing, and she has every right to that one thing, for you yourself gave her that promise. Why do you suppose she tied you up? Why do you suppose she has your carriage waiting outside for you? To take you yourself, you stubborn blind thing. She only wants you!

YOUNG KING *(Looks abashed for a minute and then begins to laugh. The others join in. A few* **COURTIERS** *and the* **MAGISTRATE** *come to the entrances to peek in):* She wanted the only worth-while thing—ha ha! Me! She wants *me*. She's staying with me. Maiden, I'll go to your hillside with you whenever you wish, so long as you become my Queen and always help me give the verdicts. *(***LORDS** *and* **LADIES** *have entered the room during this speech.)*

MAIDEN: I'll stay forever and forever, on one condition.

ALL: And that is?

MAIDEN: That he will sing the answer to the song!

ALL: Oh, who will ever her true friend be
            Whether she will or no?

MAIDEN AND KING:

            It's I will travel the roads with you
            And go wherever you go. *(Quick curtain)*

THE END

Meet the Illustrator: **David Small**

In addition to illustrating dozens of books for other people, David Small has illustrated several books that he has written. Perhaps you have noticed some of his books (*Eulalie and the Hopping Head*, *Imogene's Antlers*, and *Paper John* are three) in a bookstore or library.

Small gets ideas for stories from the drawings he makes in his sketch diaries. He draws constantly—at home, out of doors, in restaurants, even when he is riding in a car. He says, "To be a good artist you must, of course, be able to draw and paint well, but you must also exercise your brain by reading as much as you can. A really good artist develops his or her wits, imagination, and ideas as much as the ability to make pictures."

Small lives with his wife, Sherry Stewart, in a 150-year-old house on a bend of the St. Joseph River in Michigan. Their Airdale named Murphy, two canaries, and hundreds of creatures that live along the riverbank provide endless inspiration for his drawings and stories.

Responding to Literature

1. One reader enjoyed *The Wise and Clever Maiden* because it has many twists and turns in its plot, another because it has a story within a story. Do you agree that these elements make *The Wise and Clever Maiden* interesting? Tell why or why not.

2. Suppose you are the King's record keeper. List five of the most important events that took place after the King met the Maiden.

3. How does the agreement the Maiden strikes with the King change the fate of both characters?

4. Though the Maiden is never in any physical danger, she is considered brave. Why do you think this is?

5. If you were the Maiden, what would you have taken with you at the end of your stay at court? Why?

6. From what you have learned about the Maiden, do you think she will be a good queen?

Rebels from Fairy Tales

We are the frogs who will not turn to princes.
We will not change our green and slippery skin
for one so lily-pale and plain, so smooth
it seems to have no grain. We will not leave
our leap, our spring, accordion. We have
seen ourselves in puddles, and we like
our grin. Men are so up and down, so thin
they look like walking trees. Their knees seem stiff,
and we have seen men shooting hares and deer.
They're queer . . . they even war with one another!
They've stretched too far from earth and natural things
for us to admire. We prefer to lie
close to the water looking at the sky
reflected; contemplating how the sun,
Great Rana, can thrust his yellow, webbed foot
through all the elements in a giant jump;
can poke the bottom of the brook; warm
the stumps for us to sit upon; and heat
our backs. Men have forgotten to relax.
They bring their noisy boxes, and the blare
insults the air. We cannot hear the cheer
of crickets, nor our own dear booming chugs.
Frogs wouldn't ever eat men's legs.
We scorn their warm, dry princesses. We're proud
of our own bug-eyed brides with bouncing strides.
Keep your magic. We are not such fools.
Here is the ball without a claim on it.
We may begin from the same tadpoles, but
we've thought a bit, and will not turn to men.

Hyacinthe Hill

Appreciating Author's Craft

Thinking About Character Conflict and Plot

The plot of a work of fiction often moves forward from a problem to a solution. Often the problem is a conflict, a tension or struggle, between characters.

In *The Wise and Clever Maiden*, the King thinks of himself as a wise, good, and clever ruler. Everyone in his court except his advisors seems to agree. After all, he is king. However, the Maiden clearly shows wisdom and cleverness, too. Does the King think there is room at court for two wise and clever people? A conflict results. The conflict between these characters sets the plot into action, and the rest of the play shows how the conflict is worked out, or resolved. Soon after the maiden's arrival at court, as the passage below indicates, the King becomes upset.

> **YOUNG KING** (*To himself*): Look how they hang upon every word. I might as well be a slave or a statue for all they ever see me or listen to me. . .
>
> **PRIME MINISTER**: What do you suppose is the matter with the King?
>
> **MAIDEN**: That's a simple riddle to answer. He's unhappy because people have stopped calling him clever and wonderful. He wants to be praised for the things you think of for him. He wants to order us all about and he wants us to like being ordered.

Writing About Characters in Conflict

To help you understand the effect of character conflict on the plot of *The Wise and Clever Maiden*, you need to look at the King's and Maiden's actions and the reactions they cause. (For ideas about writing, look at your Writer's Handbook.)

Prewriting The chart on the next page lists actions of the King and the Maiden and how they affect the plot of the play. Copy the chart and add two more actions and reactions for the King and the Maiden.

Character	Action	Reaction
King	Declares he will marry maiden	Maiden resists
Maiden	Makes King sign an agreement	King feels outwitted

Writing Use the chart as an aid to help you write three paragraphs that compare and contrast the King and the Maiden. In the first paragraph, write about the King. Based on his actions and reactions, describe what he is like. In the second paragraph describe what the Maiden is like, based on her actions. Use the third paragraph as a conclusion. State how the King and the Maiden's differences and similarities cause a conflict.

Revising Reread your paragraphs to a partner. Ask the partner if your descriptions of the King and Maiden leave out any important details. Have your partner decide if your concluding paragraph clearly shows what the differences and similarities between the two characters are and why they cause a conflict. Revise your paper as necessary and proofread for errors. Then write your final copy.

Presenting Read your paper to the class. Ask your classmates to suggest other ways the conflict between the King and the Maiden might have been resolved.

Expressing Yourself

Choose one or more of these activities:

Become a Set Designer Design a set for the first scene of *The Wise and Clever Maiden*. Make a drawing of the stage and scenery and list the props needed for the first scene.

Write a Song What if *The Wise and Clever Maiden* were to be rewritten as a musical comedy? Write a song for the play and set it to a tune you like or one you make up.

Send a Letter to an Advice Columnist Pretend you are the king in *The Wise and Clever Maiden*. Write a letter asking for help handling your problem with the maiden. Have a friend take the part of the advice columnist and write a response.

Find Out About Royalty Many countries have kings and queens. Choose a country that has a monarch. Find out what role he or she plays in governing the country and report the results of your research to the class.

Have a Debate Debate the benefits of living at court versus life in the country. Choose the side you wish and have a friend take the other side. The class should listen to the debate and vote to decide which argument is most persuasive.

See the World from a Different Perspective Reread "Rebels from Fairy Tales," a poem told from a unique point of view. Think about how the world would look if you were a frog. Then draw a country scene from a frog's vantage point.

More Books About Courage

The Owlstone Crown by X. J. Kennedy. Bantam Books. Tim and Verity Tibbs's escape from cruel guardians is just the beginning of their trials. They follow a talking ladybug into another world where they must try to rescue their grandparents from the terrible Raoul Owlstone and his army of mechanical stone owls.

The Freedom Side by Marcie Miller Stadelhofen. New Readers Press. Rebecca Horn, a young slave in the pre–Civil War South, is approached one day by a man she does not know. The man explains that he has been sent by Rebecca's father, who escaped to Canada years before, to lead Rebecca to freedom. Rebecca must decide if she should trust this man, leave her friend and risk capture on her way to Canada.

Lou Gehrig: Iron Man of Baseball by Willard and Celia Luce. Garrard Publishing Company. Lou Gehrig was born into a poor family on New York's Lower East Side and died tragically early of a form of polio. Yet he was known for his determination and cheerfulness. This biography of one of baseball's greatest hitters will help readers understand the courageous Gehrig.

The Gift of the Pirate Queen by Patricia Reilly Giff. Dell Publishing Company. Since her mother's death, Grace O'Malley has felt responsible for the well-being of her family. Now Fiona, an Irish cousin, will care for the family. Grace is worried. Will Fiona take over and try to boss everyone? Fiona's visit helps Grace learn about courage and love.

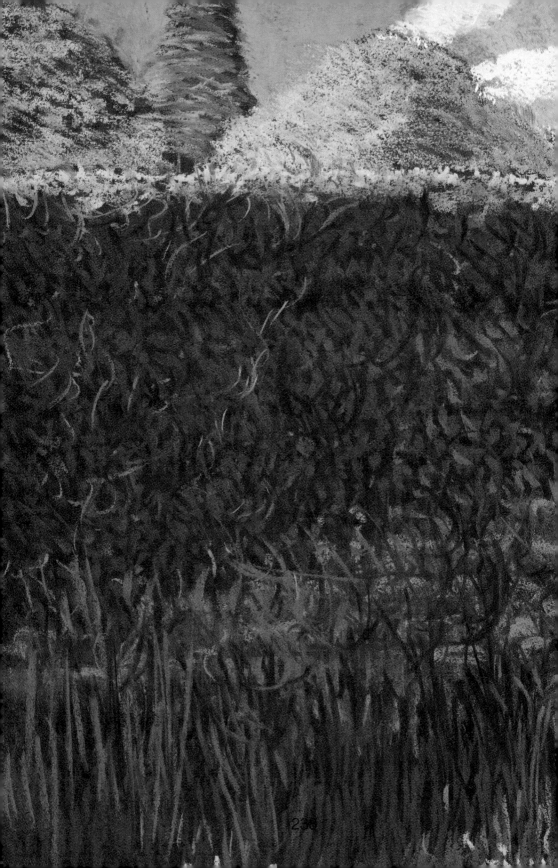

The
Secret
Garden

by Frances Hodgson Burnett

illustrated by Joel Spector

Introducing

The Secret Garden

Mary Lennox is a newcomer to Misselthwaite Manor, a huge and gloomy stone mansion on the moors of Yorkshire. One night as she tries to sleep through a raging storm, mournful crying lures her down Misselthwaite's dark corridors. What she finds is as unexpected and strange as the secret garden she has recently discovered.

The Yorkshire Moors

Frances Hodgson Burnett's novel *The Secret Garden* is set in Yorkshire in northern England. Much of the year the climate in Yorkshire is cold and damp and a fierce wind blows in off the North Sea. In the local dialect, the wind is said to "wuther."

Though Yorkshire is known for its industry and agriculture, it is the bleak beauty of the misty moors that people most closely associate with this part of England. The moors are vast, open rolling lands. Originally forests stood on these lands, but centuries ago the trees were leveled. As a result, the soil and vegetation changed. Now the land is spongy and filled with wet bogs. In the spring the moors are covered by heather, a small purplish flower, and wild grasses. Some parts of the moors are sturdy enough to support grazing sheep. Other parts are marshy hollows. Because of the dampness, the moors are often veiled in a mysterious thick mist.

Thinking About How Setting Influences Character

In literature characters are influenced by the setting, just as in life people are influenced by the environments in which they live. Characters' moods, the challenges they seek, and the joys they discover can often be traced directly to the influence of the setting. Author Burnett begins the excerpt from *The Secret Garden* by describing a stormy spring night that directly influences Mary's mood and actions.

As you're reading the excerpt on your own, decide how Mary's discovery of Colin affects her.

The Secret Garden

Mary Lennox, a sickly, spoiled child who has recently become an orphan, is sent from India to Yorkshire, England, where she is to live with her uncle, Archibald Craven. Mary rarely sees her uncle and is left to wander the immense, gloomy mansion, Misselthwaite Manor, and explore the out-of-doors on her own. Gradually she comes to enjoy the natural beauty of the moors and becomes healthier and more cheerful due partly to the attentions of Martha, the housemaid, and Ben, the gardener. Then Mary discovers a walled garden that has been locked up and forgotten since the death of her uncle's beloved wife ten years before. Mary begins to bring the garden back to life with the help of the housemaid's younger brother, Dickon. Another mystery of Misselthwaite remains unsolved, though. What is the source of the pitiful cries Mary has heard late at night?

"I AM COLIN"

You never know what the weather will do in York-shire, particularly in the springtime. Mary was awakened in the night by the sound of rain beating with heavy drops against her window. It was pouring down in torrents and the wind was "wuthering" round the corners and in the chimneys of the huge old house. Mary sat up in bed and felt miserable and angry.

"The rain is as contrary as I ever was," she said. "It came because it knew I did not want it."

She threw herself back on her pillow and buried her face. She did not cry, but she lay and hated the sound of the heavily beating rain, she hated the wind and its "wuthering." She could not go to sleep again. The mournful sound kept her awake because she felt mournful herself. If she had felt happy it would probably have lulled her to sleep. How it "wuthered" and how the big raindrops poured down and beat against the pane!

"It sounds just like a person lost on the moor and wandering on and on crying," she said.

She had been lying awake turning from side to side for about an hour, when suddenly something made her sit up in bed and turn her head toward the door listening. She listened and listened.

"It isn't the wind now," she said in a loud whisper. "That isn't the wind. It is different. It is that crying I heard before."

The door of her room was ajar and the sound came down the corridor, a far-off faint sound of fretful crying. She listened for a few minutes and each minute she became more and more sure. She felt as if she must find out what it was. It seemed even stranger than the secret garden and the buried key. Perhaps the fact that she was in a rebellious mood made her bold. She put her foot out of bed and stood on the floor.

"I am going to find out what it is," she said. "Everybody is in bed and I don't care about Mrs. Medlock—I don't care!"

There was a candle by her bedside and she took it up and went softly out of the room. The corridor looked very long and dark, but she was too excited to mind that. She thought she remembered the corners she must turn to find the short corridor with the door covered with tapestry—the one Mrs. Medlock had come through the day she lost herself. The sound had come up that passage. So she went on with her dim light, almost feeling her way, her heart beating so loud that she fancied she could hear it. The far-off faint crying went on and led her. Sometimes it stopped for a moment or so and then began again. Was this the right corner to turn? She stopped and thought. Yes it was. Down this passage and then to the left, and then up two broad steps, and then to the right again. Yes, there was the tapestry door.

She pushed it open very gently and closed it behind her, and she stood in the corridor and could hear the crying quite plainly, though it was not loud. It was on the other side of the wall at her left and a few yards farther on there was a door. She could see a glimmer of light coming from beneath it. The Someone was

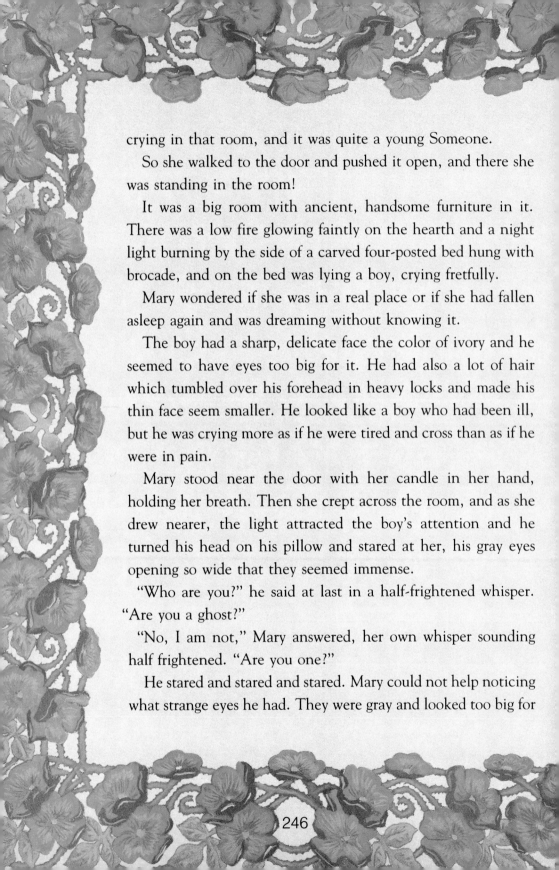

crying in that room, and it was quite a young Someone.

So she walked to the door and pushed it open, and there she was standing in the room!

It was a big room with ancient, handsome furniture in it. There was a low fire glowing faintly on the hearth and a night light burning by the side of a carved four-posted bed hung with brocade, and on the bed was lying a boy, crying fretfully.

Mary wondered if she was in a real place or if she had fallen asleep again and was dreaming without knowing it.

The boy had a sharp, delicate face the color of ivory and he seemed to have eyes too big for it. He had also a lot of hair which tumbled over his forehead in heavy locks and made his thin face seem smaller. He looked like a boy who had been ill, but he was crying more as if he were tired and cross than as if he were in pain.

Mary stood near the door with her candle in her hand, holding her breath. Then she crept across the room, and as she drew nearer, the light attracted the boy's attention and he turned his head on his pillow and stared at her, his gray eyes opening so wide that they seemed immense.

"Who are you?" he said at last in a half-frightened whisper. "Are you a ghost?"

"No, I am not," Mary answered, her own whisper sounding half frightened. "Are you one?"

He stared and stared and stared. Mary could not help noticing what strange eyes he had. They were gray and looked too big for

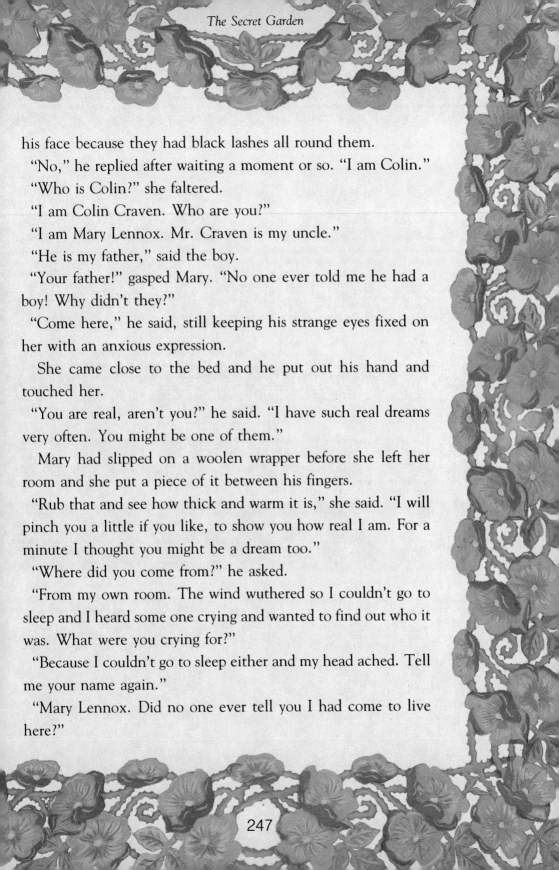

his face because they had black lashes all round them.

"No," he replied after waiting a moment or so. "I am Colin."

"Who is Colin?" she faltered.

"I am Colin Craven. Who are you?"

"I am Mary Lennox. Mr. Craven is my uncle."

"He is my father," said the boy.

"Your father!" gasped Mary. "No one ever told me he had a boy! Why didn't they?"

"Come here," he said, still keeping his strange eyes fixed on her with an anxious expression.

She came close to the bed and he put out his hand and touched her.

"You are real, aren't you?" he said. "I have such real dreams very often. You might be one of them."

Mary had slipped on a woolen wrapper before she left her room and she put a piece of it between his fingers.

"Rub that and see how thick and warm it is," she said. "I will pinch you a little if you like, to show you how real I am. For a minute I thought you might be a dream too."

"Where did you come from?" he asked.

"From my own room. The wind wuthered so I couldn't go to sleep and I heard some one crying and wanted to find out who it was. What were you crying for?"

"Because I couldn't go to sleep either and my head ached. Tell me your name again."

"Mary Lennox. Did no one ever tell you I had come to live here?"

He was still fingering the fold of her wrapper, but he began to look a little more as if he believed in her reality.

"No," he answered. "They daren't."

"Why?" asked Mary.

"Because I should have been afraid you would see me. I won't let people see me and talk me over."

"Why?" Mary asked again, feeling more mystified every moment.

"Because I am like this always, ill and having to lie down. My father won't let people talk me over either. The servants are not allowed to speak about me. If I live I may be a hunchback, but I shan't live. My father hates to think I may be like him."

"Oh, what a queer house this is!" Mary said. "What a queer house! Everything is a kind of secret. Rooms are locked up and gardens are locked up—and you! Have you been locked up?"

"No. I stay in this room because I don't want to be moved out of it. It tires me too much."

"Does your father come and see you?" Mary ventured.

"Sometimes. Generally when I am asleep. He doesn't want to see me."

"Why?" Mary could not help asking again.

A sort of angry shadow passed over the boy's face.

"My mother died when I was born and it makes him wretched to look at me. He thinks I don't know, but I've heard people talking. He almost hates me."

"He hates the garden, because she died," said Mary half speaking to herself.

"What garden?" the boy asked.

"Oh! just—just a garden she used to like," Mary stammered. "Have you been here always?"

"Nearly always. Sometimes I have been taken to places at the seaside, but I won't stay because people stare at me. I used to wear an iron thing to keep my back straight, but a grand doctor came from London to see me and said it was stupid. He told them to take it off and keep me out in the fresh air. I hate fresh air and I don't want to go out."

"I didn't when first I came here," said Mary. "Why do you keep looking at me like that?"

"Because of the dreams that are so real," he answered rather fretfully. "Sometimes when I open my eyes I don't believe I'm awake."

"We're both awake," said Mary. She glanced round the room with its high ceiling and shadowy corners and dim fire-light. "It looks quite like a dream, and it's the middle of the night, and everybody in the house is asleep—everybody but us. We are wide awake."

"I don't want it to be a dream," the boy said restlessly.

Mary thought of something all at once.

"If you don't like people to see you," she began, "do you want me to go away?"

He still held the fold of her wrapper and he gave it a little pull.

"No," he said. "I should be sure you were a dream if you went.

If you are real, sit down on that big footstool and talk. I want to hear about you."

Mary put down her candle on the table near the bed and sat down on the cushioned stool. She did not want to go away at all. She wanted to stay in the mysterious hidden-away room and talk to the mysterious boy.

"What do you want me to tell you?" she said.

He wanted to know how long she had been at Misselthwaite; he wanted to know which corridor her room was on; he wanted to know what she had been doing; if she disliked the moor as he disliked it; where she had lived before she came to Yorkshire. She answered all these questions and many more and he lay back on his pillow and listened. He made her tell him a great deal about India and about her voyage across the ocean. She found out that because he had been an invalid he had not learned things as other children had. One of his nurses had taught him to read when he was quite little and he was always reading and looking at pictures in splendid books.

Though his father rarely saw him when he was awake, he was given all sorts of wonderful things to amuse himself with. He never seemed to have been amused, however. He could have anything he asked for and was never made to do anything he did not like to do.

"Everyone is obliged to do what pleases me," he said indifferently. "It makes me ill to be angry. No one believes I shall live to grow up."

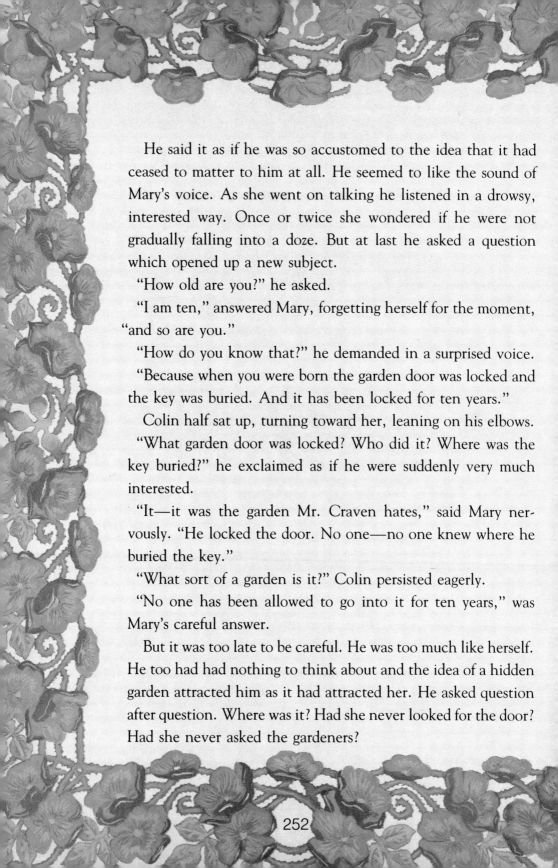

He said it as if he was so accustomed to the idea that it had
ceased to matter to him at all. He seemed to like the sound of
Mary's voice. As she went on talking he listened in a drowsy,
interested way. Once or twice she wondered if he were not
gradually falling into a doze. But at last he asked a question
which opened up a new subject.

"How old are you?" he asked.

"I am ten," answered Mary, forgetting herself for the moment,
"and so are you."

"How do you know that?" he demanded in a surprised voice.

"Because when you were born the garden door was locked and
the key was buried. And it has been locked for ten years."

Colin half sat up, turning toward her, leaning on his elbows.

"What garden door was locked? Who did it? Where was the
key buried?" he exclaimed as if he were suddenly very much
interested.

"It—it was the garden Mr. Craven hates," said Mary nervously. "He locked the door. No one—no one knew where he
buried the key."

"What sort of a garden is it?" Colin persisted eagerly.

"No one has been allowed to go into it for ten years," was
Mary's careful answer.

But it was too late to be careful. He was too much like herself.
He too had had nothing to think about and the idea of a hidden
garden attracted him as it had attracted her. He asked question
after question. Where was it? Had she never looked for the door?
Had she never asked the gardeners?

"They won't talk about it," said Mary. "I think they have been told not to answer questions."

"I would make them," said Colin.

"Could you?" Mary faltered, beginning to feel frightened. If he could make people answer questions, who knew what might happen!

"Everyone is obliged to please me. I told you that," he said. "If I were to live, this place would sometime belong to me. They all know that. I would make them tell me."

Mary had not known that she herself had been spoiled, but she could see quite plainly that this mysterious boy had been. He thought that the whole world belonged to him. How peculiar he was and how coolly he spoke of not living.

"Do you think you won't live?" she asked, partly because she was curious and partly in hope of making him forget the garden.

"I don't suppose I shall," he answered as indifferently as he had spoken before. "Ever since I remember anything I have heard people say I shan't. At first they thought I was too little to understand and now they think I don't hear. But I do. My doctor is my father's cousin. He is quite poor and if I die he will have all Misselthwaite when my father is dead. I should think he wouldn't want me to live."

"Do you want to live?" inquired Mary.

"No," he answered, in a cross, tired fashion. "But I don't want to die. When I feel ill I lie here and think about it until I cry and cry."

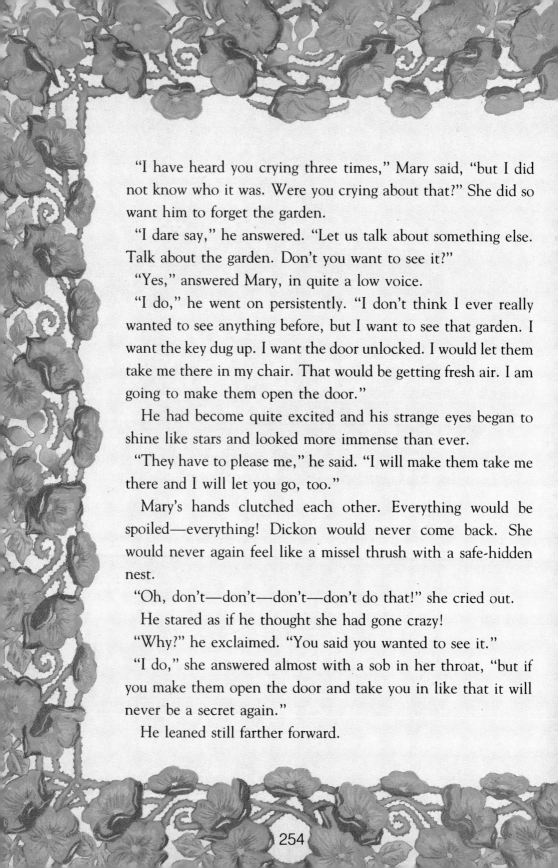

"I have heard you crying three times," Mary said, "but I did not know who it was. Were you crying about that?" She did so want him to forget the garden.

"I dare say," he answered. "Let us talk about something else. Talk about the garden. Don't you want to see it?"

"Yes," answered Mary, in quite a low voice.

"I do," he went on persistently. "I don't think I ever really wanted to see anything before, but I want to see that garden. I want the key dug up. I want the door unlocked. I would let them take me there in my chair. That would be getting fresh air. I am going to make them open the door."

He had become quite excited and his strange eyes began to shine like stars and looked more immense than ever.

"They have to please me," he said. "I will make them take me there and I will let you go, too."

Mary's hands clutched each other. Everything would be spoiled—everything! Dickon would never come back. She would never again feel like a missel thrush with a safe-hidden nest.

"Oh, don't—don't—don't—don't do that!" she cried out.

He stared as if he thought she had gone crazy!

"Why?" he exclaimed. "You said you wanted to see it."

"I do," she answered almost with a sob in her throat, "but if you make them open the door and take you in like that it will never be a secret again."

He leaned still farther forward.

"A secret," he said. "What do you mean? Tell me."

Mary's words almost tumbled over one another.

"You see—you see," she panted, "if no one knows but ourselves—if there was a door, hidden somewhere under the ivy— if there was—and we could find it; and if we could slip through it together and shut it behind us, and no one knew any one was inside and we called it our garden and pretended that—that we were missel thrushes and it was our nest, and if we played there almost every day and dug and planted seeds and made it all come alive—"

"Is it dead?" he interrupted her.

"It soon will be if no one cares for it," she went on. "The bulbs will live but the roses—"

He stopped her again as excited as she was herself.

"What are bulbs?" he put in quickly.

"They are daffodils and lilies and snowdrops. They are working in the earth now—pushing up pale green points because the spring is coming."

"Is the spring coming?" he said. "What is it like? You don't see it in rooms if you are ill."

"It is the sun shining on the rain and the rain falling on the sunshine, and things pushing up and working under the earth," said Mary. "If the garden was a secret and we could get into it we could watch the things grow bigger every day, and see how many roses are alive. Don't you see? Oh, don't you see how much nicer it would be if it was a secret?"

He dropped back on his pillow and lay there with an odd expression on his face.

"I never had a secret," he said, "except that one about not living to grow up. They don't know I know that, so it is a sort of secret. But I like this kind better."

"If you won't make them take you to the garden," pleaded Mary, "perhaps—I feel almost sure I can find out how to get in sometime. And then—if the doctor wants you to go out in your chair, and if you can always do what you want to do, perhaps—perhaps we might find some boy who would push you, and we could go alone and it would always be a secret garden."

"I should—like—that," he said very slowly, his eyes looking dreamy. "I should like that. I should not mind fresh air in a secret garden."

Mary began to recover her breath and feel safer because the idea of keeping the secret seemed to please him. She felt almost sure that if she kept on talking and could make him see the garden in his mind as she had seen it he would like it so much that he could not bear to think that everybody might tramp into it when they chose.

"I'll tell you what I *think* it would be like, if we could go into it," she said. "It has been shut up so long things have grown into a tangle perhaps."

He lay quite still and listened while she went on talking about the roses which *might* have clambered from tree to tree and hung down—about the many birds which *might* have built their nests there because it was so safe. And then she told him about the robin and Ben Weatherstaff, and there was so much to tell about the robin and it was so easy and safe to talk about it that she ceased to be afraid. The robin pleased him so much that he smiled until he looked almost beautiful, and at first Mary had thought that he was even plainer than herself, with his big eyes and heavy locks of hair.

"I did not know birds could be like that," he said. "But if you stay in a room you never see things. What a lot of things you know. I feel as if you had been inside that garden."

She did not know what to say, so she did not say anything. He evidently did not expect an answer and the next moment he gave her a surprise.

"I am going to let you look at something," he said. "Do you see that rose-colored silk curtain hanging on the wall over the mantelpiece?"

Mary had not noticed it before, but she looked up and saw it. It was a curtain of soft silk hanging over what seemed to be some picture.

"Yes," she answered.

"There is a cord hanging from it," said Colin. "Go and pull it."

Mary got up, much mystified, and found the cord. When she pulled it the silk curtain ran back on rings and when it ran back it uncovered a picture. It was the picture of a girl with a laughing face. She had bright hair tied up with a blue ribbon and her gay, lovely eyes were exactly like Colin's unhappy ones, agate gray

and looking twice as big as they really were because of the black lashes all round them.

"She is my mother," said Colin complainingly. "I don't see why she died. Sometimes I hate her for doing it."

"How queer!" said Mary.

"If she had lived I believe I should not have been ill always," he grumbled. "I dare say I should have lived, too. And my father would not have hated to look at me. I dare say I should have had a strong back. Draw the curtain again."

Mary did as she was told and returned to her footstool.

"She is much prettier than you," she said, "but her eyes are just like yours—at least they are the same shape and color. Why is the curtain drawn over her?"

He moved uncomfortably.

"I made them do it," he said. "Sometimes I don't like to see her looking at me. She smiles too much when I am ill and miserable. Besides, she is mine and I don't want everyone to see her."

There were a few moments of silence and then Mary spoke.

"What would Mrs. Medlock do if she found out that I had been here?" she inquired.

"She would do as I told her to do," he answered. "And I should tell her that I wanted you to come here and talk to me every day. I am glad you came."

"So am I," said Mary. "I will come as often as I can, but"—she hesitated—"I shall have to look every day for the garden door."

"Yes, you must," said Colin, "and you can tell me about it afterward." He lay thinking a few minutes, as he had done before, and then he spoke again.

"I think you shall be a secret, too," he said. "I will not tell them until they find out. I can always send the nurse out of the room and say that I want to be by myself. Do you know Martha?"

"Yes, I know her very well," said Mary. "She waits on me."

He nodded his head toward the outer corridor.

"She is the one who is asleep in the other room. The nurse went away yesterday to stay all night with her sister and she always makes Martha attend to me when she wants to go out. Martha shall tell you when to come here."

Then Mary understood Martha's troubled look when she had asked questions about the crying.

"Martha knew about you all the time?" she said.

"Yes; she often attends to me. The nurse likes to get away from me and then Martha comes."

"I have been here a long time," said Mary. "Shall I go away now? Your eyes look sleepy."

"I wish I could go to sleep before you leave me," he said rather shyly.

"Shut your eyes," said Mary, drawing her footstool closer, "and I will do what my Ayah used to do in India. I will pat your hand and stroke it and sing something quite low."

"I should like that perhaps," he said drowsily.

Somehow she was sorry for him and did not want him to lie awake, so she leaned against the bed and began to stroke and pat his hand and sing a very low little chanting song in Hindustani. "That is nice," he said more drowsily still, and she went on chanting and stroking, but when she looked at him again his black lashes were lying close against his cheeks, for his eyes were shut and he was fast asleep. So she got up softly, took her candle and crept away without making a sound.

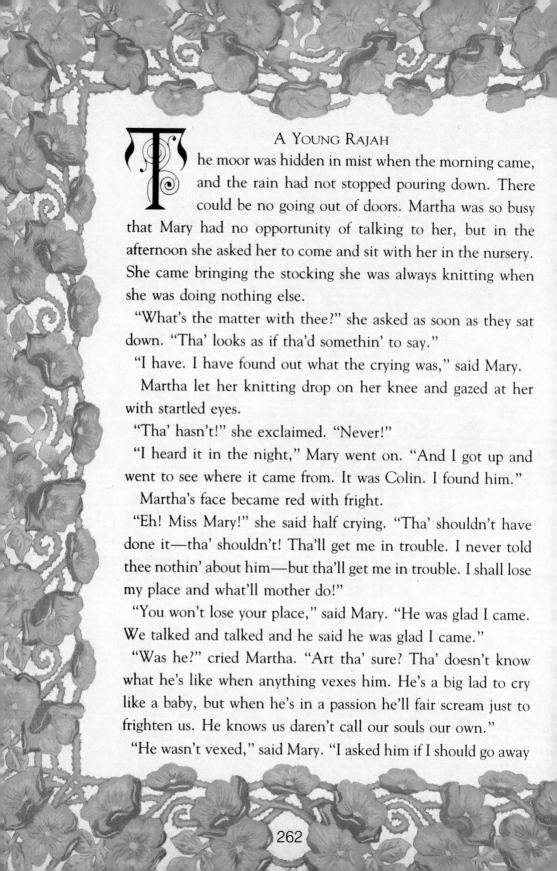

A Young Rajah

The moor was hidden in mist when the morning came, and the rain had not stopped pouring down. There could be no going out of doors. Martha was so busy that Mary had no opportunity of talking to her, but in the afternoon she asked her to come and sit with her in the nursery. She came bringing the stocking she was always knitting when she was doing nothing else.

"What's the matter with thee?" she asked as soon as they sat down. "Tha' looks as if tha'd somethin' to say."

"I have. I have found out what the crying was," said Mary.

Martha let her knitting drop on her knee and gazed at her with startled eyes.

"Tha' hasn't!" she exclaimed. "Never!"

"I heard it in the night," Mary went on. "And I got up and went to see where it came from. It was Colin. I found him."

Martha's face became red with fright.

"Eh! Miss Mary!" she said half crying. "Tha' shouldn't have done it—tha' shouldn't! Tha'll get me in trouble. I never told thee nothin' about him—but tha'll get me in trouble. I shall lose my place and what'll mother do!"

"You won't lose your place," said Mary. "He was glad I came. We talked and talked and he said he was glad I came."

"Was he?" cried Martha. "Art tha' sure? Tha' doesn't know what he's like when anything vexes him. He's a big lad to cry like a baby, but when he's in a passion he'll fair scream just to frighten us. He knows us daren't call our souls our own."

"He wasn't vexed," said Mary. "I asked him if I should go away

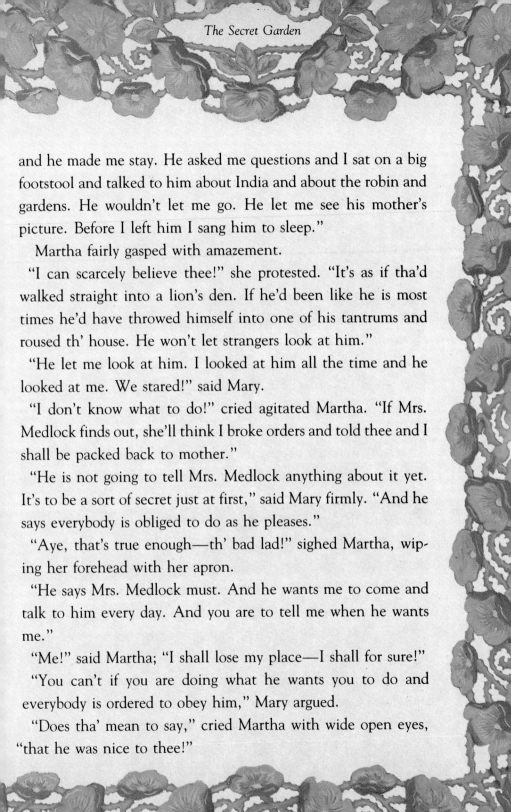

and he made me stay. He asked me questions and I sat on a big footstool and talked to him about India and about the robin and gardens. He wouldn't let me go. He let me see his mother's picture. Before I left him I sang him to sleep."

Martha fairly gasped with amazement.

"I can scarcely believe thee!" she protested. "It's as if tha'd walked straight into a lion's den. If he'd been like he is most times he'd have throwed himself into one of his tantrums and roused th' house. He won't let strangers look at him."

"He let me look at him. I looked at him all the time and he looked at me. We stared!" said Mary.

"I don't know what to do!" cried agitated Martha. "If Mrs. Medlock finds out, she'll think I broke orders and told thee and I shall be packed back to mother."

"He is not going to tell Mrs. Medlock anything about it yet. It's to be a sort of secret just at first," said Mary firmly. "And he says everybody is obliged to do as he pleases."

"Aye, that's true enough—th' bad lad!" sighed Martha, wiping her forehead with her apron.

"He says Mrs. Medlock must. And he wants me to come and talk to him every day. And you are to tell me when he wants me."

"Me!" said Martha; "I shall lose my place—I shall for sure!"

"You can't if you are doing what he wants you to do and everybody is ordered to obey him," Mary argued.

"Does tha' mean to say," cried Martha with wide open eyes, "that he was nice to thee!"

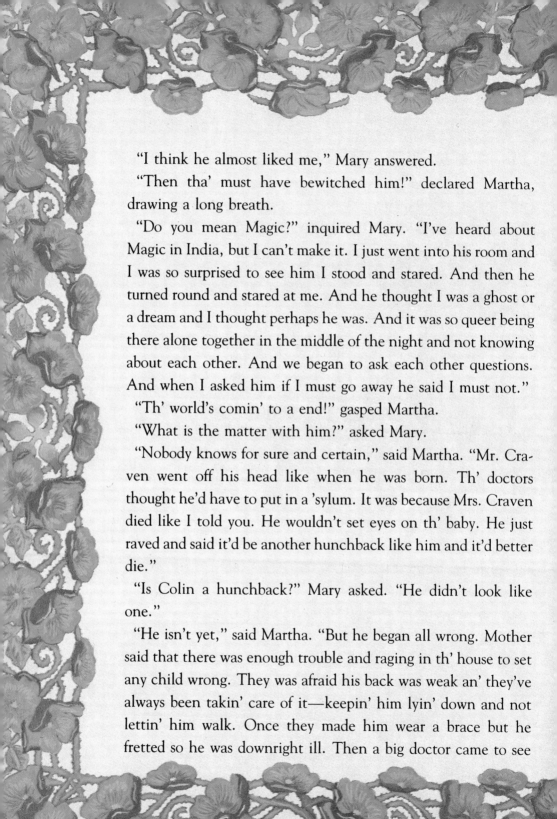

"I think he almost liked me," Mary answered.

"Then tha' must have bewitched him!" declared Martha, drawing a long breath.

"Do you mean Magic?" inquired Mary. "I've heard about Magic in India, but I can't make it. I just went into his room and I was so surprised to see him I stood and stared. And then he turned round and stared at me. And he thought I was a ghost or a dream and I thought perhaps he was. And it was so queer being there alone together in the middle of the night and not knowing about each other. And we began to ask each other questions. And when I asked him if I must go away he said I must not."

"Th' world's comin' to a end!" gasped Martha.

"What is the matter with him?" asked Mary.

"Nobody knows for sure and certain," said Martha. "Mr. Craven went off his head like when he was born. Th' doctors thought he'd have to put in a 'sylum. It was because Mrs. Craven died like I told you. He wouldn't set eyes on th' baby. He just raved and said it'd be another hunchback like him and it'd better die."

"Is Colin a hunchback?" Mary asked. "He didn't look like one."

"He isn't yet," said Martha. "But he began all wrong. Mother said that there was enough trouble and raging in th' house to set any child wrong. They was afraid his back was weak an' they've always been takin' care of it—keepin' him lyin' down and not lettin' him walk. Once they made him wear a brace but he fretted so he was downright ill. Then a big doctor came to see

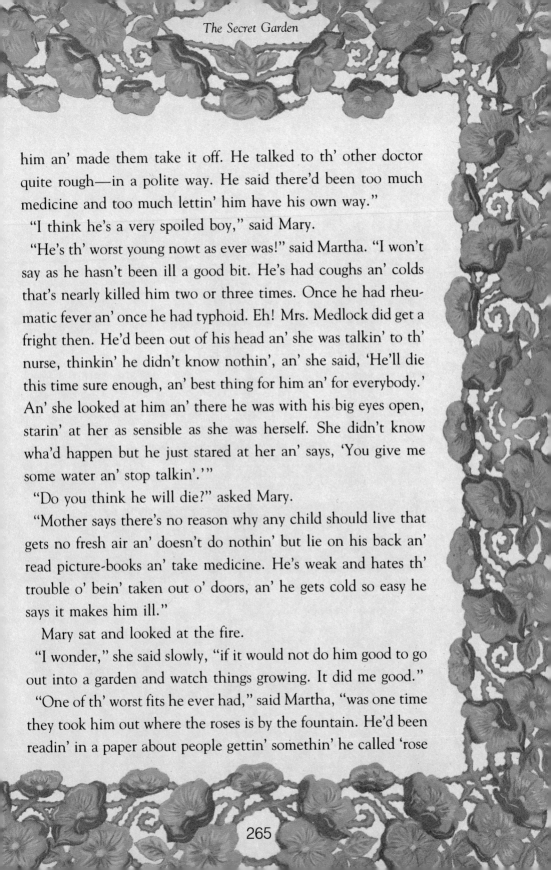

him an' made them take it off. He talked to th' other doctor quite rough—in a polite way. He said there'd been too much medicine and too much lettin' him have his own way."

"I think he's a very spoiled boy," said Mary.

"He's th' worst young nowt as ever was!" said Martha. "I won't say as he hasn't been ill a good bit. He's had coughs an' colds that's nearly killed him two or three times. Once he had rheumatic fever an' once he had typhoid. Eh! Mrs. Medlock did get a fright then. He'd been out of his head an' she was talkin' to th' nurse, thinkin' he didn't know nothin', an' she said, 'He'll die this time sure enough, an' best thing for him an' for everybody.' An' she looked at him an' there he was with his big eyes open, starin' at her as sensible as she was herself. She didn't know wha'd happen but he just stared at her an' says, 'You give me some water an' stop talkin'.'"

"Do you think he will die?" asked Mary.

"Mother says there's no reason why any child should live that gets no fresh air an' doesn't do nothin' but lie on his back an' read picture-books an' take medicine. He's weak and hates th' trouble o' bein' taken out o' doors, an' he gets cold so easy he says it makes him ill."

Mary sat and looked at the fire.

"I wonder," she said slowly, "if it would not do him good to go out into a garden and watch things growing. It did me good."

"One of th' worst fits he ever had," said Martha, "was one time they took him out where the roses is by the fountain. He'd been readin' in a paper about people gettin' somethin' he called 'rose

cold' an' he began to sneeze an' said he'd got it an' then a new gardener as didn't know th' rules passed by an' looked at him curious. He threw himself into a passion an' he said he'd looked at him because he was going to be a hunchback. He cried himself into a fever an' was ill all night."

"If he ever gets angry at me, I'll never go and see him again," said Mary.

"He'll have thee if he wants thee," said Martha. "Tha' may as well know that at th' start."

Very soon afterward a bell rang and she rolled up her knitting.

"I dare say th' nurse wants me to stay with him a bit," she said. "I hope he's in a good temper."

She was out of the room about ten minutes and then she came back with a puzzled expression.

"Well, tha' has bewitched him," she said. "He's up on his sofa with his picture-books. He's told the nurse to stay away until six o'clock. I'm to wait in the next room. Th' minute she was gone he called me to him an' says, 'I want Mary Lennox to come and talk to me, and remember you're not to tell any one.' You'd better go as quick as you can."

Mary was quite willing to go quickly. She did not want to see Colin as much as she wanted to see Dickon; but she wanted to see him very much.

There was a bright fire on the hearth when she entered his room, and in the daylight she saw it was a very beautiful room indeed. There were rich colors in the rugs and hangings and pictures and books on the walls which made it look glowing and comfortable even in spite of the gray sky and falling rain. Colin looked rather like a picture himself. He was wrapped in a velvet dressing-gown and sat against a big brocaded cushion. He had a red spot on each cheek.

"Come in," he said. "I've been thinking about you all morning."

"I've been thinking about you, too," answered Mary. "You don't know how frightened Martha is. She says Mrs. Medlock will think she told me about you and then she will be sent away."

He frowned.

"Go and tell her to come here," he said. "She is in the next room."

Mary went and brought her back. Poor Martha was shaking in her shoes. Colin was still frowning.

"Have you to do what I please or have you not?" he demanded.

"I have to do what you please, sir," Martha faltered, turning quite red.

"Has Medlock to do what I please?"

"Everybody has, sir," said Martha.

"Well, then, if I order you to bring Miss Mary to me, how can Medlock send you away if she finds it out?"

"Please don't let her, sir," pleaded Martha.

"I'll send *her* away if she dares to say a word about such a thing," said Master Craven grandly. "She wouldn't like that, I can tell you."

"Thank you, sir," bobbing a curtsy, "I want to do my duty, sir."

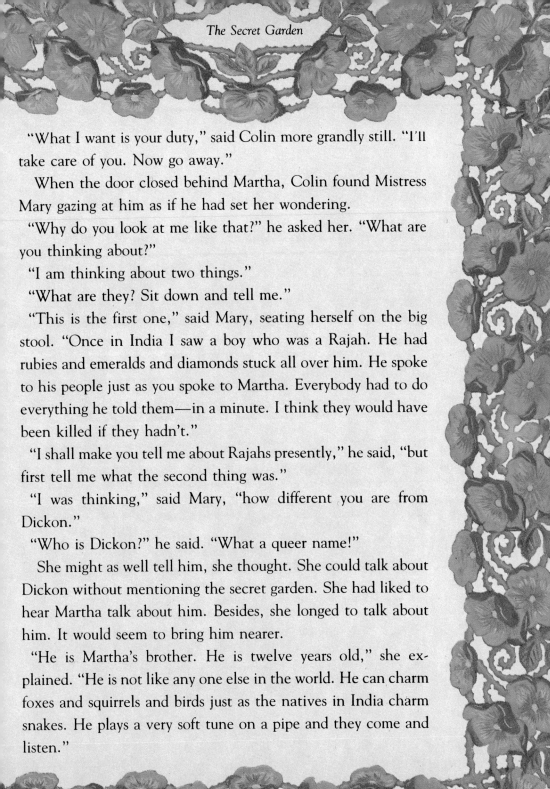

"What I want is your duty," said Colin more grandly still. "I'll take care of you. Now go away."

When the door closed behind Martha, Colin found Mistress Mary gazing at him as if he had set her wondering.

"Why do you look at me like that?" he asked her. "What are you thinking about?"

"I am thinking about two things."

"What are they? Sit down and tell me."

"This is the first one," said Mary, seating herself on the big stool. "Once in India I saw a boy who was a Rajah. He had rubies and emeralds and diamonds stuck all over him. He spoke to his people just as you spoke to Martha. Everybody had to do everything he told them—in a minute. I think they would have been killed if they hadn't."

"I shall make you tell me about Rajahs presently," he said, "but first tell me what the second thing was."

"I was thinking," said Mary, "how different you are from Dickon."

"Who is Dickon?" he said. "What a queer name!"

She might as well tell him, she thought. She could talk about Dickon without mentioning the secret garden. She had liked to hear Martha talk about him. Besides, she longed to talk about him. It would seem to bring him nearer.

"He is Martha's brother. He is twelve years old," she explained. "He is not like any one else in the world. He can charm foxes and squirrels and birds just as the natives in India charm snakes. He plays a very soft tune on a pipe and they come and listen."

There were some big books on a table at his side and he dragged one suddenly toward him.

"There is a picture of a snake-charmer in this," he exclaimed. "Come and look at it."

The book was a beautiful one with superb colored illustrations and he turned to one of them.

"Can he do that?" he asked eagerly.

"He played on his pipe and they listened," Mary explained. "But he doesn't call it Magic. He says it's because he lives on the moor so much and he knows their ways. He says he feels sometimes as if he was a bird or a rabbit himself, he likes them so. I think he asked the robin questions. It seemed as if they talked to each other in soft chirps."

Colin lay back on his cushion and his eyes grew larger and larger and the spots on his cheeks burned.

"Tell me some more about him," he said.

"He knows all about eggs and nests," Mary went on. "And he knows where foxes and badgers and otters live. He keeps them secret so that other boys won't find their holes and frighten them. He knows about everything that grows or lives on the moor."

"Does he like the moor?" said Colin. "How can he when it's such a great, bare, dreary place?"

"It's the most beautiful place," protested Mary. "Thousands of lovely things grow on it and there are thousands of little creatures all busy building nests and making holes and burrows and chippering or singing or squeaking to each other. They are so busy

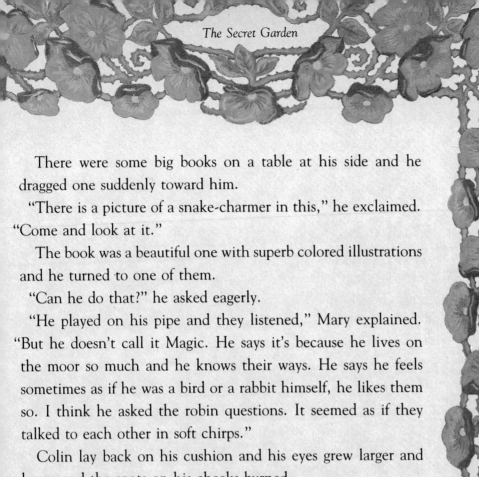

and having such fun under the earth or in the trees or heather. It's their world."

"How do you know all that?" said Colin, turning on his elbow to look at her.

"I have never been there once, really," said Mary suddenly remembering. "I only drove over it in the dark. I thought it was hideous. Martha told me about it first and then Dickon. When Dickon talks about it you feel as if you saw things and heard them and as if you were standing in the heather with the sun shining and the gorse smelling like honey—and all full of bees and butterflies."

"You never see anything if you are ill," said Colin restlessly. He looked like a person listening to a new sound in the distance and wondering what it was.

"You can't if you stay in a room," said Mary.

"I couldn't go on the moor," he said in a resentful tone.

Mary was silent for a minute and then she said something bold. "You might—sometime."

He moved as if he were startled.

"Go on the moor! How could I? I am going to die."

"How do you know?" said Mary unsympathetically. She didn't like the way he had of talking about dying. She did not feel very sympathetic. She felt rather as if he almost boasted about it.

"Oh, I've heard it ever since I remember," he answered crossly. "They are always whispering about it and thinking I don't notice. They wish I would, too."

Mistress Mary felt quite contrary. She pinched her lips together.

"If they wished I would," she said, "I wouldn't. Who wishes you would?"

"The servants—and of course Dr. Craven because he would get Misselthwaite and be rich instead of poor. He daren't say so, but he always looks cheerful when I am worse. When I had typhoid fever his face got quite fat. I think my father wishes it, too."

"I don't believe he does," said Mary quite obstinately.

That made Colin turn and look at her again.

"Don't you?" he said.

And then he lay back on his cushion and was still, as if he were thinking. And there was quite a long silence. Perhaps they were both of them thinking strange things children do not usually think of.

"I like the grand doctor from London, because he made them take the iron thing off," said Mary at last. "Did he say you were going to die?"

"No."

"What did he say?"

"He didn't whisper," Colin answered. "Perhaps he knew I hated whispering. I heard him say one thing quite aloud. He said, 'The lad might live if he would make up his mind to it. Put him in the humor.' It sounded as if he was in a temper."

"I'll tell you who would put you in the humor, perhaps," said Mary reflecting. She felt as if she would like this thing to be settled one way or the other. "I believe Dickon would. He's always talking about live things. He never talks about dead things or things that are ill. He's always looking up in the sky to watch birds flying—or looking down at the earth to see something growing. He has such round blue eyes and they are so wide open with looking about. And he laughs such a big laugh with his wide mouth—and his cheeks are as red—as red as cherries."

She pulled her stool nearer to the sofa and her expression quite changed at the remembrance of the wide curving mouth and wide open eyes.

"See here," she said. "Don't let us talk about dying; I don't like it. Let us talk about living. Let us talk and talk about Dickon. And then we will look at your pictures."

It was the best thing she could have said. To talk about Dickon meant to talk about the moor and about the cottage and the fourteen people who lived in it on sixteen shillings a week— and the children who got fat on the moor grass like the wild ponies. And about Dickon's mother—and the skipping-rope— and the moor with the sun on it—and about pale green points sticking up out of the black sod. And it was all so alive that Mary talked more than she had ever talked before—and Colin both talked and listened as he had never done either before. And they both began to laugh over nothings as children will when they are happy together. And they laughed so that in the end they were making as much noise as if they had been two ordinary healthy natural ten-year-old creatures—instead of a hard, little, unloving girl and a sickly boy who believed that he was going to die.

They enjoyed themselves so much that they forgot the pictures and they forgot about the time. They had been laughing quite loudly over Ben Weatherstaff and his robin, and Colin was actually sitting up as if he had forgotten about his weak back, when he suddenly remembered something.

"Do you know there is one thing we have never once thought of," he said. "We are cousins."

It seemed so queer that they had talked so much and never remembered this simple thing that they laughed more than ever, because they had got into the humor to laugh at anything. And in the midst of the fun the door opened and in walked Dr. Craven and Mrs. Medlock.

Dr. Craven started in actual alarm and Mrs. Medlock almost fell back because he had accidentally bumped against her.

"Good Lord!" exclaimed poor Mrs. Medlock with her eyes almost starting out of her head. "Good Lord!"

"What is this?" said Dr. Craven, coming forward. "What does it mean?"

Then Mary was reminded of the boy Rajah again. Colin answered as if neither the doctor's alarm nor Mrs. Medlock's terror were of the slightest consequence. He was as little disturbed or frightened as if an elderly cat and dog had walked into the room.

"This is my cousin, Mary Lennox," he said. "I asked her to come and talk to me. I like her. She must come and talk to me whenever I send for her."

Dr. Craven turned reproachfully to Mrs. Medlock.

"Oh, sir," she panted. "I don't know how it's happened. There's not a servant on the place tha'd dare to talk—they all have their orders."

"Nobody told her anything," said Colin. "She heard me crying and found me herself. I am glad she came. Don't be silly, Medlock."

Mary saw that Dr. Craven did not look pleased, but it was quite plain that he dare not oppose his patient. He sat down by Colin and felt his pulse.

"I am afraid there has been too much excitement. Excitement is not good for you, my boy," he said.

"I should be excited if she kept away," answered Colin, his eyes beginning to look dangerously sparkling. "I am better. She makes me better. The nurse must bring up her tea with mine. We will have tea together."

Mrs. Medlock and Dr. Craven looked at each other in a troubled way, but there was evidently nothing to be done.

"He does look rather better, sir," ventured Mrs. Medlock. "But"—thinking the matter over—"he looked better this morning before she came into the room."

"She came into the room last night. She stayed with me a long time. She sang a Hindustani song to me and it made me go to sleep," said Colin. "I was better when I wakened up. I wanted my breakfast. I want my tea now. Tell nurse, Medlock."

Dr. Craven did not stay very long. He talked to the nurse for a few minutes when she came into the room and said a few words of warning to Colin. He must not talk too much; he must not forget that he was ill; he must not forget that he was very easily tired. Mary thought that there seemed to be a number of uncomfortable things he was not to forget.

Colin looked fretful and kept his strange black-lashed eyes fixed on Dr. Craven's face.

"I *want* to forget it," he said at last. "She makes me forget it. That is why I want her."

Dr. Craven did not look happy when he left the room. He gave a puzzled glance at the little girl sitting on the large stool. She had become a stiff, silent child again as soon as he entered and he could not see what the attraction was. The boy actually did look brighter, however—and he sighed rather heavily as he went down the corridor.

"They are always wanting me to eat things when I don't want to," said Colin, as the nurse brought in the tea and put it on the table by the sofa. "Now, if you'll eat I will. Those muffins look so nice and hot. Tell me about Rajahs."

Colin and Mary come to share the secret garden. The garden has had an amazing effect on Mary; how will it affect Colin? How will Colin's father feel when he discovers what has been taking place?

Meet the Author: **Frances Hodgson Burnett**

Frances Hodgson Burnett wrote dozens of stories, plays, and novels for children and adults in the late 1800s and early 1900s. Her best-known book, aside from *The Secret Garden*, is *Little Lord Fauntleroy*.

Burnett was born in Manchester, England, and moved to the United States when she was a teenager. She became a citizen, married, and had children. In her later years, Burnett spent time in both countries.

Burnett's inspiration for *The Secret Garden* came in part from a garden at her home at Maytham Hall, Kent, England. In her garden, like Mary Lennox, Burnett made friends with a robin that became so tame it would take crumbs from her hand. Her garden was an old orchard that had returned to wilderness and was entered by a low, arched gateway with a wooden door. In it she planted roses. In 1909 while she was laying out a garden at a new home on Long Island, New York, she remembered her English rose garden and began to write *The Secret Garden*.

The Secret Garden was not immediately popular when it was first published. Perhaps some people did not like a novel in which two rather disagreeable children were main characters. But the novel gradually gained admirers and today is considered a masterpiece of children's literature.

Responding to Literature

1. One critic called *The Secret Garden* "the most satisfying children's book I know." Based on the excerpt, explain why you agree or disagree with this statement. If you disagree, which book would you choose as the most satisfying? Why?

2. Suppose you are Mary Lennox. What will you write in your journal about the crying sound and the discovery you made about it?

3. How does her discovery of Colin affect Mary?

4. Colin usually hides away from people, yet he is happy to meet Mary. Why do you think this is?

5. Reread the description of the secret garden on pages 254–257. How is the change that is happening to Mary and Colin similar to the change that is taking place in the garden?

E(HooH)E

'Who called?' I said, and the words
    Through the whispering glades,
Hither, thither, baffled the birds—
    'Who called? Who called?'

The leafy boughs on high
    Hissed in the sun;
The dark air carried my cry
    Faintingly on:

Eyes in the green, in the shade,
    In the motionless brake,
Voices that said what I said,
    For mockery's sake:

'Who cares?' I bawled through my tears;
    The wind fell low:
In the silence, 'Who cares? Who cares?'
    Wailed to and fro.

Walter de la Mare

Appreciating Author's Craft

Thinking About the Effect of Setting on Character

The setting is often a powerful influence in a work of fiction, such as a story or novel. It certainly is in *The Secret Garden.* Setting can affect a character's personality and moods. As changes in setting occur, so may changes in the character.

Colin's room is described as "a big room with ancient furniture . . . and a low fire glowing." Colin is shut away from the world. He hates fresh air and doesn't want to go outside. The setting matches Colin's mood. However, the story of the strange and wild garden Mary describes excites him.

> "I don't think I ever really wanted to see anything before, but I want to see that garden. I want the key dug up. I want the door unlocked. I would let them take me there in my chair. That would be getting fresh air. I am going to make them open the door."

As a result of learning about the garden, Colin's mood is changing from despair to hope. The new element in the setting has influenced his feelings and behavior.

Writing About the Effect of Setting on Character

If you think about the excerpt from *The Secret Garden,* you will notice how important the setting is. You can write a paragraph that describes the setting of *The Secret Garden* and tells how it influences Mary. (For more ideas about writing, look at your Writer's Handbook.)

Prewriting The following phrases from *The Secret Garden* describe the natural setting that surrounds Misselthwaite. Copy the list and add two more phrases about the outdoors.

The Outdoors

1. heavy rain
2. purple heather
3. wuthering wind
4. gorse that smells like honey

Writing How does the natural setting affect Mary? Reread the list of phrases about the outdoors. Use the list to help you write a description of the outdoors. Then tell how the setting affects Mary.

Revising Read your draft to a partner and discuss your description of the outdoors and its effect on Mary. Then revise your draft. Be sure your description is vivid and make changes based on your partner's suggestions. Proofread for errors. Finally, write your final copy.

Presenting Read your description to the class. Ask your classmates to close their eyes while you read and try to visualize the setting you describe. How do your classmates think the land around Misselthwaite Manor and the weather in Yorkshire would affect them?

Extending Your Reading

Expressing Yourself

Choose one or more of the following activities:

Design Your Own Secret Garden Find out as much as you can about plants from seed catalogs, library books, and magazines. Then choose the plants you would want in your own secret garden. Draw a plan of your garden that shows the plants you chose and how you would arrange them.

Research the Moors Find out more about the moors and the plants and animals that live there. Report your findings to the class.

Plan a Trip to Yorkshire What would you like to see if you visited Yorkshire for a week? With information you gather from travel agencies or books, put together an itinerary.

Draw Misselthwaite Manor What do you think the gloomy stone mansion looked like? Use the art material of your choice to draw or sculpt your impression of Misselthwaite.

Find the Secret Work with classmates to find the secret in the poem "Echo." Who is calling? Why is the speaker upset? After you have solved the mystery, write a newspaper account explaining it.

More Classics

The Five Little Peppers and How They Grew by Margaret Sidney. Buccaneer. Who would believe that five children and their mother could have so many good times together! The Peppers have hardly enough money to get dinner on the table, but somehow they manage surprises for birthdays and rollicking everyday moments too.

The Merry Adventures of Robin Hood by Howard Pyle. Franklin Watts. The best-known stories of England's famous hero of Sherwood Forest are told in this book. Discover how Robin cleverly outwits the Sheriff of Nottingham and shows his great skill as an archer in tales of bravery, humor, and kindness.

Mary Poppins by P. L. Travers. Revised edition, Harcourt Brace Jovanovich. Mary Poppins must certainly be the best-loved English nanny in fiction. She and her magical doings delight her four young charges and her readers, who accompany her on a number of fantastic adventures.

Hans Brinker or the Silver Skates by Mary Mapes Dodge. Putnam Publishing Group. Historic Holland, the setting for this novel, was a place where everyone skated and where windmills were as common as skyscrapers are today. Hans's story is full of exciting twists and turns.

The Door in the Wall by Marguerite De Angeli. Scholastic. Young Robin, son of a thirteenth-century English lord, is preparing to go to live in a castle and learn to be a knight when he is crippled by an illness and forced to leave his London home. The remainder of this tale relates Robin's adventures on his way to the castle and his acts of bravery once he gets there.

The Agony of Alice

by Phyllis Reynolds Naylor
illustrated by Don Madden

The Agony of Alice

Alice McKinley hopes desperately to be assigned to Miss Cole's sixth-grade class. Alice is searching for someone just like Miss Cole, someone young, pretty, and popular, after whom to model herself. Unfortunately, Alice's name appears on Mrs. Plotkin's student list, not Miss Cole's. Alice suspects that being stuck with plodding, pear-shaped, middle-aged Mrs. Plotkin is only the first disappointment of a sure-to-be disastrous year.

Growing Up

When adults look back at their childhoods, they often remember their early years as trouble free. They have forgotten that being young is not always easy or fun. Eleven-year-olds, such as Alice McKinley, are growing up. They are trying to figure out what sort of people they are—what they believe in, what they want, what is important to them. Their problems may be unimportant or amusing to the adults around them, and may even seem so to the children

themselves eventually, but at the time their difficulties seem overwhelming. (For more information about stories like *The Agony of Alice,* look up *Modern realistic fiction* in your Handbook.)

Thinking About Point of View
An author may write a story as if a character were telling it. In *The Agony of Alice,* for example, Alice seems to be telling the story. Readers see the story through Alice's eyes, from Alice's point of view. When the story is told from the point of view of one character and uses words such as *I* and *me,* the author is using the first-person point of view.

As you're reading this excerpt on your own, discover Alice's agony.

The Agony of Alice

Alice McKinley believes that if her mother were still alive or if she had a sister to give her advice she wouldn't do so many embarrassing things. Perhaps she wouldn't have joined in the Tarzan game with Donald Sheavers, or somehow avoided having to play the triangle instead of singing in the chorus. Her mother might have kept Alice from walking into the wrong dressing room and catching Patrick in his blue underwear. Alice has begun keeping a list on the back of an old poster with a "Forward" column for the grown-up things she does and a "Backward" column for her humiliations. So far, the backward column is longer. If only she could have been assigned to Miss Cole's class! Alice is sure lovely, young Miss Cole would have helped Alice change her life. Instead fate has determined that plain, uninspiring Mrs. Plotkin will be Alice's teacher. Is there any hope at all for Alice?

The Maharaja's Magic

Three weeks after school started, I was standing on the steps at recess watching the fourth graders jump rope. Charlene Verona was showing us her new designer jeans with a horseshoe on the back pocket.

"Miss Cole says she has a pair exactly like mine," Charlene said proudly. "When we have our class picnic, she's going to wear hers, and we'll be twins."

I was so jealous of Charlene at that moment I could hardly breathe. My lips were smiling, but my teeth were clamped together so hard that the fillings hurt.

"Miss Cole is so much fun!" Charlene went on. "She even let me use her nail polish yesterday after school."

I choked.

Elizabeth Price was not to be outdone, however. "I'm really glad *I* got a *man* for a teacher this year," she said. "He treats us like we're grown up. Sometimes he even calls us 'Miss' and 'Mr.' 'Miss Price, would you care to put the third problem on the blackboard?' he'll say. I heard he plays the guitar, and when you go on the overnight, everybody sings."

Right away I fantasied everyone singing around a bonfire

while Mr. Weber played his guitar, with me standing in the back with a triangle going *ping*.

And then I realized that both girls were looking at me.

"It's too bad you got Mrs. Plotkin," said Elizabeth.

The only thing I hated more than being in Mrs. Plotkin's room was being pitied, and I simply was not going to let that happen. I laughed my "Miss Cole" laugh and sort of tossed my hair.

"Oh, it's not as bad as you think," I said gaily. "Mrs. Plotkin is *so* nice, and every day, no matter what we're doing, she stops at two-thirty and reads us part of a book."

I knew that didn't sound like much compared to matching designer jeans and singing around a bonfire. The girls were looking at me strangely, and I went on: "If I could choose any class I wanted, I just might stay right where I am."

I could see they didn't quite believe me. In fact, they weren't even looking at me any longer, they were looking somewhere behind me, and I turned to see Mrs. Plotkin standing just inside the door. She smiled as she came out on the steps, holding a plant she was setting out to sun.

"What a nice thing to say, Alice!" she said. "And if I could choose any girl in the whole school to be in my room, I just might put Alice McKinley at the head of the list."

I gave Mrs. Plotkin a weak smile, and she edged on down the steps with her potted geranium. The terrible, awful truth was that now I had boxed myself into a corner. Even if Miss Cole *asked* me to be in her class, how could I switch?

The next day I tried not to look at Mrs. Plotkin at all. Every time I thought her eyes were on me, I looked away. I was the first one out the door after school. The day after that went the same. I couldn't go on not looking at her forever, though. I was already not looking at Patrick, and the crazy thing about not looking at somebody is that you are always looking at them to see if they're not looking at you.

I lived for Wednesdays, when the patrols ate in Miss Cole's room. I thought there was nothing in the world so wonderful as the perfume Miss Cole wore on her shoulders. When you walked in Mrs. Plotkin's room, you smelled lunch sacks—bananas and baloney sandwiches. You smelled chalk and raincoats and library paste. But when you walked in Miss Cole's room, you smelled gardenias or something. I mean, just standing in Miss Cole's doorway said that you were somewhere special.

It was on Wednesday, when I got home from school, that I opened an envelope marked "Occupant." I almost never get any mail. Lester gets things from the junior college, and Dad gets all the bills. Everything addressed to Occupant, they leave on the coffee table for me. Once I got a bar of free soap. Another time I got a packet of tea and a free leaf bag. This time, it was a purple card in cellophane that said, *Maharaja's Magic—the only perfume you will ever need.*

I ripped open the cellophane and pulled the card out. The perfume was really strong. I figured they must have dipped the card in *Maharaja's Magic* and then let it dry overnight. I took it upstairs and stuck it in the drawer with my tee shirts so they would smell good when I went to school the next day.

On Thursday I put on my George Gershwin tee shirt and my Niagara Falls tee shirt over that.

"Whew!" said Lester, when I sat down at the table. "What smells?"

"Your feet, probably," I told him. Lester wouldn't know gardenias from garbage.

Around nine, as I approached the school, Elizabeth Price said, "Someone's wearing *perfume!*"

"It's me," I said, before I realized it was no compliment. "It's *Maharaja's Magic.*"

"It's so strong!" said Elizabeth, making a face. "You must have used a whole bottle."

I should have gone home right then and changed. I should have taken a shower and hung all my tee shirts out to air. Instead, I walked into the classroom.

The girl who sits behind me is almost as pretty as Elizabeth Price. Her name is Pamela Jones, and until this particular morning, I thought she was my friend.

"What stinks?" said Pamela.

I didn't even have time to answer before somebody else said, "Euuyuk!"

One of the boys went over to the window and stuck his head out like he was going to be sick, and then all the boys started acting dumb. They'd take a couple steps toward me, then grab their throats and gag. The girls were giggling. I sat down at my desk and pretended I didn't notice. Mrs. Plotkin noticed, though. I could tell she was watching.

"What happened?" Pamela whispered behind me. "Did you spill something on your clothes?"

I didn't even answer.

It was probably the very worst day of my life. I couldn't go home and change at noon because then everyone would know how embarrassed I was. I played soccer instead, in hopes that all that running around would air the tee shirts out. What it did was mix some sweat with *Maharaja's Magic* so that, when I came in after lunch I smelled like the Maharaja's horse. I wanted to disappear. Mrs. Plotkin had opened a window, but the breeze just blew the perfume off me and carried it around the room.

When the bell rang at three and all the kids started for the door, I hung back. I wanted to wait until all the girls had left so I could walk home alone. I spilled my box of colored pencils on the floor on purpose and then slowly picked them up, one by one.

"Alice," said Mrs. Plotkin when the others had gone, "I wonder if you'd be interested in helping me out occasionally after school—when you're not on patrol duty, of course."

I was so grateful for an excuse to stay that I would have even cleaned the gerbil cage.

"Sure," I told her.

She said that her plants needed watering and the blackboard needed cleaning and that sometime, if I really felt like staying longer, I could rearrange the supply cupboard. I started in on the plants, then scrubbed the blackboard, and when I was pretty sure that the other girls were home, I left.

I threw the Maharaja in the garbage can and put all my tee shirts in the wash. *Wore perfume to school,* I had to write on my poster, under the "Backward" column. Then I sat out on the steps and wondered what I would be like when I was twenty. Most of the girls who were getting married and had their pictures in the paper were twenty. It told where they had gone to school and where they worked and how they were the granddaughters of the late Admiral and Mrs. Barker or somebody, and how the bride wore a gown with a scalloped neckline and tiny seed pearls. I figured that any granddaughter of a late admiral who knew about scalloped necklines was beyond doing stupid things. When *I* was twenty, if I kept on growing backwards, I would be such an embarrassment to my family that Dad would have to put me away.

The next day in English, Mrs. Plotkin announced that each year she asked her sixth graders to keep a journal. She said that journals were different from diaries because they weren't records of what happened to us so much as they were records of what we thought and felt about the things that happened. She said we were to start our journals right away, in black and white bound notebooks with lines, and turn them in at the end of May. We could write in them as often as we liked and say anything we wanted, but if we wrote something private, we should fasten those pages together with paper clips and she wouldn't read them.

"I'll bet!" said Lester at the table that night. "She probably reads those pages aloud in the teachers' lounge."

Somehow, I didn't think so. I found an old black and white notebook I'd started in third grade with only two pages used, which I carefully pulled out. Then I took my ballpoint pen with *Melody Inn* printed on one side and carefully wrote, "The Agony of Alice, page 1."

Bringing Up the Rear

I decided that if I was ever going to get Miss Cole to sort of take me on, I had to do something more than give her little presents wrapped in tissue and smear myself with perfume samples. So I opened my journal with an advertisement that I hoped Mrs. Plotkin would show the other teachers.

> WANTED: Adopted Mother
> Must be tall, smart, and beautiful
> with the initials M ____ C ____
> SALARY: love forever

I figured that Miss Cole would know right away I was writing about her, and fantasied how her eyes would grow misty and she'd call me into her room and ask how would I like to spend Thanksgiving with her and did I need any help with Christmas shopping.

When I started on the second page, though, I knew that this was the page I would paperclip, because I wrote down all the ridiculous things I had done that I wouldn't have done if I'd had a mother. It took weeks to write all the details, the horrible humiliations, but I put down everything: Donald Sheavers, Patrick in his blue underwear, the *Maharaja's Magic,* and what happened on Halloween. *Especially* what happened on Halloween.

Parkhaven School always had a parade before their big Halloween party. Pamela Jones told me all about it while we were washing out paint brushes after art class. Pamela had just finished a six-foot mural to hang in the hall outside our door. It showed all the things you could do in autumn—apple picking, nut gathering, cider making, leaf raking—painted in red and rust and bronze and gold. I had drawn an 8½ × 11 picture of a pumpkin.

"Everyone comes to school in costume," Pamela told me, "even the principal." Pamela has long yellow hair that has never been cut. It hangs all the way down her back, and she sits on it.

I stuck a brush under the running water and ran my thumb over the bristles the wrong way. Orange paint splattered my shirt. Pamela finished the brushes while I tried to clean myself off with a paper towel.

"What are you going to wear?" I asked her.

"I've got a fantastic costume from my dance recital," Pamela said. "It's a horse, and it comes in two parts. You want to wear it with me?"

I knew right away which part of the horse Pamela wanted me to be, but it didn't matter. I didn't have any ideas of my own, and when I'd asked Lester about it he said, "Just go to school without combing your hair. You can't get more gruesome than that."

"Sure," I told Pamela.

For a week before Halloween, that's all the girls talked about. Elizabeth Price's mother was making her a gypsy costume. She'd been working on it since September, Elizabeth told me. The skirt had three ruffles around the bottom in purple, pink, and green, the blouse was red, and there was a purple satin vest with sequins on it. Elizabeth even had her ears pierced so she could wear some hoop earrings.

Charlene Verona was going to come to the parade as a bottle of catsup. She said that her father had built the frame over the summer, and her sister had painted it for her. I swallowed. The nice thing about being a horse's rear end, I decided, was that no one would know who I was.

The day of the party, Dad said he would walk over to the school around one to watch our parade. I told him he didn't really have to, but Dad always tries to do what he thinks Momma would do if she were alive. The past five years he even thought up a costume for me. In first grade I was Beethoven, in second grade I was Brahms, in third, fourth, and fifth I was Schubert, Bach, and Mozart. Every year I wore the top of Dad's old tuxedo and carried a baton. The kids thought I was trying to be a magician. That's why I didn't mind being a horse this time.

When class let out at noon, most of the kids went home to change. I was practically the only one eating lunch in the all-purpose room. I stood at the front entrance and watched as people returned in their costumes. Mrs. Plotkin was dressed as a farmer. She had on a checked shirt, a kerchief, and an enormous pair of overalls. Two boys came as a pair of dice. Someone else was a box of cereal, and there was even a girl dressed as a television set. I saw the principal in a cowboy costume, and Mr. Weber dressed as a vampire, with fangs on either side of his mouth. But it was Miss Cole I was waiting for, and at last I saw her coming out of the teachers' lounge.

She was the most gorgeous sight I had ever seen. She was wearing a green and yellow kimono with a wide silk sash around her waist, white stockings, and little green slippers. Her hair was swept on top of her head and held in place with a huge spray of carnations.

I couldn't take my eyes off her. Even when Patrick went by in a Superman cape, with blue tights and his blue underwear on top of them, right out there in public, I hardly even looked at him. I wanted Miss Cole for my adopted mother more than I wanted anything else in the world. I wanted her to dress me in a green and yellow kimono and show me how to wear flowers in my hair. I wanted someone to make a fuss over me and teach me how to walk in tiny little steps and bow the way Miss Cole was bowing to some of her students.

"Come on," someone said, pulling my arm, and I turned as Pamela Jones and her mother came through the entrance holding the horse costume. I followed them to the girls' restroom. Pamela had on brown tights and tap shoes. She kept tap dancing all around the tiled floor.

Mrs. Jones smiled at me as she held out the second half of the costume, and I put my feet inside. I had to pull it up high so the legs wouldn't wrinkle.

She laughed. "You girls are going to be a riot!" The wide top was shoulder high and had snaps around it. Holding on

with both hands, I stood side by side with Pamela. We looked in the mirror and laughed. Maybe it wouldn't be so bad after all, I thought. If I couldn't wear a green and yellow kimono, it was better to be a horse's rear end than it was to be some old composer that nobody knew.

Mrs. Jones kept watch at the door, and when she saw our class lining up in the hallway, she put the horse's head over Pamela. Then I bent over and put my hands on Pamela's waist, and Mrs. Jones snapped the two parts of the costume together.

"Have fun," she said.

Gingerly, I followed Pamela out into the hall. I could hear the other kids laughing as we came. Pamela's tap shoes clicked on the corridor like hoofs, and when we got up to where I figured Mrs. Plotkin was standing, Pamela did a little tap dance while I sort of weaved around behind her and tried to hang on.

"Good heavens!" said Mrs. Plotkin, laughing. "I hope whoever is behind you has enough air."

"It's Alice," said Pamela. "She's fine."

I was fine except that I couldn't see a thing but a small patch of floor beneath my face.

The parade began to move, and I followed Pamela outside, up the sidewalk toward the street.

"Oh, look at the horse!" I heard people exclaim when we passed, and Pamela would break into her tap-dance routine while I hung on for dear life.

And then a funny thing happened. I started a little routine of my own. The fancier Pamela's dancing got up front, the sillier I acted behind. Every time we came to a corner, we'd all wait while teachers scurried by on either side to stop traffic. Pamela would tap around in a circle, and I'd stand still scratching one hind leg with the other. At the next corner while Pamela did her *shuffle-step, shuffle-step, tap heel,* I'd stand with my toes pointed in, my knees bent, bouncing up and down in time with the rhythm. And when she did her Spanish number, I'd wriggle my bottom down lower and lower until I was almost sitting on the ground. People were laughing loudly, and it sounded good.

"What are you doing back there, Alice?" Pamela asked me.

"Just having fun," I told her. I pretended I was in a Conga line. I'd take three steps and kick out my left leg. Then three steps and kick out my right.

The parade had turned around and was heading back to the school. I heard my dad's chuckle when we passed where he was standing, and I decided to give the last two blocks everything I had. As we approached the next corner, I broke into my Conga step again, kicking high as I possibly could. *One . . . two . . . three,* left leg; *one . . . two . . . three,* right. . . .

My foot made contact with something soft.

"Ouch!" a voice cried out in pain.

I knew that voice immediately, and my knees almost buckled. Skidding to a stop, I pulled at the snaps on my costume and stood up. Miss Cole was standing there rubbing her arm, her eyes smarting with the pain.

"Alice!" she said. "Why . . . ?"

I tried to speak, but couldn't. There was no excuse except that I liked the way people were laughing at us; I liked acting silly. Miss Cole turned and moved swiftly on down the line, her lips pressed tightly together. My father was looking at me from up the sidewalk.

"What's happening?" Pamela kept saying.

I couldn't possibly go on. I stepped out of my half of the costume and handed it to Pamela. Then I crossed the street and started home. Dad came running over.

"Al?" he said. "Where are you going?"

I didn't answer. He walked along beside me.

"I saw what happened," he said. "You should have explained to the teacher. She would have understood."

I wasn't worried about Miss Cole understanding, though. What I wanted was for her to *like* me, to *love* me, even, and I had to go kick her in the arm.

Dad went back to work at the Melody Inn, and I went up to my room and spent the rest of the day with a pillow over my face.

If I had a mother, I wrote in my journal that night, *I would have been a gypsy or a ballerina and none of this would have happened.*

Dinner with Marilyn

It was obvious that Miss Cole wasn't going to invite me home for Thanksgiving. She had a big bruise on her arm to remember me by, for one thing. I was afraid she might not even let me in her room. She did, though, and when I explained what had happened, she just said I could have kicked some little kid in the teeth and I ought to be more careful. She talked to me and everything at patrol meetings, but her eyes didn't seem to smile at me the way they smiled at the others. And once, when someone was teasing me, Miss Cole said jokingly, "Better watch out for Alice. She kicks."

I worked twice as hard to make it up to her. I was as helpful as I could be at our weekly patrol meetings, but I didn't get to go on duty much. Once Patrick went to a concert with his parents and I got to take his corner, and another time a patrol in Mr. Weber's class threw up. But most afternoons, if I didn't feel like walking home with Elizabeth Price and Charlene, I'd stick around Mrs. Plotkin's room. Once, just before Thanksgiving, I stayed till four o'clock and straightened her supply cupboard. I threw out an old jar of dried-up paste and poured two bottles of glue together. I divided all the construction paper into separate colors, sharpened the pencils, washed the shelves, and didn't stop until the whole cupboard was clean.

"Alice, I do believe this is the best this has ever looked," Mrs. Plotkin said.

I beamed.

She was wearing a blue dress with a white collar, and I liked her in blue because it matched her eyes.

"I found a place for everything except this brown and orange paper that's faded along one edge," I told her. "I didn't know if you wanted it mixed in with the rest or not."

"Probably not," Mrs. Plotkin said. "If you want it, it's yours."

I rolled up the paper and slipped a rubber band around it.

"I hope you're going to do something nice on Thanksgiving," she said, as I put on my coat.

"We usually go to a restaurant," I told her. "My dad can't roast a turkey."

Mrs. Plotkin laughed. "Well, believe it or not, Alice, you can get through life without ever learning to roast one. Have a good time."

"You too," I said. All the way home, though, I wondered where Mrs. Plotkin was going to celebrate Thanksgiving. I hadn't asked her. Maybe her husband was dead and she didn't have any cousins or anything. Maybe she was going to spend Thanksgiving sitting in front of the TV with a frozen dinner on her lap.

When I got home, I cut the brown and orange paper into strips, made a huge chain, and strung it around the whole living room—over the lamps, the doorway, and the back of the sofa.

"What's this for?" Lester asked.

"Thanksgiving," I told him. "Don't you know *anything*?"

Dad invited Janice Sherman from the Melody Inn to come to the restaurant with us for Thanksgiving because she's single, and then he had to invite Loretta Jenkins, the birdbrain because she's single, too. Lester said it was the worst decision Dad ever made. Loretta's a vegetarian and she kept stealing vegetables off Lester's plate to fill her up.

"What's that?" she said. "A water chestnut? I *love* water chestnuts." And she'd poke at it with her fork. "What's that? A mushroom? I *love* mushrooms." She'd wave her fork again at Lester.

I like Loretta better than Janice, though. Janice is the one in the sheet music department who wears her glasses on a chain. I think she's been in sheet music too long.

When we sat down at the table and Janice saw the bouquet of flowers in the middle, she said, "What a symphony of color!"

When the shrimp cocktails arrived, Janice said, "What a lovely overture to a meal!"

When the pumpkin pie was served, she clasped her hands and said, "The grand finale!"

"You know what, Dad?" Lester said when we'd taken them both back home. "You work with a couple of airheads."

I wondered about Mrs. Plotkin again and whether she would have come with us if I'd asked. I'll bet Lester would have liked her better than Janice or Loretta.

I told Dad it was a great Thanksgiving, though, because he was leaving the next morning for a three-day convention in New York. I went up in his room to help him pack.

"What was Thanksgiving like when Momma was alive?" I asked, as I polished his shoes with an undershirt and put them in his bag.

"Well, we always spent it with your Aunt Sally and Uncle Milt. We'd pack your high chair in the car, and your mother would feed you strained beets while the rest of us ate turkey."

I remembered watching a baby eat zwieback once in a restaurant, and it was disgusting.

"I'll bet I was a mess," I said.

"Yes, particularly when you got to the strained spinach," Dad told me, and laughed.

The thing about mothers, I was thinking, is that they like you regardless, no matter how repulsive you are. No matter how many stupid things you do. The thing about mothers, in fact, is that they keep you from doing a lot of dumb things in the first place. I couldn't imagine Elizabeth Price or Charlene Verona doing some of the stupid things I had done. It didn't seem fair that Charlene, who had a mother,

also had Miss Cole for a teacher and got to use her nail polish.

Dad left money so Lester and I could go to the Hot Shoppe the next night for dinner, but Lester's girl friend came over instead to cook for us.

She was wearing a long skirt and a blouse with puffy sleeves and she looked absolutely beautiful, almost as pretty as Miss Cole. Lester had on jeans and an old sweat shirt and was walking around in his stocking feet.

Marilyn had brought a wok with her. She showed me how to make stir-fried chicken and vegetables. It seemed as though she was unusually nice to me that night. We talked about all kinds of things, like how long it takes to get used to panty hose and how to take care of your cuticles. I didn't even know I *had* cuticles. I set the table and sliced the bread she'd made, and just before dinner, I went upstairs and put on my long blue nightgown and my best blouse over the top, so I'd look like Marilyn. If Lester married her, I realized, she'd be my sister-in-law, and I wouldn't even need Miss Cole.

"What the heck have *you* got on?" Lester said when I sat down.

"I think she looks lovely," said Marilyn. "At least she's wearing shoes."

Lester got up, slipped on his loafers, and came back to the table.

I did everything Marilyn did. I spread my napkin over

my lap, ate little tiny bites like she did, and rested my arms, not my elbows, on the table. When Lester made a joke, I even laughed delicately and tipped my head to one side. Lester looked at me strangely.

Something was wrong, though, between Lester and Marilyn. Halfway through dinner, I could just tell. When Marilyn talked to me, she smiled, but when she talked to Lester, she looked sort of sad. Lester guessed something was wrong too, and the quieter Marilyn got, the more jokes he made; but it got to the place where I was the only one who was laughing. Finally I realized that Marilyn had come over to cook our dinner because she was going to break up with Lester and she was trying to make it easy on him. I couldn't stand it anymore. I said I'd do the dishes and went out in the kitchen and closed the door, but now and then I still heard their voices.

"We're too different, Lester," Marilyn said. "It just wouldn't work."

Lester was saying something to her, but I couldn't make out what. His voice was soft and urgent, the way he talks to Dad when he needs the car. And finally Marilyn's voice again:

"I'm sorry, Les, but I just want out."

A few minutes later Marilyn stuck her head in the kitchen to say goodnight to me, and then she left. I heard the sound of her car starting up, and then Lester went up to his room.

I sat down at the kitchen table with my head in my

hands. I wasn't the only one who missed having a mother. If Momma were here right now, I bet she'd have gone up to Lester and said something nice. I thought of all the awful things I'd said to him in my lifetime and felt even worse. Finally I got up, took a can of soda pop from the refrigerator and a plate of gingersnaps, and went up to Lester's room.

I opened his door just a crack.

"Can I come in?" I asked. He didn't answer, so I went in. He was lying on his back on the bed, staring up at the ceiling. I softly crossed the room and set the soda pop and cookies beside his bed.

"I just wanted to make you feel better," I said. "I'm sorry about Marilyn."

Lester looked at me and then stared at the ceiling some more.

"Thanks," he said finally.

I sat down on the floor with my back against the wall and stayed there for a long time without saying anything. Lester didn't even seem to know I was there. Now and then he'd sigh, a lonely sigh.

"I miss her, too," I said finally.

Lester jumped when he heard me, and then he sat up. "You still here?"

"Yeah," I said. "I was thinking about Momma. I miss her, too."

"Well, I was thinking about Marilyn," he said, and lay back down.

"You want me to stay and talk?" I asked, and when he

didn't answer, I said, "There are other fish in the ocean." I'd read that somewhere; it's what you say to somebody when they lose a sweetheart. Lester still didn't answer, so I said, "Someday you'll look back on this and laugh." I'd read that, too.

Lester wasn't laughing, however. I started to say, *It's always darkest before the light,* but I didn't. I changed the subject. "What was Momma like?" I asked him. "I can't remember."

Lester put his hands behind his head. His voice was flat, but at least he was talking. "Well, she was tall, taller than Dad. She wore slacks a lot, I remember that. Long legs. Reddish-blond hair. Freckles on her arms. She used to sing songs from musicals—from *Showboat*—that was her favorite. Used to sing when she did the ironing."

I tried to imagine this mother, but somehow she didn't seem to have anything to do with me. She was tall, and I'm only average. I don't have any freckles at all, and I can't carry a tune, either.

I thought again about Marilyn and how nice she would have been as my sister-in-law.

"I'm sorry about Marilyn, Lester, I really am," I told him.

"So am I," he said, and smiled a little bit. Then he reached for the soda pop, and I realized that we had had an entire conversation without being rude to each other once.

I got out the poster that night to bring my life up to date. I had been writing in my journal regularly, but I hadn't wanted to see how long my "Backward" list was getting.

Before I could lose my nerve, I picked up the pencil and wrote, "Kicked Miss Cole," in the right-hand column. Then, under the "Forward" list, I wrote:

> Cleaned Mrs. Plotkin's cupboard
>
> Was Polite to Marilyn
>
> Was kind to Lester

For the first time, the "Forward" column was ahead.

On December first, Mrs. Plotkin collected our journals to see how we were doing. All but a few pages of mine were paper-clipped together. I didn't want her to read about Donald Sheavers. I didn't want her to know about my seeing Patrick in his underwear at the store, either. I certainly didn't want her to read about how disappointed I was that I didn't get Miss Cole for a teacher. The only other things I let her read were about how upset my father got when I confused memories of Momma with Aunt Sally, how I felt about Marilyn breaking up with Lester, and what happened on Halloween.

We had to read fifteen pages in our social studies books that afternoon, and while we were reading, Mrs. Plotkin checked through our journals. I kept lifting my eyes to see when she got to mine. All the journals looked alike on the outside, but mine was the only one with paper clips holding the pages together.

Mrs. Plotkin picked it up at last. She skipped over the paper-clipped pages and read the others slowly, taking her time. I squirmed. I was glad when she went on to someone else's journal.

At two-thirty, Mrs. Plotkin read to us aloud. She had finished *Sounder* and a book called *The Incredible Journey*, and just before Thanksgiving had started *Watership Down*. We were already on chapter five:

"'It was getting on toward moonset when they left the fields and entered the wood. Straggling, catching up with one another, keeping more or less together, they had wandered over half a mile down the fields, always following the course of the brook. . . .'"

No matter what happened to me during the day, the half hour at the end, when Mrs. Plotkin read to us, helped make up for it. When she read, her voice made pictures of the words. She read with such expression that we knew instantly what a character was feeling. The first week I was in her class, I had pretended I was doing my homework all the while she was reading. She never said anything, never paused in icy silence the way some teachers would have done. She simply read, and let the words lure me to the story. It seemed to me now impossible that I could have been so rude. It also seemed a shame that someone as kind as Mrs. Plotkin had to be so homely. *Life is unfair*, I scribbled on my desk top.

As usual, when the bell rang at three, the whole class groaned in dismay that the story was interrupted. But Mrs. Plotkin smiled as she closed the book. "We'll hear some more tomorrow," she promised. Then she handed back our journals.

I stood at my desk for a moment, thumbing through the pages to see if all the paper clips were still there. And suddenly my eye caught something that Mrs. Plotkin had written in the margin. It was on the page about Marilyn breaking up with Lester, and how we both missed having a mother.

Alice McKinley, you have a gift for words! Mrs. Plotkin had said. *Thank you for sharing that gift with me.*

I stared down at the paper, then up at Mrs. Plotkin. She was smiling. I closed my journal and smiled back, then walked quickly out the door and home, too embarrassed to stay. It was the first time in my life that I had felt embarrassed and happy, both at the same time.

Her year with Mrs. Plotkin is turning out much better than Alice first expected. Will Alice's fortunes continue to improve? Will the "Forward" column of her list continue to outpace the "Backward" column?

Meet the Author: **Phyllis Reynolds Naylor**

Phyllis Reynolds Naylor began making up stories when she was too young to write them down and has continued storytelling ever since. At sixteen her career as an author began when she earned $4.67 for a story that appeared in a Sunday-school paper. Naylor went on to write for many magazines for children and adults. After she graduated from college, she realized that she wanted to be a full-time writer. Several years later she published the first of her more than forty books.

Naylor particularly likes writing realistic books that are both sad and funny, such as *The Agony of Alice*. Her favorite of the many books she has written is *A String of Chances*, about a teenage girl named Evie Hutchins who has a difficult summer and learns to look at herself and her family in a new way.

Naylor explains her reasons for writing this way:
"Through my books I can be many different people, living many different places and doing all kinds of interesting things. I can recapture feelings from childhood or project myself into the future. Or I can take a real problem I may be experiencing and work it out on paper. Writing, for me, is the best occupation I can think of, and there is nothing in the world I would rather do."

Responding to Literature

1. In this excerpt the reader comes to know Alice McKinley quite well. Is Alice someone you would like to know in real life? Tell why or why not.

2. Imagine that you are Alice. You have decided to write to a friend who lives far away. What five events about the school year will you include in your letter?

3. Usually we say people are in agony when they are in terrible physical or mental distress. Yet the author has used the word *agony* to describe Alice's situation. Why do you think she chose this word? What is Alice's agony?

4. In time, Alice's attitude toward Miss Cole and Mrs. Plotkin begins to change. How would you describe the change? Why does it take place?

5. Do you think Alice's decision to make a list of good and bad things she does is a wise one? Why?

Abigail knew when she was born
Among the roses, she was a thorn.
Her quiet mother had lovely looks.
Her quiet father wrote quiet books.
Her quiet brothers, correct though pale,
Weren't really prepared for Abigail
Who entered the house with howls and tears
While both of her brothers blocked their ears
And both of her parents, talking low,
Said, "Why is Abigail screaming so?"

Abigail kept on getting worse.
As soon as she teethed she bit her nurse.
At three, she acted distinctly cool
Toward people and things at nursery school.
"I'm sick of cutting out dolls," she said,
And cut a hole in her dress, instead.
Her mother murmured, "She's bold for three."
Her father answered, "I quite agree."
Her brothers mumbled, "We hate to fuss,
But *when* will Abigail be like us?"

Abigail, going through her teens,
Liked overalls and pets and machines.
In college, hating most of its features,
She told off all of her friends and teachers.
Her brothers, graduating from Yale,
Said: "Really, you're hopeless, Abigail."
And while her mother said, "Fix your looks,"
Her father added, "Or else write books."
And Abigail asked, "Is that a dare?"
And wrote a book that would curl your hair. . . .

Kaye Starbird

321

Appreciating Author's Craft

Thinking About First-Person Point of View

An author determines point of view by deciding who will tell a story (the narrator) and how much the narrator will know. The author may choose to use the first-person point of view in which one character, usually the main character, tells the story using *I* and *me.* The first-person point of view is a limited one. The reader learns only the information that the character who is telling the story sees, hears, thinks, and feels. The reader doesn't know what the other characters think or feel, only what the narrator says they think or feel.

First-person point of view is very appealing to readers. Because we share the character's thoughts and feelings, we care about the character. We experience the character's troubles and share hopes and dreams. Here is an example of first-person point of view from *The Agony of Alice:*

> I wanted Miss Cole for my adopted mother more than I wanted anything else in the world. . . . I wanted someone to make a fuss over me and teach me to walk in tiny little steps and bow the way Miss Cole was bowing to some of her students.

Because the story is told from the first-person point of view, we know how badly Alice misses her mother. We feel her loneliness, too. As a result, we hope she will feel better soon.

Writing in the First-Person Point of View

One way to understand the strengths and limitations of first-person point of view is to write from that perspective. You will write a fictional journal entry, one that Alice's father, brother, Mrs. Plotkin, or Miss Cole might write. (For more ideas about writing, look at your Writer's Handbook.)

Prewriting Copy the chart and fill in the blanks to help you imagine how the characters feel about the things that happen to Alice. Lester's response to the Maharaja's Magic incident has been filled in to get you started.

	Maharaja's Magic Incident	Halloween Incident
Ben's thoughts/feelings	_____	_____
Lester's thoughts/feelings	disgusted	_____
Miss Cole's thoughts/feelings	_____	_____
Miss Plotkin's thoughts/feelings	_____	_____

Writing Review the chart and choose the character for whom you will write a journal entry. Then write the entry from that character's point of view. Don't forget to use the words *I* and *me*.

Revising Read your draft to a partner. Discuss whether your journal entry is realistic based on what you learned about that character in the excerpt. Revise your draft, incorporating your partner's suggestions. Proofread for errors before you write your final copy.

Presenting Read your journal entry to the class. Have your classmates guess which character's journal entry you are reading.

Extending Your Reading

Expressing Yourself
Choose one or more of these activities:

Make a "Forward" and "Backward" List Make your own two-column list of achievements and disasters, just as Alice did. Add to the list for a week, a month, or longer.

Draw Three Objects Make a drawing of three of the objects that were important in *The Agony of Alice*. On the bottom of the drawing write why the objects were important to the story.

Act Out a Scene With a friend, create a conversation Miss Cole and Mrs. Plotkin might have about Alice.

Write a Poem About Alice Write a poem about Alice similar to the poem "Abigail" by Kaye Starbird. Before you begin to write, think about what Alice is like. What are her goals? What makes her memorable? If you like, set your poem to music.

Make a Book List What books would you like your teacher to read aloud to the class? Choose three books. Compare your list with your classmates' lists. Perhaps your teacher will read aloud the most popular books.

More Books About Decisions

Courage, Dana by Susan Beth Pfeffer. Delacorte Press. Not everything about being a heroine is wonderful, twelve-year-old Dana Parker discovers. After saving a little boy's life, Dana is the center of attention—some of it unpleasant. When she finds herself caught in a tense situation between the school bully and a new boy, Dana knows she must decide what to do. There is an easy way out. Will she feel right about taking it?

What the Neighbors Did and Other Stories by Philippa Pearce. Thomas Y. Crowell Company. The sad, funny, curious stories in this book, all set in an English town, are about children and their decisions. What will one boy do about the grouchy neighbor who has stolen money from a junk collector? What will Charlie do when he realizes his parents will find out about the party he and his sisters had in the middle of the night?

Night Outside by Patricia Wrightson. Atheneum Publishers. When James's pet bird escapes from their apartment, James and his sister Anne know they must find him. Looking for the bird in the evening dark, the children meet some interesting people who lead them on a roundabout and mystifying search.

Harriet and the Robot by Martin Waddell. Little, Brown and Company. Harriet gives Anthea an almost-living doll for Anthea's birthday. Dolly is no ordinary toy—she's a robot. Dolly looks like a real person, but she has some mechanical problems. When Dolly comes to school, trouble and wild comedy accompany her.

Introducing

Three Tales
by Isaac Bashevis Singer

illustrated by Margot Zemach

Isaac Bashevis Singer grew up listening to Jewish folk tales told by his mother, who had heard them from her mother and grandmother. He drew on his memories, transformed by his imagination, to write these stories. Singer's tales are in his words "products of a way of life rich in fantasy and make-believe."

Life in the Countryside of Eastern Europe

Singer writes about people and places he sees in his mind's eye. The stories take place years ago in towns that never existed. Yet, the setting is not altogether imaginary, for Singer locates these towns in the Jewish communities of eastern Europe. He describes a way of life that was lived there by poor people who were religious, superstitious, and down to earth. Tradition was one of the most important things in their lives. Rabbis, the religious leaders of these towns, were greatly respected. No one dared break a holy oath. Passover and other holy holidays were celebrated with special devotion. Boys attended religious school called *cheder*. The men wore long beards. Most people worked as shopkeepers, cobblers, tailors, butchers, and peddlers.

Thinking About Folk Tales

Every culture has its folk tales, stories that were originally spoken before a group rather than written down. Though folk tales are one of the oldest forms of literature, they remain popular today, perhaps because they deal with problems that all people face at one time or another. Folk tales may be humorous or magical. They may be romantic or sad. They are filled with action and strange events, often containing a riddle to solve or a prize to capture. (For more information about this kind of story, look up *Folk tales* in your Handbook.)

Singer's stories were inspired by Jewish folk tales and share their qualities of simplicity, timelessness, humor, and emphasis on the plot, or story. The scrapes in which Singer's characters find themselves appeal to most readers. You may see yourself and people you know in Singer's characters such as Todie, Lyzer, Gronam, and Shlemiel.

As you're reading these stories on your own, ask yourself what the main characters have gained at the end of the stories they they did not have at the beginning.

Shrewd Todie and Lyzer the Miser

In a village somewhere in the Ukraine there lived a poor man called Todie. Todie had a wife, Shaindel, and seven children, but he could never earn enough to feed them properly. He tried many trades and failed in all of them. It was said of Todie that if he decided to deal in candles the sun would never set. He was nicknamed Shrewd Todie because whenever he managed to make some money, it was always by trickery.

This winter was an especially cold one. The snowfall was heavy and Todie had no money to buy wood for the stove. His seven children stayed in bed all day to keep warm. When the frost burns outside, hunger is stronger than ever, but Shaindel's larder was empty. She reproached Todie bitterly, wailing, "If you can't feed your wife and children, I will go to the rabbi and get a divorce."

"And what will you do with it, eat it?" Todie retorted.

In the same village there lived a rich man called

Lyzer. Because of his stinginess he was known as Lyzer the Miser. He permitted his wife to bake bread only once in four weeks because he had discovered that fresh bread is eaten up more quickly than stale.

Todie had more than once gone to Lyzer for a loan of a few gulden, but Lyzer had always replied: "I sleep better when the money lies in my strongbox rather than in your pocket."

Lyzer had a goat, but he never fed her. The goat had learned to visit the houses of the neighbors, who pitied her and gave her potato peelings. Sometimes, when there were not enough peelings, she would gnaw on the old straw of the thatched roofs. She also had a liking for tree bark. Nevertheless, each year the goat gave birth to a kid. Lyzer milked her but, miser that he was, did not drink the milk himself. Instead he sold it to others.

Todie decided that he would take revenge on Lyzer and at the same time make some much-needed money for himself.

One day, as Lyzer was sitting on a box eating borscht and dry bread (he used his chairs only on holidays so that the upholstery would not wear out), the door opened and Todie came in.

"Reb Lyzer," he said, "I would like to ask you a favor. My oldest daughter, Basha, is already fifteen and she's about to became engaged. A young man is coming from Janev to look her over. My cutlery is tin, and my wife is ashamed to ask the young man to eat soup with a tin spoon. Would you lend me one of your silver spoons? I give you my holy word that I will return it to you tomorrow."

Lyzer knew that Todie would not dare to break a holy oath and he lent him the spoon.

No young man came to see Basha that evening. As

usual, the girl walked around barefoot and in rags, and the silver spoon lay hidden under Todie's shirt. In the early years of his marriage Todie had possessed a set of silver tableware himself. He had, however, long since sold it all, with the exception of three silver teaspoons that were used only on Passover.

The following day, as Lyzer, his feet bare (in order to save his shoes), sat on his box eating borscht and dry bread, Todie returned.

"Here is the spoon I borrowed yesterday," he said, placing it on the table together with one of his own teaspoons.

"What is the teaspoon for?" Lyzer asked.

And Todie said: "Your tablespoon gave birth to a teaspoon. It is her child. Since I am an honest man, I'm returning both mother and child to you."

Lyzer looked at Todie in astonishment. He had never heard of a silver spoon giving birth to another. Nevertheless, his greed overcame his doubt and he happily accepted both spoons. Such an unexpected piece of good fortune! He was overjoyed that he had loaned Todie the spoon.

A few days later, as Lyzer (without his coat, to save it) was again sitting on his box eating borscht with dry bread, the door opened and Todie appeared.

"The young man from Janev did not please Basha because he had donkey ears, but this evening another young man is coming to look her over. Shaindel is cooking soup for him, but she's ashamed to serve him with a tin spoon. Would you lend me . . ."

Even before Todie could finish the sentence, Lyzer interrupted. "You want to borrow a silver spoon? Take it with pleasure."

The following day Todie once more returned the spoon

and with it one of his own silver teaspoons. He again explained that during the night the large spoon had given birth to a small one and in all good conscience he was bringing back the mother and newborn baby. As for the young man who had come to look Basha over, she hadn't liked him either, because his nose was so long that it reached to his chin. Needless to say that Lyzer the Miser was overjoyed.

Exactly the same thing happened a third time. Todie related that this time his daughter had rejected her suitor because he stammered. He also reported that Lyzer's silver spoon had again given birth to a baby spoon.

"Does it ever happen that a spoon has twins?" Lyzer inquired.

Todie thought it over for a moment. "Why not? I've even heard of a case where a spoon had triplets."

Almost a week passed by and Todie did not go to see Lyzer. But on Friday morning, as Lyzer (in his under-drawers to save his pants) sat on his box eating borscht and dry bread, Todie came in and said, "Good day to you, Reb Lyzer."

"A good morning and many more to you," Lyzer replied in his friendliest manner. "What good fortune brings you here? Did you perhaps come to borrow a silver spoon? If so, help yourself."

"Today I have a very special favor to ask. This evening a young man from the big city of Lublin is coming to look Basha over. He is the son of a rich man and I'm told he is clever and handsome as well. Not only do I need a silver spoon, but since he will remain with us over the Sabbath I need a pair of silver candlesticks, because mine are brass and my wife is ashamed to place them on the Sabbath table. Would you lend me your candlesticks?

Immediately after the Sabbath, I will return them to you."

Silver candlesticks are of great value and Lyzer the Miser hesitated, but only for a moment.

Remembering his good fortune with the spoons, he said: "I have eight silver candlesticks in my house. Take them all. I know you will return them to me just as you say. And if it should happen that any of them give birth, I have no doubt that you will be as honest as you have been in the past."

"Certainly," Todie said. "Let's hope for the best."

The silver spoon, Todie hid beneath his shirt as usual. But taking the candlesticks, he went directly to a merchant, sold them for a considerable sum, and brought the money to Shaindel. When Shaindel saw so much money, she demanded to know where he had gotten such a treasure.

"When I went out, a cow flew over our roof and dropped a dozen silver eggs," Todie replied. "I sold them and here is the money."

"I have never heard of a cow flying over a roof and laying silver eggs," Shaindel said doubtingly.

"There is always a first time," Todie answered. "If you don't want the money, give it back to me."

"There'll be no talk about giving it back," Shaindel said. She knew that her husband was full of cunning and tricks—but when the children are hungry and the larder is empty, it is better not to ask too many questions. Shaindel went to the marketplace and bought meat, fish, white flour, and even some nuts and raisins for a pudding. And since a lot of money still remained, she bought shoes and clothes for the children.

It was a very gay Sabbath in Todie's house. The boys sang and the girls danced. When the children asked their father where he had gotten the money, he replied: "It is forbidden to mention money during the Sabbath."

Sunday, as Lyzer (barefoot and almost naked to save his clothes) sat on his box finishing up a dry crust of bread with borscht, Todie arrived and, handing him his silver spoon, said: "It's too bad. This time your spoon did not give birth to a baby."

"What about the candlesticks?" Lyzer inquired anxiously.

Todie sighed deeply. "The candlesticks died."

Lyzer got up from his box so hastily that he over-turned his plate of borscht.

"You fool! How can candlesticks die?" he screamed.

"If spoons can give birth, candlesticks can die."

Lyzer raised a great hue and cry and had Todie called before the rabbi. When the rabbi heard both sides of the story, he burst out laughing. "It serves you right," he said to Lyzer. "If you hadn't chosen to believe that spoons give birth, now you would not be forced to believe that your candlesticks died."

"But it's all nonsense," Lyzer objected.

"Did you not expect the candlesticks to give birth to other candlesticks?" the rabbi said admonishingly. "If you accept nonsense when it brings you profit, you must also accept nonsense when it brings you loss." And he dismissed the case.

The following day, when Lyzer the Miser's wife brought him his borscht and dry bread, Lyzer said to her, "I will eat only the bread. Borscht is too expensive a food, even without sour cream."

The story of the silver spoons that gave birth and the candlesticks that died spread quickly through the town. All the people enjoyed Todie's victory and Lyzer the Miser's defeat. The shoemaker's and tailor's apprentices, as was their custom whenever there was an important happening, made up a song about it:

> Lyzer, put your grief aside.
> What if your candlesticks have died?
> You're the richest man on earth
> With silver spoons that can give birth
> And silver eggs as living proof
> Of flying cows above your roof.
> Don't sit there eating crusts of bread—
> To silver grandsons look ahead.

However, time passed and Lyzer's silver spoons never gave birth again.

Responding to Literature

1. Could the events in Shrewd Todie and Lyzer the Miser really have taken place? Give reasons for your answer.

2. Suppose you were a visitor to Todie and Lyzer's town. What would people tell you about Todie, Lyzer, and their dispute over the silver candlestick?

3. Though most rabbis are wise and educated men, they make mistakes from time to time as other people do. Do you think the rabbi made the correct decision in the case Lyzer brought against Todie? Tell why.

4. Everyone in town learned of Todie's victory over Lyzer. The shoemakers' and tailors' apprentices even wrote a song about the event. Why did the people enjoy Todie's triumph so much?

5. Is Lyzer's behavior likely to change as a result of his experience with Todie? Why?

The Elders of Chelm and Genendel's Key

It was known that the village of Chelm was ruled by the head of the community council and the six Elders, all fools. The name of the head was Gronam the Ox. The Elders were Dopey Lekisch, Zeinvel Ninny, Treitel the Fool, Sender Donkey, Shmendrick Numskull, and Feyvel Thickwit. Gronam the Ox was the oldest. He had a curly white beard and a high, bulging forehead.

Since Gronam had a large house, the Elders usually met there. Every now and then Gronam's wife, Genendel, brought them refreshments—tea, cakes, and jam.

Gronam would have been a happy man except for the fact that each time the elders left, Genendel would reproach him for speaking nonsense. In her opinion her highly respected husband was a simpleton.

Once, after such a quarrel, Gronam said to his wife: "What is the sense in nagging me after the elders have gone? In the future, whenever you hear me saying something silly, come into the room and let me know. I will immediately change the subject."

"But how can I tell you you're talking nonsense in

front of the Elders? If they learn you're a fool, you'll lose your job as head of the council."

"If you're so clever find a way," Gronam replied.

Genendel thought a moment and suddenly exclaimed, "I have it."

"Well?"

"When you say something silly, I will come in and hand you the key to our strongbox. Then you'll know you've been talking like a fool."

Gronam was so delighted with his wife's idea that he clapped his hands. "Near me, you too become clever."

A few days later the Elders met in Gronam's house. The subject under discussion was the coming Pentecost, a holiday when a lot of sour cream is needed to eat with blintzes. That year there was a scarcity of sour cream. It had been a dry spring and the cows gave little milk.

The Elders pulled at their beards and rubbed their foreheads, signs that their brains were hard at work. But none of them could figure out how to get enough sour cream for the holiday.

Suddenly Gronam pounded on the table with his fist and called out: "I have it!"

"What is it?"

"Let us make a law that water is to be called sour cream and sour cream is to be called water. Since there is plenty of water in the wells of Chelm, each housewife will have a full barrel of sour cream."

"What a wonderful idea," cried Sender Donkey.

"A stroke of genius," shrieked Zenivel Ninny.

"Only Gronam the Ox could think of something so brilliant," Dopey Lekisch proclaimed.

Treitel the Fool, Shmendrick Numskull, and Feyvel Thickwit all agreed. Feyvel Thickwit, the community scribe, took out pen and parchment and set down the

340

new law. From that day on, water was to be called sour cream and sour cream, water.

As usual, when they had finished with community business, the Elders turned to more general subjects. Gronam said: "Last night I couldn't sleep a wink for thinking about why it is hot in the summertime. Finally the answer came to me."

"What is it?" the Elders chorused.

"Because all winter long the stoves are heated and this heat stays in Chelm and makes the summer hot."

All the Elders nodded their heads, excepting Dopey Lekisch, who asked: "Then why is it cold in the winter?"

"It's clear why," replied Gronam. "The stoves are not heated in the summer, so there is not heat left over for the winter."

The Elders were enthusiastic about Gronam's great knowledge. After such mental effort, they began to look towards the kitchen, expecting Genendel to appear with the tea, cakes, and jam.

Genendel did come in, but instead of a tray she carried a key, which she gave to her husband, saying: "Gronam, here is the key to the strongbox."

Today of all days Gronam was confident that his mouth had uttered only clever words. But there stood Genendel with the key in her hand, a sure sign that he had spoken like a fool. He grew so angry that he turned to the Elders and said: "Tell me, what foolishness have I spoken that my wife brings me the key to our strongbox?"

The Elders were perplexed at this question and Gronam explained his agreement with Genendel, that she should give him the key when he talked like an idiot. "But today, didn't I speak words of high wisdom? You be the judges."

The elders were furious with Genendel. Feyvel Thickwit spoke out. "We are the Elders of Chelm, and we understand everything. No woman can tell us what is wise and what is silly."

They then discussed the matter and made a new law: whenever Genendel believed that her husband was talking like a fool, she was to come in and give the key to the Elders. If they agreed, they would tell Gronam the Ox to change the subject. If they did not agree, she was to bring out a double portion of tea, cakes, and jam and three blintzes for every sage.

Feyvel Thickwit immediately recorded the new law on parchment and stamped it with the seal of Chelm, which was an ox with six horns.

From that day on, Gronam could talk freely at meetings, since Genendel was very stingy. She did not want the elders of Chelm to gorge themselves with her beloved blintzes.

That Pentecost there was no lack of "sour cream" in Chelm, but some housewives complained that there was a lack of "water." But this was an entirely new problem, to be solved after the holiday.

Gronam the Ox became famous all over the world as the sage who—by passing a law—gave Chelm a whole river and many wells full of sour cream.

Responding to Literature

1. Do you think the discussions Gronam has with the other Elders are funny? Why or why not?

2. What might Genendel write in a letter to her sister about the Elders and the meeting at which they decided to call water sour cream?

3. Genendel has a plan to keep Gronam from uttering foolishness. Even though Gronam agrees that the plan is a good one, it fails. Why does this happen?

4. Clearly, Genendel is much smarter than Gronam and the other Elders, yet she has no say in governing Chelm. Why do you think this is?

5. The author is trying to tell readers something about government in general in this story of the Elders of Chelm. What might Singer's message be?

When Shlemiel Went to Warsaw

Though Shlemiel was a lazybones and a sleepyhead and hated to move, he always daydreamed of taking a trip. He had heard many stories about faraway countries, huge deserts, deep oceans, and high mountains, and often discussed with Mrs. Shlemiel his great wish to go on a long journey. Mrs. Shlemiel would reply: "Long journeys are not for a Shlemiel. You better stay home and mind the children while I go to market to sell my vegetables." Yet Shemiel could not bring himself to give up his dream of seeing the world and its wonders.

A recent visitor to Chelm had told Shlemiel marvelous things about the city of Warsaw. How beautiful the streets were, how high the buildings and luxurious the stores. Shlemiel decided once and for all that he must see this great city for himself. He knew that one had to prepare for a journey. But what was there for him to take? He had nothing but the old clothes he wore. One morning, after Mrs. Shlemiel left for the market, he told the older boys to stay home from cheder and mind the younger children. Then he took a few slices of bread, an onion, and a clove of garlic, put them in a kerchief, tied it into a bundle, and started for Warsaw on foot.

There was a street in Chelm called Warsaw Street and Shlemiel believed that it led directly to Warsaw. While still in the village, he was stopped by several neighbors who asked him where he was going. Shlemiel told them that he was on his way to Warsaw.

"What will you do in Warsaw?" they asked him.

Shlemiel replied: "What do I do in Chelm? Nothing."

He soon reached the outskirts of town. He walked slowly because the soles of his boots were worn through. Soon the houses and stores gave way to pastures and fields. He passed a peasant driving an ox-drawn plow. After several hours of walking, Shlemiel grew tired. He was so weary that he wasn't even hungry. He lay down on the grass near the roadside for a nap, but before he fell asleep he thought: "When I wake up, I may not remember which is the way to Warsaw and which leads back to Chelm." After pondering a moment, he removed his boots and set them down beside him with the toes pointing toward Warsaw and the heels toward Chelm. He soon fell asleep and dreamed that he was a baker baking onion rolls with poppy seeds. Customers came to buy them and Shlemiel said: "These onion rolls are not for sale."

"Then why do you bake them?"

"They are for my wife, my children, and for me."

Later he dreamed that he was the king of Chelm. Once a year, instead of taxes, each citizen brought him a pot of strawberry jam. Shlemiel sat on a golden throne and nearby sat Mrs. Shlemiel, the queen, and his

children, the princes and princesses. They were all eating onion rolls and spooning up big portions of strawberry jam. A carriage arrived and took the royal family to Warsaw, America, and to the River Sambation, which spurts out stones the week long and rests on the Sabbath.

Near the road, a short distance from where Shlemiel slept, was a smithy. The blacksmith happened to come out just in time to see Shlemiel carefully placing his boots at his side with the toes facing in the direction of Warsaw. The blacksmith was a prankster and as soon as Shlemiel was sound asleep he tiptoed over and turned the boots around. When Shlemiel awoke, he felt rested but hungry. He got out a slice of bread, rubbed it with garlic, and took a bite of onion. Then he pulled his boots on and continued on his way.

He walked along and everything looked strangely familiar. He recognized houses that he had seen before. It seemed to him that he knew the people he met. Could it be that he had already reached another town, Shlemiel wondered. And why was it so similar to Chelm? He stopped a passer-by and asked the name of the town. "Chelm," the man replied.

Shlemiel was astonished. How was this possible? He had walked away from Chelm. How could he have arrived back there? He began to rub his forehead and soon found the answer to the riddle. There were two Chelms and he had reached the second one.

Still it seemed very odd that the streets, the houses, the people were so similar to those in the Chelm he had left behind. Shlemiel puzzled over this fact until he suddenly remembered something he had learned in cheder: "The earth is the same everywhere." And so why shouldn't the second Chelm be exactly like the first one? This discovery gave Shlemiel great satisfaction. He wondered if there was a street here like his street and a

348

house on it like the one he lived in. And indeed he soon
arrived at an identical street and house. Evening had
fallen. He opened the door and to his amazement saw a
second Mrs. Shlemiel with children just like his. Everything was exactly the same as in his own household.
Even the cat seemed the same, Mrs. Shlemiel at once
began to scold him.

"Shlemiel, where did you go? You left the house alone.
And what have you there in that bundle?"

The children all ran to him and cried: "Papa, where
have you been?"

Shlemiel paused a moment and then he said; "Mrs.
Shlemiel, I'm not your husband. Children, I'm not your
papa."

"Have you lost your mind?" Mrs. Shlemiel screamed.

"I am Shlemiel of Chelm One and this is Chelm Two."

Mrs. Shlemiel clapped her hands so hard that the
chickens sleeping under the stove awoke in fright and
flew out all over the room.

"Children, your father has gone crazy," she wailed. She
immediately sent one of the boys for Gimpel, the healer.
All the neighbors came crowding in. Shlemiel stood in
the middle of the room and proclaimed: "It's true, you all
look like the people in my town, but you are not the same.
I come from Chelm One and you live in Chelm Two."

"Shlemiel, what's the matter with you?" someone cried.
"You're in your own house, with your own wife and
children, your own neighbors and friends."

"No, you don't understand. I come from Chelm One. I
was on my way to Warsaw, and between Chelm One and
Warsaw there is a Chelm Two. And that is where I am."

"What are you talking about. We all know you and you
know all of us. Don't you recognize your chickens?"

"No, I'm not in my town," Shlemiel insisted. "But," he
continued, "Chelm Two does have the same people and
the same houses as Chelm One, and that is why you are

mistaken. Tomorrow I will continue on to Warsaw."

"In that case, where is my husband?" Mrs. Shlemiel inquired in a rage, and she proceeded to berate Shlemiel with all the curses she could think of.

"How should I know where your husband is?" Shlemiel replied.

Some of the neighbors could not help laughing; others pitied the family. Gimpel, the healer, announced that he knew of no remedy for such an illness. After some time, everybody went home.

Mrs. Shlemiel had cooked noodles and beans that evening, a dish that Shlemiel liked especially. She said to him: "You may be mad, but even a madman has to eat."

"Why should you feed a stranger?" Shlemiel asked.

"As a matter of fact, an ox like you should eat straw, not noodles and beans. Sit down and be quiet. Maybe some food and rest will bring you back to your senses."

"Mrs. Shlemiel, you're a good woman. My wife wouldn't feed a stranger. It would seem that there is some small difference between the two Chelms."

The noodles and beans smelled so good that Shlemiel needed no further coaxing. He sat down and as he ate he spoke to the children.

"My dear children, I live in a house that looks exactly like this one. I have a wife and she is as like your mother as two peas are like each other. My children resemble you as drops of water resemble one another."

The younger children laughed; the older ones began to cry. Mrs. Shlemiel said: "As if being a Shlemiel wasn't enough, he had to go crazy in addition. What am I going to do now? I won't be able to leave the children with him when I go to market. Who knows what a madman may do?" She clasped her head in her hands and cried out: "God in heaven, what have I done to deserve this?"

Nevertheless, she made up a fresh bed for Shlemiel; and even though he had napped during the day, near the smithy, the moment his head touched the pillow he fell fast asleep and was soon snoring loudly. He again dreamed that he was the king of Chelm and that his wife, the queen, had fried for him a huge panful of blintzes. Some were filled with cheese, others with blueberries or cherries, and all were sprinkled with sugar and cinnamon and were drowning in sour cream. Shlemiel ate twenty blintzes all at once and hid the remainder in his crown for later. In the morning, when Shlemiel awoke, the house was filled with townspeople. Mrs. Shlemiel stood in their midst, her eyes red with weeping. Shlemiel was about to scold his wife for letting so many strangers into the house, but then he remembered that he himself was a stranger here. At home, he would have gotten up, washed, and dressed. Now in front of all these people he was at a loss as to what to do. As always when he was embarrassed, he began to scratch his head and pull at his beard. Finally, overcoming his bashfulness, he decided to get up. He threw off the covers and put his bare feet on the floor. "Don't let him run away," Mrs. Shlemiel screamed. "He'll disappear and I'll be a deserted wife, without a Shlemiel."

At this point Baruch, the baker, interrupted. "Let's take him to the Elders. They'll know what to do."

"That's right! Let's take him to the Elders," everybody agreed.

Although Shlemiel insisted that since he lived in Chelm One, the local Elders had no power over him, several of the strong young men helped him into his pants, his boots, his coat and cap and escorted him to the house of Gronam the Ox. The Elders, who had already heard of the matter, had gathered early in the morning to consider what was to be done.

As the crowd came in, one of the Elders, Dopey Lekisch, was saying, "Maybe there really are two Chelms."

"If there are two, then why can't there be three, four, or even a hundred Chelms?" Sender Donkey interrupted.

"And even if there are a hundred Chelms, must there be a Shlemiel in each one of them?" argued Shmendrick Numskull.

Gronam the Ox, the head Elder, listened to all the arguments but was not yet prepared to express an opinion. However, his wrinkled, bulging forehead indicated that he was deep in thought. It was Gronam the Ox who questioned Shlemiel. Shlemiel related everything that had happened to him, and when he finished, Gronam asked; "Do you recognize me?"

"Surely. You are wise Gronam the Ox."

"And in your Chelm is there also a Gronam the Ox?"

"Yes, there is a Gronam the Ox and he looks exactly like you."

"Isn't it possible that you turned around and came back to Chelm?" Gronam inquired.

"Why should I turn around? I'm not a windmill." Shlemiel replied.

"In that case, you are not this Mrs. Shlemiel's husband."

"No, I'm not."

"Then Mrs. Shlemiel's husband, the real Shlemiel, must have left the day you came."

"It would seem so."

"Then he'll probably come back."

"Probably."

"In that case, you must wait until he returns. Then we'll know who is who."

"Dear Elders, my Shlemiel has come back," screamed Mrs. Shlemiel. "I don't need two Shlemiels. One is more than enough."

"Whoever he is, he may not live in your house until everything is made clear," Gronam insisted.

"Where shall I live?" Shlemiel asked.

"In the poorhouse."

"What will I do in the poorhouse?"

"What do you do at home?"

"Good God, who will take care of my children when I go to market?" moaned Mrs. Shlemiel. "Besides, I want a husband. Even a Shlemiel is better than no husband at all."

"Are we to blame that your husband left you and went to Warsaw?" Gronam asked. "Wait until he comes home."

Mrs. Shlemiel wept bitterly and the children cried too. Shlemiel said: "How strange. My own wife always scolded me. My children talked back to me. And here a strange woman and strange children want me to live with them. It looks to me as if Chelm Two is actually better than Chelm One."

"Just a moment. I think I have an idea," interrupted Gronam.

"What is your idea?" Zeinvel Ninny inquired.

"Since we decided to send Shlemiel to the poorhouse, the town will have to hire someone to take care of Mrs. Shlemiel's children so she can go to market. Why not hire Shlemiel for that? It's true, he is not Mrs. Shlemiel's husband or the children's father. But he is so much like the real Shlemiel that the children will feel at home with him."

"What a wonderful idea!" cried Feyvel Thickwit.

"Only King Solomon could have thought of such a wise solution," agreed Treitel the Fool.

"Such a clever way out of this dilemma could only have been thought of in our Chelm," chimed in Shmendrick Numskull.

"How much do you want to be paid to take care of Mrs. Shlemiel's children?" asked Gronam.

For a moment Shlemiel stood there completely bewildered. Then he said, "Three groschen a day."

"Idiot, moron, ass!" screamed Mrs. Shlemiel. "What are three groschen nowadays? You shouldn't do it for less than six a day." She ran over to Shlemiel and pinched him on the arm. Shlemiel winced and cried out, "She pinches just like my wife."

The Elders held a consultation among themselves. The town budget was very limited. Finally Gronam announced: "Three groschen may be too little but six groschen a day is definitely too much, especially for a stranger. We will compromise and pay you five groschen a day. Shlemiel, do you accept?"

"Yes, but how long am I to keep this job?"

"Until the real Shlemiel comes home."

Gronam's decision was soon known throughout Chelm and the town admired his great wisdom and that of all the Elders of Chelm.

At first, Shlemiel tried to keep for himself the five groschen that the town paid him. "If I'm not your husband, I don't have to support you," he told Mrs. Shlemiel.

"In that case, since I'm not your wife, I don't have to cook for you, darn your socks, or patch your clothes."

And so, of course, Shlemiel turned over his pay to her. It was the first time that Mrs. Shlemiel had ever gotten any money for the household from Shlemiel. Now when she was in a good mood, she would say to him: "What a pity you didn't decide to go to Warsaw ten years ago."

"Don't you ever miss your husband?" Shlemiel would ask.

"And what about you? Don't you miss your wife?" Mrs. Shlemiel would ask.

And both would admit that they were quite happy with matters as they stood.

Years passed and no Shlemiel returned to Chelm. The Elders had many explanations for this. Zeinvel Ninny believed that Shlemiel had crossed the black mountains and had been eaten alive by the cannibals who live there. Dopey Lekisch thought that Shlemiel most probably had come to the Castle of Asmodeus, where he had been forced to marry a demon princess. Shmendrick Numskull came to the conclusion that Shlemiel had reached the edge of the world and had fallen off. There were many other theories. For example, that the real Shlemiel had lost his memory and had simply forgotten that he was Shlemiel. Such things do happen.

Gronam did not like to impose his theories on other people; however, he was convinced that Shlemiel had gone to the other Chelm, where he had had exactly the same experience as the Shlemiel in this Chelm. He had been hired by the local community and was taking care of the other Mrs. Shlemiel's children for a wage of five groschen a day.

As for Schlemiel himself, he no longer knew what to think. The children were growing up and soon would be able to take care of themselves. Sometimes Shlemiel would sit and ponder. Where is the other Shlemiel? When will he come home? What is my real wife doing? Is she waiting for me, or has she got herself another Shlemiel? These were questions that he could not answer.

Every now and then Shlemiel would still get the desire to go traveling, but he could not bring himself to start out. What was the point of going on a trip if it led nowhere? Often, as he sat alone puzzling over the strange ways of the world, he would become more and more confused and begin humming to himself:

> *"Those who leave Chelm*
> *End up in Chelm.*
> *Those who remain in Chelm*
> *Are certainly in Chelm.*
> *All roads lead to Chelm.*
> *All the world is one big Chelm."*

Meet the Author: **Isaac Bashevis Singer**

When Isaac Bashevis Singer, a small lively old man with bright blue eyes, sits down in his apartment in New York City to write, he does so in a language called Yiddish. Yiddish was the first language Singer heard in Radzymin, Poland, where he was born. Yiddish was developed in the tenth century. It came from a form of old German and borrowed from other languages as it traveled with Jews around the world. Before World War II, Yiddish was spoken by eleven million people. Now only four million speak Yiddish. When an interviewer asked Singer why he likes to write in a language most people can only read in translation, he said, "I like to write ghost stories and nothing fits a ghost better than a dying language. The deader the language, the more alive is the ghost. Ghosts love Yiddish, and as far as I know, they all speak it."

As a young boy, the son of a rabbi, Singer was filled with endless questions. His childhood questions and experiences remain vivid to him. Perhaps this is one reason Singer, a Nobel Prize-winning author of dozens of books for adults, expecially enjoys writing for children. Singer has said that children are the best readers of genuine literature. "The young reader demands a real story, with a beginning, a middle, and an end, the way stories have been told for thousands of years."

Responding to Literature

1. Which of the characters in the three Singer stories would you most like to move in to the house next door to you? Why?

2. Imagine that you are the town crier in Chelm. Finish this announcement, "Hear ye, hear ye, Shlemiel has returned but . . ."

3. Shlemiel is without a doubt a lazybones and sleepy-head. He is so dense that he never discovers the mistake that changes his life. What would you say to convince Shlemiel that there is only one Chelm?

4. Singer's stories take place long ago. List five details that tell you these stories are about days gone by.

5. What have Todie, Gronam, and Shlemiel gained at the end of the stories in which they appear that they did not have at the beginning?

Yarns
from "The People, Yes"

They have yarns
 Of a skyscraper so tall
  they had to put hinges
   On the two top stories
    so to let the moon go by,
 Of one corn crop in Missouri when the roots
  Went so deep and drew off so much water
   The Mississippi riverbed that year was dry,
 Of pancakes so thin
  they had only one side,
 Of "a fog so thick
  we shingled the barn
   and six feet out on the fog,"
 Of Pecos Pete straddling a cyclone
  in Texas and riding it to the west coast
   where "it rained out under him,"
 Of the man who drove a swarm of bees
  across the Rocky Mountains and the Desert
   "and didn't lose a bee."
 Of a mountain railroad curve
  where the engineer in his cab can touch the caboose
   and spit in the conductor's eye,
 Of the boy who climbed a cornstalk
  growing so fast he would have starved to death
   if they hadn't shot biscuits up to him,
 Of the old man's whiskers:
  "When the wind was with him
   his whiskers arrived a day before he did,"

Of the hen laying a square egg
   and cackling, "Ouch!" and of hens laying eggs
      with the dates printed on them,
Of the ship captain's shadow:
   it froze to the deck
      one cold winter night,
Of mutineers on that same ship
   put to chipping rust
      with rubber hammers,
Of the sheep-counter
   who was fast and accurate:
      "I just count their feet and divide by four,"
Of the man so tall
   he must climb a ladder
      to shave himself,
Of the runt so teeny-weeny
   it takes two men and a boy
      to see him,
Of mosquitoes:
   one can kill a dog,
      two of them a man,
Of a cyclone that sucked cookstoves
   out of the kitchen, up the chimney flue,
      and on to the next town,
Of the same cyclone picking up wagon-tracks
   in Nebraska and dropping them
      over in the Dakotas,
Of the hook-and-eye snake
   unlocking itself into forty pieces, each piece two inches long,
      then in nine seconds flat snapping itself together again,

Of the watch swallowed by the cow:
　　when they butchered her a year later the watch was running
　　　　and had the correct time,
Of horned snakes, hoop snakes that roll themselves
　　where they want to go, and rattlesnakes
　　　　carrying bells instead of rattles on their tails,
Of the herd of cattle in California
　　getting lost in a giant redwood tree
　　　　that had been hollowed out,
Of the man who killed a snake
　　by putting its tail in its mouth
　　　　so it swallowed itself,
Of railroad trains whizzing along
　　so fast they reached the station
　　　　before the whistle,
Of pigs so thin
　　the farmer had to tie knots
　　　　in their tails
　　　　　　to keep them from crawling
　　　　　　　　through the cracks in their pens,
Of Paul Bunyan's big blue ox, Babe,
　　measuring between the eyes
　　　　forty-two ax-handles and a plug
　　　　　　of Star tobacco exactly,
Of John Henry's hammer
　　and the curve of its swing
　　　　and his singing of it
　　　　　　as "a rainbow round my shoulder." They have yarns . . .

Carl Sandburg

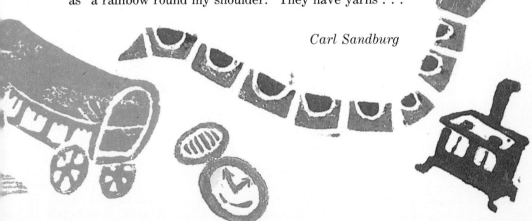

361

Appreciating Author's Craft

Thinking About Folk Tales

I B. Singer's stories are based on the folk tales he knew as a boy and share many of the qualities common to these tales. Folk tales often involve impossible or unlikely events. For example, in "Jack and the Beanstalk," Jack plants a seed and the beanstalk sprouts up to the sky. In Singer's "Shrewd Todie and Lyzer the Miser," at least one character thinks it possible for spoons to give birth. Todie tells his wife that he got money when a cow flew over the roof and dropped a dozen silver eggs. Exaggeration helps make Singer's tales and the folk tales which inspired them humorous and magical.

Riddles or problems to solve play a part in many traditional folk tales and in Singer's stories. For example, Shlemiel's problem becomes so exaggerated that this dialogue occurs.

> As the crowd came, one of the Elders, Dopey Lekisch, was saying, "Maybe there really are two Chelms."
> "If there are two, then why can't there be three, four, or even a hundred Chelms?" Sender Donkey interrupted.

Exaggeration and problem solving that leads to ridiculous answers, elements often found in folk tales, help make "When Shlemiel went to Warsaw" a humorous and enjoyable story.

Writing a Tale

You will write a humorous tale that centers on the problem of one character. Your story will start with a common event or problem and end with an exaggerated solution. (For more ideas about writing, look at your Writer's Handbook.)

Prewriting Think about the exaggerated action in Singer's stories. Notice that the action starts with a common event and moves to a humorous explanation.

Then think of an ordinary event and how it might be exaggerated in an amusing way. Add your event to the chart.

Event	Exaggeration
Todie borrows spoons	Todie says the spoons gave birth
Summer is hot	Stoves in the winter make summer hot
Shlemiel gets turned around on his journey to Warsaw	Shelmiel decides there must be two Chelms

Writing Reread the chart. Focus on the event and exaggeration you added. Choose a character to participate in the event you listed. Use the information to write a tale of a few paragraphs starting with, "Once upon a time" or "Long, long ago." Have the final paragraph of your tale include a lesson your character learned.

Revising Reread your draft with a partner. Does your story have a beginning (the event), a middle (the exaggeration), and an end (the lesson)? If not, revise your draft to add a few lines to include these elements. Then proofread your draft and write your final copy.

Presenting Read your tale to the class. Ask your classmates if they understood and enjoyed the humor based on exaggeration in your story.

Extending Your Reading

Expressing Yourself

Choose one or more of the following activities:

Learn About Yiddish As you have learned, Isaac Bashevis Singer's stories were written in a language called Yiddish and then translated into English. Some names in his stories, for example Shlemiel and Shmendrick, are Yiddish words. Find out all you can about this language. Make a list of the Yiddish words in the stories you read and their definitions.

Collect Folk Tales Do you know anyone who has heard folk tales from parents or grandparents? Find someone who enjoys telling folk tales and make a tape of the person telling a favorite tale.

Compare Folk Tales Work with a group to gather books of folk tales from various countries. Display the books you have collected in your classroom.

Read Some Yarns Aloud Reread the poem on pages 359–361. Look through books of tall tales to find some of the yarns described in the poem and read one or several tall tales aloud to the class. Work with a partner, if you like.

Make a Book of Tales Collect the tales your classmates have written, choose several students to illustrate them, and assemble the tales in book form to place in the class library. Share your stories with another classroom.

More Books About Days Gone By

Bo Rabbit Smart for True by Priscilla Jaquith. Philomel Books. For two hundred years, the Gullah people have lived in South Carolina and Georgia and have told stories about animals, such as Bo Rabbit, who knew how to get nearly anything he wanted and how to trick almost anyone. But what about Snake, who is tricky enough to hypnotize a bear? Can he match wits with Bo Rabbit?

The Old Banjo by Dennis Haseley. Macmillan Publishing Company. As a boy and his father work on their farm, they wonder about the old musical instruments left by someone who lived there before them. The instruments are dusty and broken, but they have their own lives and begin to play faintly, as if they are talking with each other. They remember the old days in their own magical way . . .

Coyote Tales by Hettie Jones. Holt, Rinehart and Winston. One of the most famous tricksters of the old days is Coyote, about whom the Indians of North America told many stories. Here are four tales about this smartest of animals. Who but Coyote could steal the summer right out from under the nose of a watchful man? Who else could destroy the monster Iya?

A Gift for Mama by Esther Hautzig. The Viking Press. This story takes place in Vilna, a city in Poland, in the early part of this centrury. Sara has always made presents for her mother, but this Mother's Day she wants to earn money to buy slippers for her. Can Sara earn enough money? What will mother think of the store-bought gift?

In the Year of the Boar and Jackie Robinson

by Bette Bao Lord
illustrated by Marc Simont

In the **Year** of the **Boar** and **Jackie Robinson**

The year is 1947 and the Brooklyn Dodgers are locked in a race for the National League pennant. Throughout Brooklyn baseball fans are gathered around their radios listening to announcer Red Barber. Unfortunately, unruly triplets keep one fan, Shirley Temple Wong, from concentrating on the radio. Shirley, a young Chinese immigrant, finds that the triplets cause her more problems than the Cardinals cause the Dodgers. However, the desperate Shirley has a plan to pacify the triplets.

Brooklyn in 1947

Bette Bao Lord's novel *In the Year of the Boar and Jackie Robinson* is a work of historical fiction. (For more information about this sort of story, look up *Historical fiction* in your Handbook.) It takes place in Brooklyn, the largest of New York City's five boroughs, or sections, in the time just after World War II. The neighborhoods of Brooklyn are filled with immigrants from many nations. These new arrivals bring their old cultures with them. For example, Chinese immigrants such as Shirley's family still follow the Chinese calendar. To them, 1947 is also the Year of the Boar.

One thing draws these immigrants together and gives them a common bond. One thing makes them proud to live in Brooklyn—their beloved Brooklyn Dodgers. For years Brooklyn has loved to hate its "bums," as they call their losing team. But 1947 is different. The Brooklyn Dodgers make history.

The Dodgers decide to bring the first Black player, Jackie Robinson, to the major leagues. Branch Rickey, the Dodgers president, knows that Robinson is a sensational player and believes Robinson has the character necessary to "break the color barrier" in America. Robinson, who had been a star football, basketball, track, and baseball player at UCLA (the University of California at Los Angeles), responds with one of the greatest rookie seasons on record. His inspired play helps lift the Brooklyn Dodgers to a National League title. For those who have always lived in Brooklyn, this is a joyful event. To the new Americans who live there, Robinson's triumph is a fantasy come true, a sign of the opportunities for the underdog and the newcomer in America. Jackie Robinson is everyone's hero!

Thinking About Elements of Humor

In the Year of the Boar and Jackie Robinson has many funny parts. What does author Lord do to amuse her readers? First, she creates a situation between Shirley and the triplets that has many comic possibilities. One baby is hard to care for, but three are impossible! Events follow one after another so quickly the reader is almost dizzy. Lord's use of words is funny too. Her unusual comparisons make us smile.

As you're reading this excerpt on your own, think about the various winners you meet in the story.

In the **Year** of the **Boar** and **Jackie Robinson**

Sixth cousin adopts the name of a famous American film star, Shirley Temple, as she and her mother leave Chungking, China, to join her father in Brooklyn, New York. Though Shirley is eager to move, she knows she will miss her relatives, especially fourth cousin, her dearest friend, and Precious Coins, the baby of the clan.

America holds many challenges and brings some surprises to Shirley as she struggles to understand her adopted country. One of Shirley's greatest enthusiasms is baseball—the all-American game.

Secrets

A secret, like a chore, always seems to lead to another, one even more troublesome than the first. Shirley's secret began the night of the final encounter between the Dodgers and the Cardinals. Her team led the league by 4½ games, but their opponents were the defending champions and still had a chance to take the pennant. It wasn't going to be easy, not with Harry Brecheen pitching for the Cardinals. He had been the hero of the last World Series. Even before the players took the field, Red Barber's voice was hoarse with excitement.

Suddenly her mother claimed Shirley's attention. "Have you done all your homework?"

"Yes."

"Then, you won't mind doing something for Mrs. O'Reilly, will you?"

"Now?"

"Now."

"Do I have to?"

"I think it is an opportunity . . ."

Rats! Another opportunity.

"Mrs. O'Reilly has asked you to baby-sit tonight. The poor woman has not been able to go to church to do her good works since the babies came. Now that you are grown up and they live only downstairs, Mrs. O'Reilly thought you might like to earn some money."

Money? That was different.

"Does Mrs. O'Reilly have a radio?"

Mother nodded, smiling.

Well, then. It was a golden opportunity.

The moment Shirley walked into the apartment, Mrs. O'Reilly picked up her pocketbook and was ready to go. "Dinner's on the table. Their diapers are in their room. I should be back in about two hours. Any questions?"

Shirley could not think of any. The radio was in plain sight, on the table next to the armchair.

"Be good, boys, won't you? Shirley's here to take care of you."

Sean, Seamus and Stephen stopped pushing their toy cars around the floor to look up with identical sweet smiles and wave.

"Bye-bye, Mommy."

"Bye-bye, Mommy."

"Bye-bye, Mommy."

As soon as the door closed, Shirley turned on the radio and twisted the dial until she found the familiar sounds of the ball park. Nothing had happened in the first inning.

Better get acquainted, she told herself and kneeled on the floor to say hello. But she got no response to Hi, Sean, Hi, Seamus or Hi, Stephen. The three merely crawled around, crying "Beep-beep, beep-beep, beep-beep." When they sat perfectly still, each triplet was indistinguishable from his brothers. Now, in orbit, they were an endless multitude. The effect was far from relaxing.

Grabbing the nearest, Shirley tried to station him in a high chair. The baby weighed less than Precious Coins, but was a lot more grief. He drooled with delight at Shirley's foolish struggle to thread him into the chair. If the legs were in position, the head was turned the wrong way. If the head faced the right direction, the legs dangled over the table. If she begged the child to bend, he stiffened. If she begged him to straighten, he slouched, almost slipping through her hands. Compared to this, dressing an octopus would have been a cinch.

One seated, two more to go. In each case, the battle was prolonged and silent.

When all three were safely in their chairs, Shirley was exhausted, and Joe Garagiola hadn't beaten the throw but had spiked Jackie Robinson's foot instead and given all Dodger fans one more reason to hate the Cardinals. The stands were in an uproar. But nothing compared to the cries that now emanated from the triplets, each outdoing the other.

"My chair. I want my own chair."

"My chair. I want my own chair."

"My chair. I want my own chair."

Shirley didn't even know which one was Sean, Seamus or Stephen, much less their chairs.

"Okay. Okay." Shirley hurried to reverse the seating that had taken her an inning to accomplish.

"Beep-beep, beep-beep, beep-beep."

Stamping her foot, she shouted, "Which is your chair?"

All three pointed to the one facing the kitchen.

"That mine."

"That mine."

"That mine."

Third Uncle was right. Money did not rain from the skies. But no baby was going to defeat her. She picked up the nearest one and sat down at the table. With one hand tight around his belly, she fed him with the other. The process was messy, like pitching coal onto a moving train.

Meanwhile Robinson came to bat and almost got into a fight with the catcher, Garagiola. If it hadn't been for the umpire, there would have been a riot in St. Louis. Shirley longed for just such an official to keep the peace among Sean, Seamus and Stephen. When one was not spitting out food, another was tugging at her skirt, while the third screamed for his car, which had rolled underneath the sofa.

By the fifth inning, she had finally restored the dining room to its original condition. Now with one man on base, her hero smacked the ball right out of the park. She yelled hooray. The boys did too. But when she had stopped, they kept on yelling.

"Hooray! "Hooray! "Hooray!"

"Please stop, please, please don't shout anymore."

She might as well have been speaking Chinese.

Somehow she managed to peel off their clothing, stuff them into pajamas, and put them to bed. Then, muttering thanks to the Goddess Kwan Yin, she flung her weary self into the armchair to seek solace in the uninterrupted enjoyment of the last inning.

No sooner had she done so than a chorus of cries issued from the bedroom.

"Sean's wet."

"Sean's wet."

"Sean's wet."

"Which one of you is Sean?"

Silence. Drooling.

Undoing the buttons from neck to toe, she looked for signs of Sean, wishing that they were dressed like Chinese babies, with a handy slit in their pants. How much simpler life had been in Chungking, when all she had had to do was lift Precious Coins' legs over a chamber pot.

By the time Sean was found and sanitized, the game was over. The Dodgers had won, 4 to 3, but Shirley was much too beaten to enjoy the victory.

Within moments, Mrs. O'Reilly returned. Her sons were snoring peacefully. Not a limb moved. The warriors had fought the good fight and deserved a rest.

Shirley earned three dimes that shone in her palm as brightly as medal for valor. She couldn't wait to show them to her parents.

The next day, Father presented her with a piggy bank. "Now that you're earning money, you deserve a proper place to keep it."

While her proud parents watched, Shirley lovingly deposited the coins in the china pig.

Thereafter, twice a week, Mrs. O'Reilly did her good works, and twice a week, Shirley wrestled with Sean, Seamus and Stephen. For a while, the coins that jingled ever more loudly in the pig drowned out the taunts of the Terrible Threesome. But as the magic number—any combination of Dodger wins or Cardinal losses needed for the Dodgers to win the National League pennant—dwindled from 7 to 6 to 5 to 4 to 3, Shirley fretted. More and more, she longed to exchange the chaos of the downstairs apartment for the quiet of her own. The boys were no fans of the Dodgers, or of Shirley.

Drastic measures were called for. Before she went to baby-sit again, Shirley secretly substituted buttons for the coins in the piggy bank. Then, at Mr. P's, she armed herself with a fabulous array of candy. *Amitabha!* Bribery worked magic.

Sucking sweets, the Terrible Threesome was no more. In their stead, the Tame Trio.

Bursting into her own apartment in triumph, Shirley found her mother still working on the accounts for the Señora and her father mixing paint. As usual, they stopped what they were doing to witness the grand ceremony of feeding the pig. Mother gave her a quick squeeze. Father patted her on the shoulder.

"Go on, Shirley. Go on."

"No. Wait," announced Father as he pulled a small blue book from his back pocket to give Shirley. On it were stamped many numbers and her name in gold.

"What is it?"

"Your own savings account at the Brooklyn National Bank. Open it."

On the first line was a deposit of $5.00, a week's grocery money.

"Now every time the pig is filled, you can go to the bank yourself and make a deposit. And every penny in the account will go to help pay for your college education."

"College?"

"Yes. It is not too early to plan. College is expensive, but it is the most valuable treasure a person can have. With a proper education, you can aspire to do anything you desire in America. Be a doctor or a teacher or . . ."

"An engineer?"

"Of course."

Passing her finger over the name in gold, Shirley pictured herself as a grown-up, saving a life on the operating table, teaching a class, building a bridge. The images thrilled her, for she saw them so clearly in her parents' eyes.

She wanted to tell them all that was in her heart, but how do you express such feelings? Americans, she knew, would simply say, "I love you." But Chinese never used the phrase. It was too obvious, too direct. Like a present on one's birthday rather than those her father gave for no reason at all. Americans would also kiss. They did it all the time, even in public. That also seemed wrong. Without her saying a word, her parents knew how she felt and this she understood. It was the essence of being Chinese. But Shirley wanted to find a special way, her own way. What could it be?

Mother came to the rescue by handing her the pig. She gave it the customary three shakes. This never failed to make her parents laugh. Suddenly, Shirley remembered the trick she had played, bribing the boys. This time when the dimes dropped, the sound was hollow. Counterfeit.

In the morning the shame had not gone away. It cast a stillness within her like the hush of new snow. She began to see things she had failed to see before. Once again, her parents had slept through the alarm. But only now did she realize it was because of the long hours they worked. Worked to build a new life for them in America. Worked without complaint, always with cheer. How could she have deceived them so?

Shirley confessed everything to Emily.

"You'll feel much better when the buttons are replaced."

"How?"

"I'll share my school meals with you until you have saved enough."

"You will?"

"That's what friends are for."

But things thoughtlessly done are never so easily undone. This Shirley learned the next time she babysat. Expecting candy and having none, the boys took turns unplugging the radio. Three against one was no contest. And so she missed the crucial game—the game that clinched the pennant for the Dodgers.

The World Series

Brooklyn went berserk. The Dodgers were the champs of the National League. Jackie Robinson was voted "Rookie of the Year" by *The Sporting News*. Nothing else mattered but the World Series.

Each day during the Series, at the sound of the school bell, Shirley and her classmates dashed to Mr. P's to cheer their team. This was no game. This was war. Huddled on empty soda crates, they sweated out each play. A Yankee hit, a blow to the stomach. A run, a mortal wound. A Dodger steal, a seizure of enemy territory. A score, a hero's welcome.

When the Yankees won the first two games easily, Tommy made the mistake of saying, "De Bums played like amateurs." No one spoke to him after that except Shirley, who sensed his tough talk masked a loyalty as passionate as the others'. "You didn't mean it, did you?"

"Sure, I meant it. Amateurs. Girl amateurs, to boot."

The next game was the longest ever played in the history of the World Series—over three hours of hard hitting and fielding and running at Ebbets Field. If it had gone into extra innings, Shirley's heart would have stopped. The Dodgers finally edged the Bronx Bombers, 9 to 8. Relief swooped through the crowd like the news of a snowstorm on the morning when a report not yet written was due.

After the fourth game, "Cookie" was on the lips of everyone. It had nothing to do with chocolate chips. It had everything to do with a player named Lavagetto. He was called off the bench to pinch-hit with two outs in the ninth, two Dodgers on base after walks, and the enemy leading by one run. The Yankee pitcher was one out away from becoming a phenomenon so rare that it had never been seen before—the first man to pitch a no-hitter in the World Series. Lavagetto swung and missed. Shirley prayed. He swung again. At the crack of the bat, everyone jumped to his feet and did not breathe until the ball hit the concrete wall to drive in the winning runs. The Series was tied.

In the last inning of the fifth game, Mabel shook Shirley like a bottle of catsup, shouting, "Do it again. Bust this one outta the park, Cookie!" Unbelievable as it seemed, once again it was the Yankees 2 to 1, with two outs and Lavagetto at bat. But history would not repeat itself. He fanned. And the kids who had rallied at Mr. P's disappeared as silently as dandelion heads in the breeze.

Tommy almost got himself killed before a pitch was thrown in the sixth game on Sunday. "It's over. De Bums are through.

Back in Yankee territory, they got as much chance as a guppie swallowing a whale." Even Shirley thought he had gone too far. She helped to push him out the door.

The game was endless. Thirty-eight men played before it was over. Maria set a record too. She chewed Mr. P clean out of gum. The Dodgers led throughout most of the game, but everyone knew the Yankees were luckier than mice in a cheese factory. They could not relax until Red Barber announced a Brooklyn victory. Not even when there was only one out to go, Yankees trailing 5 to 8. Especially not when Joe DiMaggio was swinging the bat with two men on base. He had already smacked a home run earlier and could get lucky again.

DiMaggio connected, walloping one 415 feet to left center. At that instant Shirley hated him. Then a miracle. A miracle that banished every unkind thought and filled her with wonder. Gionfriddo, charging from left field to the edge of the bullpen, reached behind the fence and robbed DiMaggio of his sure home run and a tied game.

Screeching and leaping, the fans at Mr. P's gave a good imitation of monkeys stung by a swarm of bees. Even the boxes of soap and cereal, jars of peanut butter and mustard, hopped. Forgetting thirty-nine generations of Confucian breeding, Shirley hugged anyone in reach.

Mr. P swept her up in his arms and twirled to a song he bellowed out in Greek. Everybody started to clap in time. Around and around, faster and faster, until finally in happy exhaustion, he plopped her on the counter to mop his face with his apron. Mabel and Joseph took the floor. Like a yo-yo, the captain flung Joseph out and snatched him back. Mabel sure could jitterbug. Finally to Irvie's horror, Maria pulled him off the freezer and as he stood stiff as an icicle, she tap-danced about, nudging him with a shoulder, patting him on the cheek, closer and closer till they were nose to nose, and he fled into the street.

Only then did Shirley notice Tommy, outside, darting from car to car, kissing the hoods like a proud new papa. Any other day, it might have seemed strange. Not today. The Series was tied and the Dodgers had been reborn.

Next, the Dodgers face the Yankees for the World Championship. Shirley, too, has new challenges to face. Also awaiting her are an honor she could never have imagined and a thrilling surprise.

Meet the Author: **Bette Bao Lord**

When Bette Bao Lord was eight, she left her home in Shanghai, China to join her diplomat father in Brooklyn, New York. The Bao family expected to live in the United States for two years, but troubles in China caused the move to become a permanent one. Young Bette spoke no English and had to make her way in a society very different from the one she had known. Bette, like all immigrants, had to learn to become an American. At the same time, because she loved and respected her family and its values, she tried to keep her Chinese roots alive. Sometimes Bette felt that she was benefiting from this blend of cultures. At other times, she felt caught in the middle— neither Chinese nor American.

Bette Bao Lord drew upon her childhood experiences to write *In the Year of the Boar and Jackie Robinson*. This is what author Lord has to say about her reasons for writing the novel. "Something awful happens to a lot of folks who stuff their feet into high-heeled shoes, who sprout stubble on their cheeks. They forget. No matter how they try, they no longer can recall what it was like to be young. The fun of it. The fright of it. And that, after all, was what I wanted to write about: the fun and fright of being a Chinese immigrant dumped into the fifth grade at P.S. #8 without speaking a word of English, without knowing another soul. So I decided not to write the story of Shirley Temple Wong for the likes of them—grown-ups who overlook people shorter than they, grown-ups who overrule people less hairy then they. I wrote IN THE YEAR OF THE BOAR AND JACKIE ROBINSON for the brave who continually dream anew."

Lord's first fictional work was *Spring Moon*, a book for adults published in 1981. *Spring Moon* tells the story of five generations of a Chinese family and the changes that took place in traditional Chinese values over the past century. The novel was on the best-seller lists for many months and has been published in twelve languages. Currently, *Spring Moon* is being made into a movie produced by Chinese and Americans working together.

Bette Bao Lord is married to Winston Lord, the American ambassador to China. She enjoys her job as ambassador's wife, since she has spent so much of her life promoting better understanding between Americans and Chinese. Lord is a somewhat untraditional ambassador's wife. At a recent embassy party, for example, the guests listened to a leading Chinese singer performing (in Chinese) "Seventy-Six Trombones," a song from the American musical *Music Man*. Certainly, on this occasion at least, Lord had blended the two cultures and come up with something new.

Responding to Literature

1. Author Bette Bao Lord has written a novel that is both serious and comic. Did Shirley's troubles with the triplets make you laugh? Why or why not?

2. Suppose someone were interviewing Shirley for a book about immigrants to the United States. What important experiences would Shirley tell the interviewer?

3. There are several interesting characters in *In the Year of the Boar and Jackie Robinson*. Which ones would you call winners?

4. Author Lord sets up a comic situation by having Shirley take care of unruly triplets. What does she do in her writing that makes the scenes with Shirley and the triplets even funnier?

5. Shirley and her parents love their new land, but they miss their homeland and its ways. What is one difference between Chinese and American ways of behaving?

We Have Our Moments

Sometimes   we leap and land.
Sometimes   we trip   and fall.
Sometimes   we catch the other team   before they score.
Sometimes   we jump too soon   and get faked out of our
                                                                socks.

      We can be sharp on the pick-off play   at third.
Or
        we can have rocks in our heads and miss that
                                                softly batted ball,
                                                and miss that
                                                                one
                                        sweet   chance   to
                                                                save
                                                                the
                                                                day.

I lose. I win. We lose.   We win.
The team   finishes   in last place.
The team is
                in the play-offs at last
                and past defeats fade
                                        fast.
We   have   our   moments.

                            Arnold Adoff

Appreciating Author's Craft

Thinking About Humor

Writing a funny story requires more than telling jokes. Humor in fiction is carefully crafted in a variety of ways. The writer sets up a situation in which funny things can happen. That is what Bette Bao Lord does in *In the Year of the Boar and Jackie Robinson* when she brings Shirley together with the triplets.

The conflict between Shirley and Sean, Seamus, and Stephen leads to comedy. The "Terrible Threesome" resist everything Shirley does for them. They spit their food, they roll underneath the sofa, they scream when she begs for quiet.

Humorous comparisons and a careful choice of words add to the comical account of Shirley's trials. Most readers will smile at these sentences: "Screeching and leaping, the fans at Mr. P's gave a good imitation of monkeys stung by a swarm of bees." "Compared to this, dressing an octopus would have been a cinch."

A funny story is made up of amusing events and a humorous style, or way of telling the story.

Writing Humorous Instructions

Perhaps you would like to try writing humor. You might write instructions for someone who has accepted a job babysitting for the "Terrible Threesome." (For ideas about writing, look at the Writer's Handbook.)

Prewriting The web on the next page shows how one funny idea can lead to another. Add some other funny possibilities to the web.

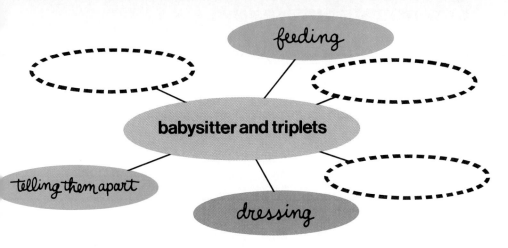

feeding

babysitter and triplets

telling them apart

dressing

Writing Read this scene in which the action happens almost like a play-by-play account in a baseball game.

> Grabbing the nearest, Shirley tried to station him in a high chair. . . . He drooled with delight at Shirley's foolish struggle to thread him into the chair. If his legs were in position, the head was turned the wrong way. If the head was in the right direction, the legs dangled over the table. If she begged the child to bend, he stiffened.

Based on the ideas you added to the web, write a set of instructions for a babysitter who has the difficult task of caring for Sean, Seamus, and Stephen. For example, you might write instructions for putting on the triplets' shoes. Be sure to title your instructions and write the steps in order. You may wish to number the steps.

Revising Read your instructions to the person who sits next to you in class. Did your partner understand the instructions? Did they make your partner laugh? Change the instructions to make them clearer or funnier, based on your partner's suggestions. Proofread for errors. Then write your final copy.

Presenting Choose classmates to play the babysitter and the triplets. Have these people act out the instructions as you read them aloud.

Extending Your Reading

Expressing Yourself
Choose one or more of the following activities:

Interview Immigrants Talk to people born in another country about their experiences when they first moved to the United States. Tape record your conversation if possible and play the tape for your classmates.

Learn About Jackie Robinson Why is the name Jackie Robinson one of the best-known in baseball? Read a book or magazine article about this famous ball player. Report what you learn to the class.

Write a Letter to a Newcomer What would you say about the place you live to someone who was planning to come to live there? Write a letter telling a newcomer the things he or she would need to know about your community.

Make a Diagram Suppose you were trying to explain baseball to someone who had never heard of the game. Draw a diagram of a baseball field. Label all the positions.

Write a Commercial Organize a group of friends to write a television or radio commercial to persuade people to read _In the Year of the Boar and Jackie Robinson_. Describe the excerpt in such a way that everyone will want to rush to a library or bookstore to find the book.

Find the Chinese Year Find out the Chinese year in which you and the other members of your family were born. Make a chart of Chinese years and illustrate it.

More Books About Winners

Bigmouth by Maggie Twohill. Bradbury Press. Bunny Squill believes she is a winner, but her friends and family are not so sure. Bunny is smart and lively, but she doesn't know when to stop talking and start listening. Her bad habit lands the entire family in trouble. Shocked nearly speechless, Bunny changes her ways and slowly learns how to come out on top.

The Mechanical Doll by Pamela Stearns. Houghton Mifflin Company. When a merchant gives the King of Shen a mechanical dancing doll, the king is enchanted. Not so his favorite flute player, Hulun, who breaks the doll in a fit of jealousy and is banished forever. How can Hulun ever find a way to return to his king? The mechanical doll holds the answer to Hulun's question.

The Future of Hooper Toote by Felice Holman. Charles Scribner's Sons. Hooper Toote is a perfectly ordinary boy in all ways except one—he can generally be found floating several inches above the ground. When the Toote family moves to New York City, Hooper's special quality can no longer go unnoticed. It is up to Hooper to decide whom to trust, an eccentric scientist, NASA, or his new friends, and how to lead the life he would really like.

Baseball's All-Time All-Stars by Jim Murphy. Clarion Books. The author selects players for two "all-time, all-star" baseball teams. The book includes statistics about these players and information about their accomplishments. Die-hard baseball fans will want to compare their dream team with author Murphy's.

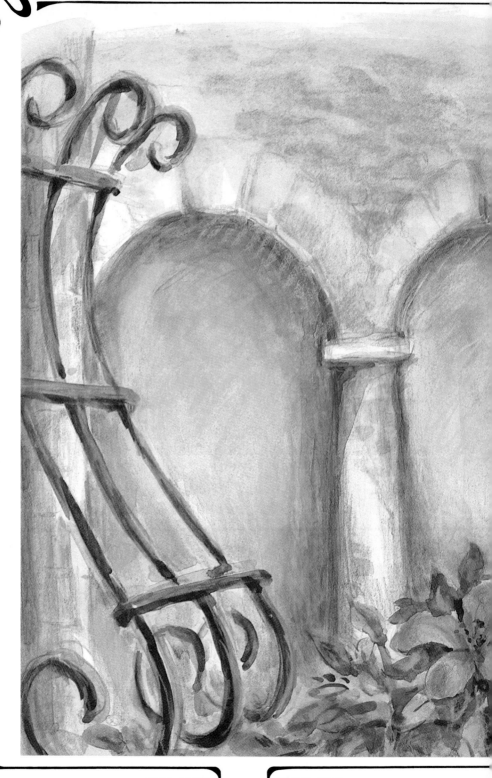

The Dragons of the Queen

by Mary Stolz

illustrated by Ann Grifalconi

Introducing

The Dragons of the Queen

Edith and George Kenilworth, lifelong residents of a town near Boise, Idaho, are vacationing in Mexico. It is the first time they have ever been in a foreign country—in fact, it is the first time they have ever been more than a few miles from Boise. Now they find themselves stranded in a small Mexican village without a hotel room for the night. Tired, hungry, and increasingly irritable, the Kenilworths do not realize that the adventure of their lives awaits them.

South of the Border

Each year thousands of tourists from the United States visit Mexico, the country that lies beyond its southern border. Some of these visitors speak Spanish, the official language of Mexico, and attempt to get to know the Mexican people and explore their country. Other tourists make no attempt to speak Spanish and do not take the time to understand a land and people different from their own.

In *The Dragons of the Queen,* author Mary Stolz helps her readers appreciate life in a Mexican village. She describes the traditional small square at the center of town with its blooming flowers and trees. We spy the pink plaster church across from the square. We hear its bells singing, and the echo of

answering bells from other churches in the distance. We see the villagers relaxing at the end of the day, lounging in the sun on the park benches, laughing and speaking with one another. We see the moonlight gleam on yucca plants in the desert at night and hear a fountain of gently flowing water.

Stolz makes *The Dragons of the Queen* seem real by adding some Spanish words to her characters' dialogue. English-speaking readers may recognize some of these words, such as "señor," which means "sir," "ocupado," which means "occupied," and "por favor," which means "please."

Thinking About How Character Influences Plot

A plot is the series of events that moves a story's action forward. There can be no plot, of course, without characters to act out these events. A well-written story closely links the personality of its main characters to the development of the plot. In *The Dragons of the Queen*, Doña Pascuala's unusual personality has a great effect on the plot of the story.

As you're reading this story on your own, decide how their meeting with Doña Pascuala changes the Kenilworths' lives.

The Dragons of the Queen

T he queen was not a real queen and the dragons were not real dragons. But to the people of the town, Doña Pascuala, who lived in a castle with dragons to guard her, was a descendant of kings. The castle was an old *hacienda,* and it was crumbling. When strangers asked what held it together, Doña Pascuala would answer proudly "Tradition, dignity, and vines."

Doña Pascuala was a hundred and two years old. She wore a crown on her black hair. Nobody knew whether it was a real crown or just a ring of glitter she had found somewhere sometime during her one hundred and two years. Still, she held her head high and the crown flashed when she moved. She looked a royal woman as she moved through the walks and gardens of her time-eaten castle with the seven dragons frothing at her heels.

The dragons were named Luis, Paco, Salvador, Esteban, Manuel, Velas, and Harald. Harald was from north of the border and his blood lines were not good. But he was loyal to the queen and could make more noise than all the other dragons together, so everyone accepted him as an oddity.

One evening, as on all evenings, the bells were ringing the sun down behind the far hills and all the birds of the desert were flying in to roost on the roofs and eaves and trees of the village square. This time a large automobile came down the hilly cobbled streets and parked in front of the *posada.*

"*Posada,*" said the man at the wheel. He was a chauffeur.

The people in the back seat looked at each other. They were Mr. and Mrs. George Kenilworth from just outside Boise, Idaho. They did not speak Spanish, the language spoken in Mexico, which is where they were this evening in the dusk in their big car.

"*Posada,*" said the chauffeur again and translated for them: "Hotel."

"I know that by now," Mr. Kenilworth muttered crossly.

His wife said, "Really, George. I do not wish to spend the night in this dreary little town."

"It's too far to go on tonight. Having the car break down was very bad luck. We'll just have to make the best of it. Be brave, my dear."

"Very well," she said, looking brave. "Go and get us rooms," she said to the chauffeur.

"*Por favor,*" said Mr. Kenilworth. He had picked up a few words of Spanish, in spite of not trying. "*Por favor* means please," he said to his wife.

"George, how wonderful you are. First thing we know, we'll be speaking like natives."

They laughed together.

"Why learn Spanish?" George had often said during their trip. "The only person we ever get to talk to is our driver."

"And he does all the talking for us," his wife would add.

They were a lazy couple, but cheery enough if all went smoothly—by which they meant if everything went their way.

Tonight everything was not to go their way.

The bells rang and the starlings sang and the woman covered her ears. "Isn't there some way to stop them?" she pleaded.

"Can't think of any," said Mr. Kenilworth. "However, my dear, I'll do what I can." He got out of the car.

He stood in the square and looked around.

There was a large rectangle of trees in a garden in the square, and the trees were bursting with blackbirds, all calling their evening song in harsh tones. Across the square, a great pink plaster church resounded with ringing, swinging bells, and from other parts of the town smaller churches pealed smaller songs.

The more he watched and listened, the more Mr. Kenilworth realized that he wasn't going to be able to do anything about any of it. But still he did not get back into the car. He looked about him at the flowers in the garden, pearly and purple and scarlet and gold. He looked at the populace lounging on benches, taking their ease in the setting sun. He watched the children going by, hand in hand, talking rapidly to one another.

"Spanish, of course," George muttered to himself. He felt put out that children could speak a language he could not. As they went past they looked at him and giggled. He got back into the car.

"You're right," he said to his wife. "It's a terrible town." After a moment he added, "Pretty though. Have to give it that."

His wife seemed surprised. She looked out of the window for the first time. She saw people lounging easily on benches in the park, and brilliant flowers springing in the garden, and the pink plaster church decorated like an anniversary cake. She saw the children going by, hand in hand.

Now that the birds were still, the bells silent, the town growing quiet in the deep rose evening, she was ready to say it was pretty. Sort of pretty. Since they had to spend the night here, there was little use in continuing to say how awful it was.

Anyway, they'd only spend one night.

The driver came out of the hotel.

"Ah, Paco," said the man eagerly. "I hope you got us good rooms? The very best?"

"I got you no rooms at all, *señor*," said Paco, lifting his shoulders.

"What's this?" said Mrs. Kenilworth.

"There are no rooms, *señora*."

"How can there be no rooms," George demanded, "when we have to spend the night here? What do you mean—no rooms?"

"*Señor*, I mean their rooms are all filled, *ocupado*. There is nothing for you. *Nada*. Nothing."

"I think I'm going to faint," said the woman.

"Edith, be brave," said her husband. "Let me take care of this." He strode into the hotel.

Paco, the driver, peered into the car, curious to see if the woman had fainted. She had not. She was fanning her face with a perfumed handkerchief. She looked very, very annoyed.

Paco straightened and leaned against the fender, waiting for the *señor* to come out again, which he did, quickly, his face dark and furious.

"There aren't any rooms!" he said, as if it were the first any of them had heard of it.

"Where's another hotel, Paco?" said Mrs. Kenilworth.

"No other hotel, *señora*," Paco said brightly. "*Posada Santa Teresa*. That's it. *Ningún otro*."

"Well, what are we supposed to do?" George Kenilworth demanded. "I suppose we'll have to push on for the border."

"Oh, no, *señor*," said Paco. "Not at night. For one thing, I am tired. For two things, I am afraid of the dark. For three things—"

"All right, all right. But what do we do?"

Paco pinched his chin thoughtfully. "I could myself sleep on a bench over there in the park. But I do not think—no, I do not think that would do for you and the *señora*."

"I don't think that either," said George Kenilworth firmly. "Mrs. Kenilworth and I cannot sleep in the park on a bench. You'll have to come up with another idea."

Paco tugged gently at his earlobe. "You might maybe sleep in the castle."

Edith Kenilworth brightened. "Castle?"

"What castle?" said Mr. Kenilworth suspiciously.

"*Señor*," said Paco, speaking slowly, in a tone of awe. "There is in this town a castle—a *hacienda* in truth, but still a castle— hundreds of years old, and a queen lives there. She has seven dragons to guard her, and she has one hundred and two years." He stopped.

"Well? Well?" said Mr. Kenilworth. "What has this to do with us? You mean Her Royal Highness takes roomers?"

"She sometimes is so kind as to put up with wayfarers," Paco said guardedly.

"I'll bet. And what's the going rate for rooms in a castle when the only hotel is full up?" George Kenilworth's normally pleasant face was not so pleasant now. He was tired, hungry, and sure he was about to be taken. A castle! A queen! Dragons!

"No rates," said Paco, shaking his head. "The queen does not charge for her hospitality."

"Then what's the catch?"

"Catch, *señor?*"

George looked helplessly at his wife.

"What Mr. Kenilworth is asking," said Mrs. Kenilworth to Paco, "is—ah—why? Why is the queen so kind as to sometimes put up wayfarers for nothing?"

"Because she is so kind," said Paco, looking from one to the other of his exhausted charges, as if wondering if he had not used the correct words. "Kind," he repeated. "Only—"

"Ah–hah!" said George. "I knew it. Now it comes. Only what, Paco?"

"Only, *señor*—the queen has to like you. That is to say, no one is turned away from the castle if the hotel is full up, but you may not dine with Doña Pascuala, or talk with her, or even see her if she does not like you."

George Kenilworth took out a handkerchief and wiped the top of his head. "How will she know if she likes us if she doesn't see us?" he asked irritably.

"She has her ways," Paco said mysteriously.

"Peepholes in the castle stronghold," said Mrs. Kenilworth, who was beginning to look forward to the adventure.

"Just get us to the castle, Paco," said Mr. Kenilworth wearily. "I don't care if she talks to us or dines with us or even looks at us—just so we get something to eat and a place to sleep."

"Dragons," Mrs. Kenilworth mused. "What do you think, George? Not gila monsters surely?"

"Probably some carved junk in the driveway," George grumbled. "The country's full of images and if they aren't plumed serpents, they're undoubtedly dragons. I wish we'd gone to Yellowstone."

Mrs. Kenilworth took his hand and patted it as the car wound slowly up the cobbled hill and into the desert along a rutted road that in the headlights scarcely looked a road at all—just a flattened place in a rocky landscape.

After what seemed a long time, Paco turned in between a pair of stone pillars that started up without seeming purpose, for there was no wall or fence or even driveway for them to mark. They were just there—like two stone trees in the desert—and beyond them the dark, harsh, flat land went on.

Just when Mr. Kenilworth had concluded that the two stone pillars were all that was left of the castle, Paco said heartily, "¡Entrada!"

"Entrada to what?" Mr. Kenilworth demanded. He sounded irritable but was in truth more hungry than angry and more tired than hungry. All I want, he thought, is to lie down.

"Why, the entrance," said Paco. "At any moment now we will be at the castle itself." He turned around. "May I say, with all respect, señor y señora, that when we arrive it is maybe more better for me to talk?" The car swerved and Mrs. Kenilworth squealed. "A thousand pardons," said Paco, giving his attention again to the road.

"Why can't we speak for ourselves?" Mr. Kenilworth asked. "I am accustomed to speaking for myself."

"Doña Pascuala," said Paco, dropping his voice as if he were already in her royal and ancient presence, "is a most waning lady of one hundred and two years. She is able to bear only the lowest, softest of sounds. It has something to do," Paco said apologetically, "with her ears."

"You mean I yell?" George Kenilworth said loudly. "I like that. What do you think of that, Edith? Now let me tell you, Señor Paco," he went on, his voice rising on each syllable, "I am not accustomed to—"

"George," said Mrs. Kenilworth. "George." She patted his hand again. "Let us do as Paco says. We are in his hands. For my part, I shall be happy to have him do the talking. Only to lie down—to rest—to have a roof over our heads—"

"*¡Aquí!*" said Paco. "Look, *señor, señora!* The castle!"

And there it was—a long, low, stone *hacienda* of many years and much neglect. In the moonlight it did resemble a castle, with its arches and stone traceries, its terraced weed-rank lawns, its great size indistinct and uncertain in the shadows. Tall, plumy jacaranda trees grew everywhere and great-leaved rope-thick vines gripped the walls and thrust into the very foundations of the building. Somewhere in the night a fountain was splashing and a bittersweet scent lay lightly on the warm air.

In one far window a flickering light burned. Otherwise, the castle seemed asleep in the milky moonlight.

"She's retired. She's in bed," said Mrs. Kenilworth with a sob in her voice. "We'll have to go away!"

"No, no," said Paco. "It is all right, *señora*. I will rouse the queen."

"But—"

"She reads in her room, that is all. Doña Pascuala says that at one hundred and two years, sleep is only a brief messenger of the future and easily dismissed. Until, of course," he added sadly, "the day of no dismissal comes."

He got out of the car, went up to the great carved wooden doors, and pulled at an iron bell that sprang up and down, ringing and resounding, echoing in the night.

"I thought she didn't like loud noises," Mr. Kenilworth complained, putting his hands to his ears. As he spoke, a din burst forth that sent Mrs. Kenilworth into her husband's arms, where she cowered, her face against his chest.

"What is that?" she moaned.

"Sounds like a pack of mad dogs. Hungry mad dogs at that."

"*Los dragones,*" said Paco proudly. "Here they come. The dragons of the queen!"

Down the colonnaded arcade came a rippling silver mass of what looked to Mrs. Kenilworth like huge caterpillars. She shrank closer against her husband's big chest and closed her eyes.

Mr. Kenilworth, of stouter stuff, faced the onrushing horde, which sorted itself into a pack of yelping pewter-colored Pekingese dogs. Behind them, halting every few yards to lift his head and bay earnestly, was a huge brown-and-white hound-like creature with no tail.

Behind them all, fluttering in black tatters, came a small figure leaning on a silver cane. She wore a crown of glitter on her black thick hair and carried a kerosene lantern that swung as she walked, throwing shadows wildly to one side and then the other.

"Oh, my gosh," said Mr. Kenilworth. "Here comes Her Highness."

Mrs. Kenilworth peered fearfully down the arcade.

"Well, I never—" she gasped. "I never—"

Paco, as the queen approached, made a low bow.

"*Buenas noches, Doña Pascuala,*" he said in a reverent voice. "*¿Cómo está?*"

"*Muy bien, gracias, Paco. ¿Y usted?*" Her voice was strong and vibrant, and it lifted above the clamor of the dragons.

"*Muy bien, señora, gracias.* Here we have *Señor y Señora* Kenilworth from the United States of America. The *posada*, alas, is unable to accommodate them. They are tired and in need of food."

"Ah, a thousand pities," said Doña Pascuala.

"She has a voice like an oboe," said Mr. Kenilworth. "I expected a flute."

He spoke in a whisper, but Doña Pascuala apparently had nothing wrong with her hearing. She smiled as if pleased.

The Pekingeses yelped, the hound dog bayed, and starlings, made restless by the invasion, began to scream.

"What was that about not liking loud noises?" Mr. Kenilworth muttered to Paco.

Paco shrugged and then said cheerfully, "I see, *señor*, that even at one hundred and two years one is able to change. A wonderful prospect, is it not?"

"What're the prospects for a meal and a night's lodging?" said George, still in a voice meant to be obscured by the frenzied dragons and starlings.

"They are excellent," said Doña Pascuala. "Come, Mr. and Mrs. Kenilworth. I will show you to your room, and then we shall all meet in the *sala* for food and conversation."

"Oh, but we wouldn't dream of putting you to any trouble—that is, of keeping you up—that is—"

Bed! George Kenilworth was thinking. We have to get to bed!

"A pleasure. An honor," said Doña Pascuala. "I sleep but little and relish any opportunity for the exchange of views. Come."

Mr. and Mrs. Kenilworth did not look at each other.

The queen led her entourage down the colonnaded arcade, along a narrow hallway lined with pictures they could not see, across a great shadowy tiled patio where the fountain was splashing in a stone basin, through an entrance at the other side, up a broad flight of stairs, down a wide hallway.

Paco, with the bags, followed Mr. and Mrs. Kenilworth. Behind him came the dragons, quiet now except for the clatter of their toenails on slate and tile. The lantern threw their silhouettes, and those of the small tattered queen, the two big North Americans, and lively Paco, up and down and sideways on walls and floors.

"Here we are," said Doña Pascuala, throwing open a door just as Mrs. Kenilworth began to think she and her husband had gotten into a dream of endless walking by lantern light in Mexico—or maybe in Eternity.

The room into which they stepped was vast in feeling, but the lantern light did not penetrate its reaches.

"Paco," said Doña Pascuala imperiously, "light the candelabra and then await our guests in the hall to show them down. I shall leave you now," she said to Mr. and Mrs. Kenilworth, "to see that Lola prepares dinner. You must be very hungry."

"Yes, but Your Highness, at this hour—dinner—that is to say—just a snack—"

The queen was gone.

Paco lighted the candles and glided out, closing the door behind him soundlessly. Mr. and Mrs. Kenilworth now looked at each other.

"Is it a dream?" said Mrs. Kenilworth at last. "George, do tell me we're back at home and about to wake up at any moment."

He shook his head. "We're awake," he said, then added, "barely. You and I, my dear, are in a Mexican castle, being entertained by royalty." He yawned and said, "Royalty that is apparently willing to stay up all night."

"I can't," said Mrs. Kenilworth.

"We must. Anyway, Edith," he said, and seemed all at once to shed his fatigue, "what an experience, eh? Nothing like this ever happened to us before. Nothing—magical like this—mysterious."

Indeed, in all their years nothing like this had ever happened to them before. Looked at in a certain way, it might be said that nothing had ever happened to them at all.

They had been born and had grown up in a little town just outside Boise. They'd married and raised children, and their children had married and moved away. Still Mr. and Mrs. George Kenilworth never left the outskirts of their home town.

Then on a day a couple of months earlier, Mr. Kenilworth had announced at dinner that they were going to take a trip.

"A trip?" Mrs. Kenilworth had said somewhat fearfully. "A trip where? And why, George?"

"Why? Because we've never been anyplace, that's why," George had said firmly. He didn't seem as certain when it came to the question of where. "Where would you like to go?"

"The—the Grand Canyon, maybe?"

"Snowed in this time of year."

"We could wait."

"No, no," George had said loudly. "Now is when I got this idea, and now is when we should do it. Who knows, if we wait, we might never go at all."

This was rather what Mrs. Kenilworth had in mind, but she said to herself that if this was what George wanted, it was what he should have.

"To—to—to Europe, maybe?" she'd said and had been relieved when George shook his head.

"That's too far away." He'd sounded alarmed. "Europe. My gosh. Hey, I've got it! We'll go to Mexico. That's the ticket. I mean, after all, it's attached to our own country. We wouldn't have to go across the ocean or anything. Mexico," he repeated. "Just the thing."

But still they'd been reluctant to start off on such an adventure—just the two of them—until George read about how one could go to Mexico City and hire a driver who would take car and passengers anywhere they wished to go at any pace. You didn't need to know a word of Spanish, for the driver would do all the talking. George, who was not a good driver in Idaho, was confident he'd be a terrible driver south of the border, and neither of them had any Spanish. But this plan solved all their problems.

And so for over a month they had been touring in the capable hands of Paco, who would shortly deposit them in San Antonio, Texas, where he was to pick up another couple and drive them back down to Mexico City. The Kenilworths had seen the ancient pyramids and the jungles of Yucatan, the silversmiths of Taxco, the beaches at Acapulco, and a monastery at Yanhuitlan. They felt indeed that they had seen Mexico roundly and well, but they planned to come back one day for the things and places they'd missed.

But who ever would have expected this? Until this night there had never been any trouble about room reservations. For that matter they had reservations for the night—only not in this

408

town. Today for the first time something had gone wrong with the car—something severe that even Paco had been unequal to. For hours the Kenilworths had waited by the roadside while Paco trudged off to a garage they'd passed an hour before breaking down, and then for hours they'd waited while the mechanic Paco brought back with him had labored to get their engine working. He'd been good at his job, and the engine was running smoothly again. But now Mr. and Mrs. Kenilworth were a long way from their room reservations here in a castle with an old queen and her dragons.

Mrs. Kenilworth moved cautiously about the room. "This place is tremendous, George." She looked at the great bed canopied with worn velvet, at the huge dark wardrobe, at one carven chair, and the single table. "Can she really be a queen?"

"The last queen of Mexico was Carlota. Actually she was an empress. Probably the villagers just call Doña Pascuala a queen for a courtesy title, or something. Because she's so old maybe. Maybe she's awfully rich."

"She can't be rich. This place is falling apart."

"Maybe she's got royal blood in her veins. That's a possibility. Lots of Mexicans are descended from Spanish aristocracy."

"Just think of it," said Mrs. Kenilworth. Then so as not to sound too impressed, she added, "But why do they call those dogs dragons?"

George lifted his shoulders. "Pekes sort of look like dragons, don't they? With those squashed faces and fringy curled tails? And they seem to guard the place all right. Funny color, aren't they? Like silver. Seven silver dragons and a queen a hundred and two years old with a crown on her head. Who'd ever believe it?"

"Six silver dragons. That other one's a mutt. How do you suppose he got into the queen's guard?"

"Hey, look," said George. "Here's a bathroom. Bigger than our rumpus room I think." He turned on a faucet. A spider fell out and walked down the marble tub. George laughed and looked around, holding one of the candles up. "Edith, there's grass growing in this bathroom. It's coming up between the tiles."

"There's a pitcher and basin in here," she called. "And a thermos of ice water. And, George, the bed linen must be fifty years old. It's the most beautiful I've ever seen."

"I'm beginning to think," he said, "that maybe that breakdown was the luckiest part of our trip. I mean, look at us. Look at all this." He stepped out on the balcony, first testing to be sure it wouldn't come away from the house. "Look, Edith."

The balcony faced the desert, where yucca plants gleamed like fans in the moonlight. Below them the fountain tossed and fell with a musical sound in its great stone bowl, and far off a coyote wailed and was answered by another coyote and yet another. In the dark and densely foliated gardens, iguanas clacked. "They sound like someone nailing up copper gutters," George said. He said it every time they heard the iguanas, and Mrs. Kenilworth always agreed because it was what they sounded like. An owl flew past, silhouetted for a soft swift moment against the moon.

Mr. and Mrs. Kenilworth, standing hand in hand on the balcony, sighed and marveled that they should be here.

"She must like us," George said at length. "Paco says she only converses with people that she takes to."

"He said she didn't like noise too," Mrs. Kenilworth pointed out. "In my opinion, she's probably lonely up here in the wilderness and willing to talk to anyone. It stands to reason, at one hundred and two she doesn't get around much anymore. I do hope," she added, her eyes on the huge comfortable-looking bed with its fragrant fresh old linen, "that she doesn't want to talk all night."

"We can always sleep," George said briskly. "When will we get to talk with a queen again?"

Paco knocked softly at the door. *"Señor, señora—la comida está servida."*

George and Edith followed him back down the wide hallway and the great staircase, across the patio, through another arcade, and into a great *sala*.

At the far side a little fire burned in a vast hearth, before which the dragons lay on a frayed and glowing ruby rug. There were candles on a mantel and on a table set for dinner. There were four high–backed, carved, massive chairs covered with dark red velvet and tarnished fringe. In one of these sat Doña Pascuala, looking small, upright, and majestic. There was no other furniture at all in the great room, but above the mantel was an oil painting of a beautiful young woman wearing a white *mantilla* and sitting before this very hearth in the very chair now occupied by Doña Pascuala. Six silver Pekingeses lay on what appeared to be the same ruby rug.

Edith and George Kenilworth stood still, looking from the picture on the wall to Doña Pascuala.

She smiled. "It is I. Painted eighty years ago. Was I not beautiful?"

"Very beautiful, Your Highness," said George softly. "Like a flower."

"No titles, please. Doña Pascuala I am called. Paco, Lola may serve us, *por favor*."

The food was hot and spicy and delicious. After their fast of nearly a day, George and Edith did not restrain their appreciation, but Doña Pascuala took only a little to drink. She turned and turned the stem of her glass and regarded them peacefully.

"Well, but Your Highness—I mean Doña Pascuala," George said at length. "How did you come to be a queen? I mean, what's back of it all?" Edith's foot nudged his, and he said hastily, "Excuse me for being nosy, *señora*. It's just—well, I can't help being curious."

"The town calls me a queen," said Doña Pascuala, lifting her

frail shoulders in a gesture of acceptance. "Some are and some are not queens. Who is to say or be sure? I can say that my family tree, which goes back to the twelfth century, has thirteen crowns on it. Thirteen crowns," she repeated with dreamy pride, then grew silent.

They saw that the mystery of her queenship was to remain a mystery, and George decided it was just as well. He said many times after that night that some things in life ought to be mysterious and remain mysterious.

Doña Pascuala, however, was glad to talk of anything else. She told them about the painting and how the painter had posed her here so many years ago with the remote ancestors of Luis, Paco, Salvador, Esteban, Manuel, Velas, and Harald.

"Harald?" said Mrs. Kenilworth. "Surely not."

"Ah. Ah, yes." Doña Pascuala smiled. "I keep forgetting that he is not descended from silver dragons, as he forgets it himself, and that he is not alas, represented in the portrait."

"Who is he descended from?" George asked, looking at tailless Harald, who stared pensively back.

"*¿Quién sabe?* Who knows? He came to the *hacienda* one day, starving and faint. Someone had dropped him from a passing car no doubt," she said sternly. "Some unspeakable type who didn't want him anymore and took this means of disposal. I fed him, and he attached himself to my guard. He has been most stalwart. In the beginning, I confess, I thought to give him away. He spoils the symmetry, you know." She regarded her small glistening cohorts with their flat, idol faces, and then looked at Harald, looming among them like an old stump starting out of the sea. "But no one would take him. He eats too much, and his voice is too deep. And he wouldn't leave me anyway," she said confidently.

"How come you called him Harald?" George asked.

"He was named for a guest of the time. And it is such a northern-sounding name, is it not? Harald. It fairly breathes chill climes."

"But Harald clearly considers himself a Mexican," said Edith.

At this repetition of his name, Harald leaped to his feet and began to howl. Doña Pascuala implored him to be silent. Paco rushed into the room and begged him to desist. But Harald continued to call out that someone had named him and him alone, and he wanted to know the reason why.

"*¡Silencio! ¡Silencio!*" cried Doña Pascuala. "*¡Silencio, Harald amigo!*"

But Harald kept on howling.

"Down boy!" said George Kenilworth without thinking.

Harald, in midhowl, grew still and sat.

"I'm not sure how Mexican he feels," said Doña Pascuala. "In all these years he has never learned a word of Spanish. And I never remember, in my frenzy to silence him at these times, how to say 'Down Boy.'"

At this Harald looked surprised, then flattened himself on the rug, nose on his paws. The Pekes sat in a circle around him, silent and watchful.

Mr. and Mrs. Kenilworth, their fatigue quite gone, sat with Doña Pascuala and listened to her oboelike voice as she told of past splendors in the *hacienda.* What balls and parties, what weddings and funerals, what christenings there had been. What music and dancing, what weeping and laughter, what joy and what loss. Her words wove a century of love and revolution and challenge and change.

"And now," she said at length, "here I am, quite alone, save for Lola and my seven faithful guardians."

"There is the town," George said. "They—the people of the town—revere you."

"Of course," said Doña Pascuala gracefully. "There is the town which I love. Upon which I depend, you understand. But the town is down there, and I am up here, alone on the hill. That is why it is good, now and then, that the *posada* fills up and I have the privilege of entertaining a wayfarer or two at my table, of exchanging views about the world."

Although in truth there had been no real exchange and Doña Pascuala had spoken only of a world now past, Mr. and Mrs. Kenilworth nodded agreement. Perhaps they had given Doña Pascuala something—their rapt attention, their high regard, their inexpressible astonishment at being here. But they were only two among the many wayfarers who had found and would find themselves enmeshed in fascination within her castle walls. For them she would remain forever unique—a glittering puzzle in their forthright, everyday lives.

In parting from her, Mr. Kenilworth bowed deeply, almost with the grace of Paco, and Mrs. Kenilworth very nearly curtsied.

"*Buenas noches, amigos,*" said Doña Pascuala, then laughed. "*Buenos días,* I should say."

Indeed, the air stirring the long faded damask draperies was touched with morning freshness, and the sky outside the French doors was pale.

When Mr. and Mrs. Kenilworth got to their room, the candles that had been tall were guttering, sending up streamers of scented smoke before flickering out. Wordlessly the two travelers prepared for bed, thinking that nothing they could dream would be as strange as what they had just experienced.

They woke in the afternoon to the sound of a bell.

"George," said Edith, poking him. "George, what's that?"

"Church bell," he mumbled.

"I know. But are they—isn't it tolling?"

"Sure enough," said George, sitting up. "Somebody died." He went to the window. "Edith," he called. "Edith, come here. Look there."

Winding slowly down the hill on a cart drawn by an old ivory-yellow horse was a small coffin. Behind the cart walked Paco, Lola, and the seven dragons. As the cortege progressed, people came out of their houses and followed it. They tossed flowers on the cart as it rattled down the road toward town.

"Can it be—it must be," Edith Kenilworth whispered. "It's Doña Pascuala. She has died since we saw her."

"Must be," George said softly. He sighed.

"How sad," said Mrs. Kenilworth.

"Oh, no. No, Edith. Remember what she said? That to someone who has one hundred and two years, death is no stranger. Death is a father arriving to take his child home from the party."

They recalled how she'd laughed. "My father comes rather late than soon, does he not? But he will come," she'd concluded peacefully. "Yes, he will come. And the party has been splendid."

"I wonder why no one woke us," George said.

"Because we aren't part of things here," said his wife. "They never thought of us."

"Not even Paco."

"No, not even Paco. He was so proud of Doña Pascuala, wasn't he?"

"Well, let's get dressed, Edith. Let's hurry to join the procession and do her honor." He looked from the balcony across the desert where many cactus flowers were blooming. The sun was gentle, the sky azure and untroubled.

"She has a good day for her journey, the little queen," said Mr. Kenilworth.

In the square the cart pulled up before the pink plaster church, the townsmen carried the coffin into the dark cool nave, resting it on a bier before the altar. Then, in a slow line, the people of the village filed past Doña Pascuala to bid her *adiós.*

Out in the sun again, George and Edith Kenilworth found Paco on a bench.

"What happens now, Paco?" said Mr. Kenilworth.

The slender shoulders lifted and fell. "Now *senõr?* Now no town in all Mexico has a queen."

"What will happen to the castle?" asked Edith.

"Ah, *qué cosa,* the castle! Well, *señora,* the castle will now fall apart. Don Jorge, *el doctor,* will get the portrait of Doña Pascuala. Don Fernando, the *licenciado*—lawyer—will take what furniture there is since it all belongs to him anyway—"

"To the lawyer?" said George Kenilworth. "Not to Doña Pascuala?"

"*Señor,* many, many, many years ago, Doña Pascuala came to the end of her last *peso.* Her father squandered an untellable fortune—all the riches his ancestors had left him—in one life-time, and he left his daughter with nothing. *Nada.* Not a *peso.* So Don Fernando—this Don Fernando's grandfather, you understand—took over the *hacienda* and let Doña Pascuala stay there and provided for her needs, which she was most graceful to accept. And his son did the same, and his son the same, and we sometimes thought that his son would do the same. Indeed, I feel we had all come to think that Doña Pascuala would, in truth, and in defiance of nature, live forever. And now she is gone," he said mournfully.

"What happens to the dragons?"

Paco straightened and looked more cheerful. "Ah, *los dragones.* Long ago Doña Pascuala made disposition of her dragons for when she should be gathered to her fathers and they left behind. Don Fernando takes two, Don Jorge two, Don Luis one, and I, myself, am to have my namesake Paco. He will ride beside me in my big car and keep me company when I am alone."

"Do you think perhaps some of your passengers will object?" said Mr. Kenilworth. "Not everybody likes dogs, you know, Paco."

"*Señor*—if they object, I will get different passengers. Besides, who could be anything but proud to ride in the company of such a shining object, descended from nobility? Now, if it were that Harald—" He turned out his hands and lifted his eyes.

"But then, what will happen to Harald?" cried Mrs. Kenilworth.

"*Señora,* this is a sad cruel world we live in. It grieves me to say that—well, that no one knows what will happen to Harald. Even Don Fernando cannot think what disposition to make of him, and Doña Pascuala made her wishes clear before the arrival of Harald. How sad that she never got around to arranging for his future."

"Then what will his future be?" Mr. Kenilworth demanded.

"*¿Quién sabe?* He lived by his wits before the queen took him into her guard. No doubt he can live by his wits again."

"You mean you'll just turn him out? The way the people did who abandoned him in the first place?"

"*Señor,*" said Paco patiently, "this is a poor town. Harald is too big. He's too noisy. He eats too much. Besides, he does not understand Spanish."

Indeed, in some way of his own, Harald seemed already to have sensed his loss of place. Inside the church the six silver Pekingeses sat still and sturdy around the queen's bier. But Harald was out in the square, wandering from place to place, looking from face to face. At length, he sat down, lifted his head, and began to howl.

"*¡Silencio!*" cried several of the villagers. "*¡Estese quieto!*"

Harald's melancholy voice filled the square, set the starlings shrieking and the children laughing. His loud and wavering lament mingled with the tolling of the bells.

"*¡Silencio! ¡Silencio!*"

But Harald kept on wailing.

"Down boy!" said George Kenilworth.

Harald grew still. He turned and looked at the church, then walked slowly, head down, to sit between Mr. and Mrs. Kenilworth. He did not seem especially hopeful—just uncertain of what else to do.

George and Edith Kenilworth studied the big boney brown-and-white dog. They looked at each other and then at Paco, who stared up at the spire of the pink plaster church.

"Well," said George Kenilworth. "Well. How do you like that?"

Mrs. Kenilworth sighed. "I guess we've been left a bequest by the queen."

"I guess we have at that."

Paco regarded his two passengers proudly. He wondered if they knew how they had changed since meeting the queen. Mrs. Kenilworth didn't order him around now. Mr. Kenilworth didn't look as if people spoke Spanish only to annoy him. They did not appear to feel that everything was going well only as long as it went their way. Don Fernando had often told him that all her life long the queen had been able to touch people as if with a wand, and here, on her very last night, she had woven her magic for Harald's sake. And, yes, for the sake of the North Americans too.

How happy she must be, Paco went on to himself, looking up at the sky where Doña Pascuala must surely be looking down on her town.

When the Kenilworths got home to the town outside Boise, they never told even their best friends that their homely, sweet-tempered, loud-voiced, rather gluttonous new pet had come right out of a royal guard of honor.

"For one thing," George pointed out to his wife, "no one would believe us. For two things, we'd be laughed at. For three things—"

"For three things," Mrs. Kenilworth would go on, "we had something magical and mysterious happen to us, and Harald is part of that mystery and magic. I don't think people should talk about magical and mysterious happenings, except to each other."

They would sit for a while, remembering the darkened castle with its vines and jacaranda trees and the iguanas clacking in the darkness. They would recall that small figure in fluttering black tatters, coming toward them in the lantern light—crown aglitter—with the seven dragons frothing at her heels.

Harald, between them, would sigh in his sleep, turning his boney head from side to side, as if he too recalled other, grander times, when he had been a dragon and served a queen.

When he began to snort and whimper and mumble through his dreams, Mr. Kenilworth would say *"¡Silencio, Harald! ¡Silencio!"*

Harald, who had finally learned a word of Spanish, would grow still—happy to hear in this foreign land the accent of the town he dreamed of.

Meet the Author: **Mary Stolz**

During Mary Stolz's forty-year career, she has written dozens of books, books that have been published in thirty languages and issued in Braille. Though Stolz always enjoyed writing, her career as an author began because an illness forced her to stay inside for several months. Since she couldn't do what she really wanted to do—ride horses—she began writing a novel. That novel, *To Tell Your Love,* was accepted by a publishing company.

Stolz's goal in writing is to entertain her readers, to " . . . keep them turning the pages . . ." She adds, "All writers don't delight all readers, obviously. But we find each other, the one who's right for the other. The many who are right for the one. Along the line, of course, you owe your readers other things: honesty, humane feelings."

Children frequently write to Stolz asking for advice about becoming an author. What does she tell them? "Read a lot and write a lot, read a lot, write a lot," the simple recipe that has worked so well for Stolz herself.

Responding to Literature

1. Author Mary Stolz says that her goal is to entertain her readers, to "keep them turning the pages." Do you think she has achieved her goal? Why or why not?

2. The Kenilworths have definite opinions about Mexico and the Mexican people at the beginning of the story. Their opinions change as the story proceeds. Explain the events that cause the Kenilworths to change their minds.

3. Doña Pascuala has a powerful effect on the Kenilworths. How does their meeting with "the queen" change the Kenilworths' lives?

4. Some people might say that it makes no difference whether or not Doña Pascuala is a real queen. Do you agree? Tell why.

5. Mary Stolz, the author of *The Dragons of the Queen,* makes her story realistic in many ways. List two of the ways.

Travel

The railroad track is miles away,
   And the day is loud with voices speaking,
Yet there isn't a train goes by all day
   But I hear its whistles shrieking.

All night there isn't a train goes by,
   Though the night is still for sleep and dreaming,
But I see its cinders red on the sky,
   And hear its engine steaming.

My heart is warm with the friends I make,
   And better friends I'll not be knowing;
Yet there isn't a train I wouldn't take,
   No matter where it's going.

Edna St. Vincent Millay

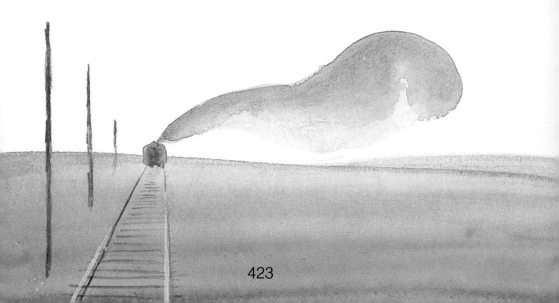

Appreciating Author's Craft

Thinking About How Characters Affect Plot

In *The Dragons of the Queen,* as in every story, the author has created characters whose personality has an effect on the plot. For example if Mr. Kenilworth had not become restless, the Kenilworths would not have traveled to Mexico and the meeting with Doña Pascuala would not have taken place.

The Kenilworths are the kind of people who see only the surface of Mexican life at first because "They were a lazy couple, but cheery enough if all went smoothly—by which they meant if everything went their way." Since things are *not* going their way at the start of the story, they are loud, rude, and unaware of the beauty that surrounds them. Author Mary Stolz lets the Kenilworths' personality traits affect the development of the plot. If Stolz had made the Kenilworths easygoing people who liked surprises and adventures, *The Dragons of the Queen* would have a different plot.

Writing About How Characters Affect Plot

Pretend you are one of the characters in the story. Think about how your personality affects what happens in the story. You will write a biographical paragraph showing how your actions make a difference to the plot. (For more ideas about writing, look at your Writer's Handbook.)

Prewriting Make a balloon for each of the major characters in *The Dragons of the Queen.* Reread to find clues about the personality of each character. Put clue words into the balloons. You may use these words to help you write your biographical paragraph.

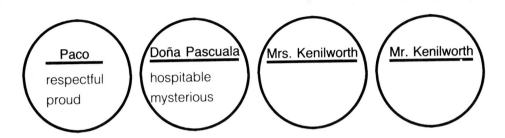

Paco	Doña Pascuala	Mrs. Kenilworth	Mr. Kenilworth
respectful	hospitable		
proud	mysterious		

Writing Now imagine yourself one of the characters in the story. Use the bank of words for that character to help you compose a biographical paragraph. Have your character tell how the plot was affected by your character's personality. Write your paragraph in the first person. For example, if you write about Doña Pascuala, you may start with this sentence: _My name is Doña Pascuala._

Revising Read your draft to a partner, leaving out the name of the character. Does your partner recognize the person you are describing? Correct any parts of your paragraph that are unclear. Proofread your draft for errors. Then write the final copy.

Presenting Read your biographical paragraph to a group of classmates, leaving out the name of the character. Ask those who have read _The Dragons of the Queen_ to guess who you are describing.

Extending Your Reading

Expressing Yourself
Choose one or more of the following activities.

Read a Map   Use a road map to calculate the distance from Boise, Idaho, to Mexico City. How many days would you need to drive from Boise to Mexico City?

Be a Tour Guide   Pretend you are guiding a group of tourists through the area in which you live. What would you point out to them so they would appreciate their visit?

Create Your Own Village   Working in a group, make a model in clay, papier-mâché, or other material of your choice of the village visited by Mr. and Mrs. Kenilworth. Base your model on details from the story.

Cook Mexican Food   Read a cookbook or talk with someone who cooks Mexican food. Choose a dish and prepare it for your family. Report the result of your efforts to classmates.

Gather Information About Mexico   Visit a travel agency and write to the Mexican tourist office or consulate in your area asking for information about Mexico. If there is an area of Mexico in which you are particularly interested, ask about that. Bring the materials you receive to class and share them with your classmates.

Compare Trains   In the poem "Travel," the poet writes about a train with a steam engine. Have you ever seen one? What sort of fuel do modern engines use? Gather information to answer these questions. If you like, draw a picture of an old-fashioned steam engine.

More Books by Mary Stolz

Lands End   Harper & Row. Josh Redmond, an only child, loves the beautiful, lonely area of Florida where he lives. That doesn't mean, though, that he isn't happy to see the Arthurs move nearby—especially since the Arthur family includes a zoo veterinarian, several children, a grandfather, and wild animal pets.

A Wonderful, Terrible Time   Harper & Row. Mady and Sue Ellen are used to their racially mixed city neighborhood where no one has much money, but when the two friends have a chance to go to camp in the country, everything changes. For Mady and Sue Ellen their time at camp is a most important one—both wonderful and terrible.

Cat Walk   Harper & Row. Most barn cats are content with their lives on the farm, but one kitten isn't. His travels lead him out of the barn and through a series of homes and adventures, until he at last find his favorite place to stay.

The Noonday Friends   Harper & Row. Franny Davis is so busy taking care of her little brother she can only see her friend Simone at lunch time and on weekends. When Franny's father, who would rather paint pictures than anything else, loses his job, it seems Franny is headed for more work and fewer good times. However, wonderful surprises await her.

The Bully of Barkham Street   Harper & Row. Unfortunately, Martin Hastings deserves his reputation as the neighborhood bully. He doesn't want to misbehave, but somehow things always end up badly. When Martin tries to change, he discovers that a bad reputation is much harder to get rid of than it was to acquire in the first place.

BLIND OUTLAW

written and illustrated by

Glen Rounds

BLIND OUTLAW

Many years ago in the American West, cattle and horses wandered freely across the open range. When cowboys rounded up wild horses, the bravest and most skilled ranch hands would try to break, or tame, them. Horses that could not be gentled for riding were called outlaws. *Blind Outlaw* is the story of one such horse and his meeting with an exceptional young boy.

Cowboys and the Old West

Blind Outlaw by Glen Rounds presents an accurate account of the lives of cowboys in the Old West. At the time of the Civil War, huge herds of Texas longhorn cattle roamed the plains. Cowboys rounded up as many as five thousand head of cattle and herded them across the plains to market. The pace was slow, no more than ten miles could be covered in a day, and the trip was long, sometimes as long as one thousand miles. Trail drives were hard on cowboys, and lonely too. Trail drives meant many weeks in the saddle chasing stray cattle and driving the herd. They meant cold nights sleeping on the ground. They often meant water shortages, attacks by wolves, injuries, or wildfires. Despite these hardships, many men wanted nothing more than to be cowboys. By the end of the 1800s, much of the open range had been fenced in for ranches, and the railroads were closing in on cattle territory. The days of long trail drives were over.

Cowboys became heroes to many people because the life of a cowboy seemed so uncomplicated and free and cowboys came to symbolize the early days of the United States. Cowboy songs, such as "Home on the Range," became and have remained popular. People who had never ridden a horse enjoyed dressing like cowboys.

Blind Outlaw will help you appreciate what the everyday life of cowboys was really like. You will discover how the range offered a home for anyone who knew how to handle a horse and a rope.

Thinking About a Novel's Theme

Every work of fiction has one or more themes, or central ideas, that tie it together. If you ask the question, "What does this story mean?" when you read a novel such as *Blind Outlaw,* you may discover the novel's theme. A well-written work of fiction will explore a theme, such as "friendship may be found in unexpected places" or "everyone must have hope," in a way that teaches the reader something new and important about these ideas.

As you're reading this novel on your own, decide why the Boy seems to have a magical effect on the Horse.

BLIND OUTLAW

*O*ddly enough, during all the long summer the Boy and the Blind Outlaw were around the ranch, neither was ever known by name.

The Boy had some sort of impediment in his speech and could only make wordless sounds. So while he most probably did have a name, there was no way of knowing what it was.

And if in his mind the Boy had a name for the Horse, it stayed as much a mystery as his own.

To this day when their story is told, they are simply called the Boy and the Blind Outlaw.

1

The Horse

It was about the middle of a late spring morning when the Horse came in sight from the far side of the bare ridge and stood for a while on the highest part.

He appeared to be four or five years old, compactly built and with a rough coat somewhere between blue-gray and mouse color. He wore no owner's brand, and the only distinctive mark on him was the strange mask-like patch of darker color covering his forehead and upper muzzle. The untidy tangles and mats of cockleburs and mud in his long tail and mane marked him as a range horse, and not one that had simply strayed off from some ranch or farm.

For a time he stood quietly on the crest with his head held high, his sharply pointed ears flicking forward and back as he snuffed through widened nostrils, testing the tiny air currents that drifted up the sun-warmed slope from the flat below.

The faint sound of magpies quarreling came from somewhere out of sight, and nearby a big fly buzzed loudly as he went about his morning's business. There was a smell of sage and old winter grass as well as the fainter scent of newly turned earth from where a gopher was repairing or enlarging his burrow.

But none of these things appeared to disturb the Horse, and before long he started unhurriedly down the slope.

He moved with a certain caution, his steps almost catlike as he set each hoof carefully down before moving the next. With his head held low, he seemed to be intent on each small sound or scent coming to him from the grass ahead.

Nonetheless he walked without hesitation, and from a little distance a bystander would not have known that the Horse was blind. Apparently, with long practice, he had learned to "read" the world around him with surprising accuracy by scent and sound instead of by sight.

Coming down onto the little flat where the first green

grass was just beginning to appear in small scattered patches, the Blind Horse began to graze. Pushing his muzzle deep among the last year's stems, he sniffed out the hidden tender tufts without trouble, greedily cropping each one, then moving on in search of the next.

But as he fed, his ears and nose continually brought him news from both close by and far off. He took no notice when an early rising grasshopper flew out from under his nose with a sudden raspy whir. Nor was he startled by the occasional quick scurrying of field mice in nearby tussocks.

But when a rattlesnake, sunning himself on a nearby patch of bare ground, wakened and started slowly gathering his coils, the Horse threw up his head at the first dry scaly rustle. With his ears pointing stiffly forward, he quickly located the source of the small sounds, and identified the snake by his rank scent.

Since the snake was out of striking distance, the Horse stood without moving—but listening intently. And for a little while the snake seemed to be waiting also. Then, when the Horse made no threatening move, the snake relaxed his coils and began to crawl slowly away in the direction of a nearby patch of buckbrush. Pointing his

ears to follow the tiny rustlings as the snake wound his
way through the high grass, the Horse waited until both
the scent and the sounds had disappeared. Then he went
back to his interrupted feeding.

Later in the morning, as the sun warmed the air and
set larger air currents drifting lazily this way and that, he
caught a faint whiff of the warm furry scent of a coyote.
Unlike the big gray wolves that were still fairly common
in that country, the coyote hunted only small creatures,
and the Horse seemed to follow the animal's progress
with only neighborly interest.

The coyote trotted up to an old buffalo skull some
distance from the Horse. After sniffing carefully, he
raised a leg and added his mark to the ones already
there, then started searching the high grass for his
breakfast.

With his nose busily twitching and his big ears braced
forward to catch the slightest scurry or rustle in the grass,
the coyote moved stealthily from tussock to tussock. The
Horse continued to stand quietly where he was, following
the coyote's progress by the strengthening or weakening
of his scent and the small excited sniffings and snufflings
as he thrust his muzzle deep into tangles of old grass,

searching for possible game.

Now and again there would be the sound of sudden movement as the coyote leaped high in the air to snap at a flying grasshopper, or pounced to pin an unlucky mouse under his paws. But both sounds and scent grew gradually fainter as he finished his business on the flat and finally disappeared into a shallow gully on the other side.

As the heat of the day increased, the Horse too moved off the flat, working his way slowly up the slope of the ridge ahead. On top an updraft made a little breeze strong enough to keep the biting flies away. And there the Horse settled down to rest and doze the afternoon away.

The sun was only a couple of hours high in the west when he stirred again. The small afternoon wind had sprung up and carried with it the faint smell of water. Facing in the direction, the Blind Horse left the ridge, crossed another shallow valley and the hogback of the far side of that. Coming into a sagebrush flat, he moved more cautiously than before to avoid stumbling over the low tough bushes.

But he soon caught the warm smell of range cattle and dust from a deep stock path winding through the sage.

Turning into that, he found the going easier, and the smell of the water grew stronger. When he came at last to the water hole, the cattle had already finished drinking, and he could smell and hear them grazing some way off.

Sniffing his way carefully across the wide band of trampled mud around the edges of the small pond, he drank, then moved off in the opposite direction from the grazing cattle. A colder wind was beginning to blow in fitful gusts, and there was the smell of rain in the air. Moving with the wind behind him, the Horse worked his way out of the sagebrush and up a shallow draw until a small thicket of box elder trees and plum bushes blocked his way. These and the sides of the draw offered him some protection from both wind and rain, so he settled down for the night.

For several days the Blind Horse drifted steadily but without hurry across the range. And in spite of his blindness, he seemed to have no difficulty in finding good grass or the location of the widely scattered water holes.

As he grazed, he sometimes caught the scent of fresh horse tracks in the grass, and one afternoon he came

close to a small band of range horses. But even though
he stayed in their neighborhood for several days,
following them at a distance on their daily trips to water,
he was never allowed to join them.

So it happened that one morning he was grazing some
distance from a water hole where the band was drinking,
when he heard men's voices and the creak of saddle
leathers from a ridge behind him.

Throwing up his head and facing in the direction of
the sounds, he snorted. Then, catching the scent of the
men themselves, he wheeled away and broke into a run.

In his panic he ran directly toward the water hole and,
before he realized his danger, he had stumbled and fallen
to his knees in the treacherous mud. Struggling to his
feet, the Blind Horse lunged and splashed his way
through the mud and water and onto the dry ground on
the other side. But now he was in the middle of the
milling band of range horses, crashing heavily against
first one and then another.

By that time the riders were close behind and on
either side of the confused horses, shouting and swinging
long rope ends to drive the band ahead of them. Each
time the Blind Horse tried to turn aside, a whistling rope

or a horse and rider blocked his way. So there was
nothing for him to do but run blindly with the rest. As
they turned this way or that to avoid washouts or other
obstacles, he was carried along by the press of horses on
either side. He stumbled over sagebrush or little gullies
from time to time, but luckily he did not fall.

After the first wild rush, the horses, guided by the
riders on either side and pushed on by the ones behind,
were allowed to settle down to an easy trot. For a while
the men drove them straight across country, but after a
few miles they were turned onto a wide stock trail that
wound up an easy slope to a ridge above. At the top, the
path led through the wide opening between a pair of
wing fences fanning out from the gate of a stout pole
corral some distance down the slope. Seeing the fences,
the horses in the lead tried to turn back but the ones
behind, driven by the shouting riders, forced them ahead
and through the gate.

As soon as they were all inside, the heavy gate was
shut and the men went away. For a while the horses
milled aimlessly about, looking for a way out. But the
fence had no weak spots, and gradually they settled down
to uneasy waiting.

Some of the bolder ones, overcoming their fear of the clanking windmill, even went cautiously to the water trough to drink. But the Blind Horse backed into a corner of the corral and stood there trembling, his coat darkened in great patches of nervous sweat.

2

The Boy

The Boy was already at the ranch when the Blind
Horse was brought in with the others off the range.

He had appeared there sometime in the early spring, as
nearly as anyone now remembers, with the old Buggy
Salesman. The old man would start out from the railroad
driving a good team hitched to a new buggy, and with
two or three more of various styles hitched on behind in
trailer fashion. He'd travel from town to town and ranch
to ranch, peddling his buggies as others peddled extracts,
cough cures, needles, or liniment.

But as is the case even with automobile dealers today,
his dealings were not always for cash. He not only took
old buggies and even old sets of harnesses in place of
money, but often traded for horses as well. An old buggy
could be hitched on behind the remaining new ones, and

one or two extra horses could be tied alongside the team he was driving. But, as his second-hand horse herd grew, he would hire someone to drive them along behind.

The Boy had drifted into the old man's camp one morning, somewhere the other side of Miles City, Montana, and had been earning his keep by wrangling the little bunch of loose horses, washing road dust off the new buggies before they were shown to prospective customers, and helping with camp chores. The Buggy Salesman had no idea where he came from or what his name was—he simply called him Boy.

He wasn't much to look at, and it was hard to judge his age. He might have been a big ten-year-old or a small fifteen for all anyone could tell. He wore a battered Stetson, well past its best years and obviously a hand-me-down from some long gone Texan. His boots, too, were Fort Worths well along into advanced age—and big enough that he'd be able to grow into them for some years yet without danger of their pinching his feet. The saddle on the potbellied old horse he seemed to own had been made in Miles City years before the Boy was born. His mismatched spurs, too, were Montana style—short iron shanks and sharp rowels the size of dimes instead of

the long goosenecks and "dollar rowels" of the southern ranges. So to judge his origins from his gear was impossible.

During his layover at the ranch, the old man sold all his loose horses to a passing trader and no longer needed a wrangler. So when he left, the Boy stayed on as a sort of chore boy.

At first the Ranch Owner and the men around the ranch thought it was strange that, while he didn't appear to be sullen by nature, he never answered when spoken to. But the old Buggy Salesman explained that, while the Boy could hear and understand what was said to him, for some reason or other he was unable to speak. He could make some sounds, but nothing more.

However, he seemed to understand animals and birds, and in some fashion was able to communicate with them. When he first came to the ranch, he had a tame magpie that he talked to in a strange wordless fashion that the bird seemed to understand.

Later he found a nest of baby rabbits whose mother had probably been taken by a coyote or hawk. He put them in a box filled with rags and fed them diluted condensed milk with a medicine dropper until they were big enough to forage for themselves. As they got older, they followed him about as he did the ranch chores and, for some reason, neither the cats nor the ranch dogs ever bothered them.

The coyote pup a passing cowboy had given him later also became a familiar sight around the ranch, following the Boy and the young rabbits. And the day old Ring, the one-eyed vicious-tempered ranch dog, tangled with a porcupine, he lay without a snarl or whimper while the Boy removed the painful quills one by one from his cheeks and muzzle.

But whoever he was and wherever he came from, the Boy was a good worker. He wrangled the saddle horses, chopped and carried wood, hauled water, and did the hundred-and-one small jobs that have to be done around any ranch. And after a while, nobody paid attention to the fact he could not speak.

3

The Horsebreaker

When the Ranch Owner and the Cowboy, who spent his spare time breaking new horses to fill out the remuda, walked down to look over the wild ones that had just been brought in, the Boy and his animals followed close behind them.

Sitting on the top rail of the corral, the two men watched the horses milling around below, judging their tempers, looks and condition. When they agreed on one that would possibly make a good saddle horse, it was separated from the others and run into another pen by the men down on the ground.

They had picked out several before the Horsebreaker pointed to the Blind Horse still standing alone in the corner of the corral.

"What about the mouse-colored one with the dark

patch on his face?" he asked.

"He doesn't look like one of ours," the Ranch Owner told him. "He must be a stray."

"I've looked at him on both sides," one of the cowboys told him, "and he doesn't have a brand on him anywhere."

Any animal on the range that carries no owner's brand belongs to whoever picks him up and, after carefully looking the stray over again, the Ranch Owner said, "All right, run him into the pen with the others. If he turns out all right, and nobody comes looking for him, we'll brand him later."

And as he climbed down from the fence he spoke again. "Turn the rest loose and run them back out onto the range," he said. And he and the Horsebreaker walked away.

Right after breakfast next morning, the Horsebreaker had one of the new horses run into the round roping corral for its first lesson. After the gate was closed, he stood for a while by the scarred snubbing post in the center, quietly talking to the horse as it circled the corral looking for a way out. Making no sudden moves, the man waited for the horse's first panic to pass.

Then, moving away from the post with the coil of his rope in his left hand and tailing the opened noose from his right, he waited for the horse to pass him. With a sharp side-arm swing, he flipped the loop neatly over the animal's head and twitched it snug around its neck.

The horse, feeling the rope tighten, snorted and reared high onto his hind legs, then lunged away. But by taking a couple of turns of the rope around the post, the Horsebreaker easily stopped the horse's rush, slowly taking up the rope's slack to bring him closer and closer to the snubbing post.

Most horses quickly learn that fighting the rope only draws the choking noose tighter. So this one was soon standing braced at the end of the rope, breathing heavily while the Horsebreaker talked softly to him. When the man moved, the horse would snort and lunge again, but each time the struggle was shorter, until at last he stood quietly while the man undid the turns of his rope from the snubbing post, flipped the noose free from the horse's head, and turned him loose for the day, his first lesson finished.

One after another, the Horsebreaker dealt with several more of the wild horses as he had the first and, as soon

as they stopped fighting the rope, he turned them loose.

And then the mouse-colored Stray, in his turn, was run through the gate. When he smelled the man, he did as the others had done, and whirled toward the fence. But instead of turning to follow it around the circle, he crashed straight into it, then reared in a frantic attempt to climb over. Falling back, he scrambled to his feet and again crashed headlong into the fence.

When the Horse showed no sign of giving up his attempts to crash through or climb the fence, the Horsebreaker at last cast his loop over his head and twitched it snug. As he felt the noose tighten around his neck, the Horse made a hoarse bawling sound and reared high on his hind legs. The rope around the snubbing post held fast, however, and the Horse crashed heavily onto his back. When he'd gotten to his feet again, he faced the man, braced himself, and pulled backwards until his neck was stretched to what looked like the breaking point.

With his weight against the rope pulling the choking noose tighter and tighter against his windpipe, the Horse stood braced with his nostrils distended and his tongue showing between his half-opened jaws. He breathed in

great hoarse, rasping sobs that gradually became weaker until at last he went slowly to his knees.

Seeing the horse weaken, the man by the post loosened the rope a little. With the pressure of the noose gone, the Horse drew in a few great whistling breaths, then struggled to his feet and again threw himself backwards against the rope.

And again, when the tightening noose choked him to his knees, the man gave him slack.

Time after time the struggle was repeated. The Stray's coat was black with sweat and his tongue, when it showed, was smeared with corral dirt, but still he showed no signs of giving up.

The Boy had been watching through the fence since the Horse had been brought into the corral with the Horsebreaker, and now a cowboy and the Ranch Owner, on the way to the ranch house for dinner, stopped by also.

The Horse was on his knees again, so the Horsebreaker gave him a little slack in the rope and turned to where there others sat on the fence.

"This is the worst spooked horse I ever worked with," he said, wiping sweat from his face. "I'd guess somebody

has abused him badly some time or other. He's got scars around his head as if he'd been beaten with a chain or some such thing.

"He's pure outlaw now," the Horsebreaker went on, "He fights the rope 'til he chokes himself down, then as soon as I give him a little air, he gets up and starts all over. And before I got the rope on him, he almost managed to climb the fence. He just isn't going to give up."

"Too bad," the Ranch Owner said. "He's a right likely looking horse."

By now the Horse, still breathing in great gasps, was struggling back to his feet, and the Horsebreaker spoke again.

"How about coming in here and hog-tying him for me when he chokes down this time?" he asked. "I want to look at him close before I turn him loose for good."

So when the Horse went to his knees, the Horsebreaker left the rope tight while the others quickly tied his feet together and gently pushed him onto his side, where he lay helpless.

The Horsebreaker loosened the noose from the Horse's neck, then spent some time examining his head and

muzzle. Getting to his feet he said, "Besides being outlaw, that Horse is blind."

"Blind?" the Ranch Owner asked. "You sure?"

"Yep," the Horsebreaker told him. "I'd begun to suspect it from the way he acted, and just now I looked real careful. He's blind as a bat."

For a little while, the men stood watching the Horse as he struggled weakly against the ropes around his feet.

"It's too bad," the Ranch Owner finally said. "But it doesn't seem right to turn him back on the range, him being blind. Maybe we ought to shoot him?"

The Ranch Owner felt a touch on his arm and turned to find the Boy beside him. Pointing at the Horse and then to himself, he seemed to be trying to say something.

"What's he trying to say, do you reckon?" the Ranch Owner asked.

"I think he wants the Stray," the Horsebreaker said. "You know how he is about animals."

"You think you could tame that Horse, is that it?" the Ranch Owner asked the Boy, who nodded his head.

For a while longer, the men stood there without saying anything, while the Boy anxiously watched both the Horse and their faces. They looked at the Boy, at the

tame magpie on his shoulder, and at the half-grown coyote lying on the ground with the young rabbits.

After a bit the Horsebreaker nodded and half to himself, he said, "You know, he just might do it."

The Ranch Owner thought for a while longer, then turned to the Boy and said, "Spooked like that Horse is, I don't see how even you could break him. And even if you did, what good would a blind horse be to anybody? He's too big to keep just for a pet like your other animals."

The Boy made no answer, simply stood there making soft noises to himself and the Horse lying hog-tied on the ground. After a while, the Ranch Owner spoke again.

"All right," he said to the Horsebreaker, "let the Horse up and put him in one of the corrals by himself."

And turning to the Boy, he went on, "If you think you can gentle that Blind Outlaw in your spare time, he's yours. And the day you can ride him up to the house, I'll give you a bill of sale for him."

4

Boy and Horse

So the Blind Horse was separated from the others—
and put into an unused corral by himself. The Boy still
had his chores to do, but nonetheless he found dozens of
excuses to go by just to look at the Horse, or to see that
the water trough was full.

After supper he came back, with his small animals
following, and brought hay from the stack yard to put by
the water trough. Then, climbing to the top rail of the
corral fence, he sat for a long time, whittling on a stick,
while crooning and chirping in his soft wordless way to
the Horse or to the magpie perched on the post nearby.

Across the corral, the Blind Horse stood backed into a
corner, shifting his feet nervously as he faced the place
where the Boy sat. Now and again he cleared his nostrils
with a soft snorting sound as he delicately sniffed the air

to sort out the strange scents of the Boy, the young coyote, and the small rabbits.

He flung up his head and pointed his ears at each unfamiliar ranch sound—the squeal of a horse from the nearby pasture, the slam of a screen door, or the sounds of voices from the bunkhouse. But after a time, when the Boy made no move to leave his perch on the fence, the Horse seemed to relax a little. He occasionally switched his long burr-matted tail or stamped a foot to dislodge a fly. But his sharp pointed ears were always set to catch the Boy's soft voice as it went on and on, sounding strangely like some small bird talking to itself.

When the dusk had thickened until the Boy could see the Horse only as a light-colored blur against the fence, he climbed quietly down the outside of the corral. With his animals following him, he went back to the bunkhouse, and the Horse was left alone.

During the next few days the Horsebreaker and the other cowboys used any handy excuse to go by the corral, hoping to see how the Boy who couldn't speak would go about taming the Blind Outlaw. But as far as they could tell, he was in no hurry to begin, and there was no way they could ask what his plan was.

Each morning he brought more hay and made sure the

water trough was full. And he went through the corral a
dozen times a day on one errand or another, simply
coming in one gate and going out the other without
stopping or making any move toward the Horse.

The Horse, whenever he heard the Boy's footsteps and
caught his scent, would back into the far corner and
stand with his head high, nostrils wide and ears flicking
forward and back as he listened for the creak of the
opening gate. And as the small procession passed him,
he turned his head, sniffing and listening to follow their
progress. But when they seemed intent on some business
of their own, he made no other move.

For several days this went on—the Boy making his
trips through the Blind Horse's corral at odd times during
the day, and sitting on the top rail from suppertime until
dark. The Horse still stayed watchfully in his corner
whenever the Boy and the animals were about, but as
the days went on he showed less and less sign of
nervousness.

Then one night after supper the Boy brought his old
saddle horse from where he'd been grazing in the little
horse pasture and turned him loose in the corral. The old
horse walked over to the Blind One in the corner and,
stretching his neck far out, touched noses with him to

get his scent. Then he went to the water trough for a drink before picking over the hay on the ground.

Later the Boy went to the bunkhouse and brought back his bedroll and pushed it between the lower bars before climbing to his usual perch on the top rail. There the Boy made his wordless sounds to the horses and the small animals while he busily braided narrow strips cut from soft boot leather to make one of the quirts he sold to passing cowboys. The Blind Horse, from his corner, divided his attention between the Boy's voice and the movements of the old saddle horse.

The Blind Horse in his corner spent the night awake, stirring nervously at the slightest sound from where the Boy and the small animals slept. At first daylight the Boy got up and rolled his bed, placing it neatly beside the fence before going to the water trough to wash. While he was doing these things, he made his usual wordless sounds to himself, but seemed to pay no attention to the Blind Horse, and when he was finished he led the old horse, with the small animals following, out through the gate.

From then on the Boy not only made his usual trips through the corral during the day, but spent every night there as well. While he worked quietly at his leather

work before bedtime, the soft conversational sounds that were not words went on and on. The small animals, going about their own affairs, often passed close to the Blind Horse's feet. The Horse heard the sounds they made and recognized, without alarm, their warm furry smells. But he threw up his head with ears sharply forward at any sound of movement from where the Boy sat on the fence.

For some days the Horse backed into his corner whenever the Boy and his animals appeared. But before long he began to cock his ears forward in interested fashion as he followed the sounds of the little processions through his corral, or listened to the sound of the Boy's voice in the evenings. He still remained watchful, starting at any strange sound, but before long he began to move freely around the corral in the nights after the Boy had gone to bed. Often he followed the older horse as he searched under the bottom rail of the fence for odd tufts of grass. And now he spent much of every night dozing on his feet, waking only when he heard the Boy stir in his sleep. During the day he sometimes cautiously approached the bedroll beside the corral fence, nuzzling lightly as he sniffed the now familiar scent of the boy.

And evenings, when the Boy brought the old saddle

horse into the corral for the night, the Blind Outlaw, instead of backing into his corner, now often stood quietly a little distance off. He'd seem to listen interestedly to the Boy's voice and the small sounds as he took off the old horse's halter and neatly coiled the lead rope.

Then one night the Boy, while scratching and petting the old horse, took three or four carrots from his pocket and fed them to him one by one. Hearing the crisp crunching sounds as the old horse ate them, the Blind One suddenly stretched his head forward, ears flicking and his nostrils wide. Snuffling softly, trying to catch the faint scent of the carrots, he cautiously shifted his feet this way and that but without coming any closer. Still listening and testing the air, he waited where he was until the Boy had gone back to his place on the top rail. Then cautiously, a short step at a time, turning his head often to listen for any movement from the Boy, he went to where the old horse stood and snuffled in the dust, searching out tiny bits the other had dropped.

A range-raised horse usually pays no attention to carrots, apples and such things, so now the Boy was sure that before he turned outlaw this one had been someone's pet, accustomed to being fed tidbits of one kind and another.

From then on the Boy brought some treat from the garden or the kitchen each night. And while the other crunched the crisp bits, the Blind One listened and snuffed the air as before. And each night he came a little closer, but always poised to back away at any unusual sound of movement.

So far the Boy had seemed to ignore the Blind Horse. But one night when, keeping the old horse between them, he had come closer than usual, the Boy quietly flipped a carrot out in his direction. At the sound the Horse whirled away and stood snorting softly some distance off.

But later, while the Boy went on feeding other bits to the old horse, the Blind One cautiously sniffed his way to where the carrot had dropped and picked it up. Stepping back, he stood crunching it until it was gone, then sniffed about in the dust for more.

Each night after that the Blind Horse came a little closer, but always kept the old horse between himself and the Boy. And when he heard the treat drop in front of him, he'd reach down without hesitation and pick it up.

Then one night the Boy took a piece of dried apple from his pocket but, instead of tossing it to the Horse as he had been doing, he simply reached under the old horse's neck and held it toward the other.

The Horse stretched his neck forward, blowing softly through his nostrils as he caught the sweet apple scent. He stamped, shifting his feet one way and another, coming a few inches, then backing off, but stayed out of reach. So after a bit the Boy fed the piece to the old horse and climbed with his leatherwork to his usual place on the top rail.

While he watched, the Horse sniffed about for the treat he'd expected to find on the ground, then went to search out the tiny scraps the old horse had dropped.

The next night and the one after that, the Horse stood nervously nearby, sniffing and tossing his head while the old horse was fed all the small bits the Boy had brought. But the third night, his greed finally overcame his caution. This time, when the Boy reached past the old horse, holding out a piece of jelly bread, the Horse inched toward him and gently took it from his fingers before stepping back out of reach.

When the Horse had finished the bread, the Boy coaxed him back to take a piece of dried apple and, later, some bits of dried apricot from his hand. But still he would not come close enough to be touched, staying always on the far side of the older horse.

5

Brush and Currycomb

Sometimes the Boy would be away from the ranch
from morning until night, helping repair fences, greasing
windmills, or cleaning out springs. During those days the
Blind Horse would move restlessly around his corral,
often going over to sniff at the Boy's bedroll by the
fence, or standing at the gate with his ears cocked in the
direction of the bunkhouse.

And when the Boy came in after supper, bringing the
old horse with him, the Blind Horse would come part way
across the corral to meet them. Stopping a little way off,
he'd stand flicking his ears and listening to the sounds of
the saddle being taken off, or sniffing at the small
animals as they came past him. And when he heard the
rustling as the Boy reached in his pockets for the things
he'd brought from the kitchen, he'd cautiously move
closer. Every night he took his share from the Boy's

fingers, but only when the old horse stood between them. He still wouldn't let himself be touched and, at all other times, kept his distance.

Then one rainy night, the Boy spread his bedroll in the shed at the end of the corral, where the older horse had already taken shelter. Before he went to sleep, he saw the Blind Horse standing out in his usual place, seeming not to mind the light drizzle. But in the night, wakened by the feel of a warm breath on his face, he looked up without moving and found the Outlaw standing over him in the dark, gently sniffing his face, hair, and bedding. In the morning, however, the Horse was back in his usual place.

From then on, whenever the Boy went through the Horse's corral in the daytime, he gave his soft birdlike call before he reached the gate but, instead of going straight on through, as he had been doing, now he would stop for a bit just inside. Clucking and chirping to the Horse, he'd take a cold biscuit or a bit of dried apple out of his pocket and hold it out.

As long as the Boy made no move to come close, the Horse would stand quietly, his neck stretched forward, trying to catch the scent of what it was the Boy was holding in his hand. Sometimes he'd shift his feet a

little, blowing softly but, without the other horse there, he would not come close.

The Boy would carry on this odd, one-sided, wordless conversation for a while, then carefully toss the treat toward the Horse's feet before making some signal to the small animals lolling in the dust nearby and leading them out through the other gate.

The Horse would wait until he heard the far gate close, then step forward to sniff out whatever the Boy had dropped on the ground. But he was losing much of his distrust and, in the evenings, with the old horse between them, he was taking tidbits from the Boy's hand with less and less caution. And he was becoming more and more greedy for the little snacks.

So now even without the old horse there, the Boy was able to coax him a little closer each day until at last he'd not only taken the things from the Boy's fingers, but would nuzzle and nibble at his pockets when they were being doled out too slowly. And the day the Boy first reached up and lightly scratched him behind the ears, he seemed not to notice.

From then on the strange relationship between the Boy and the Blind Outlaw developed rapidly. Whenever he heard the Boy coming toward the corral, the Horse

would nicker softly and trot to the gate to meet him. After giving out whatever bits he'd brought, the Boy would stand for a while rubbing the Horse's forehead and stroking the velvety muzzle, the familiar sound of his soft voice going on and on.

The Horse seemed to listen intently to the Boy's voice, flicking his ears backwards and forward. And when he walked away, the Horse would follow close behind, often nudging his back or shoulder in friendly fashion with his muzzle.

Sometimes after supper, the Ranch Owner and the Horsebreaker came down to sit a while on the top rail, talking quietly to each other while they watched the Boy and the Horse below. If he was alone in the corral, the first sound or scent of the men would send the Blind Horse to his place in the far corner, where he would stand, snorting and nervously shifting his feet. But with the Boy there, he seemed less fearful. And as long as they stayed quiet on the fence, seeming not to threaten him, he gradually came to ignore them.

One such night, the men found the Boy and the Horse playing what seemed to be a strange game of follow-the-leader. While they watched, the Boy scratched and stroked the Horse's head for a while, then, after making

a curious chirping signal, he turned and walked away while the Horse stood where he was, with his ears cocked sharply forward.

After taking a few steps, the Boy stopped, turned, and chirped again. The Horse, when he heard the small sound, walked forward and stopped directly in front of the Boy, rubbing his forehead against his chest and nibbling gently at his shirt. After another soft chirping sound to the Horse, the Boy walked off in another direction, and this time, the Horse walked beside him.

For some time the men watched as the Boy and the Horse walked this way and that—starting, stopping, turning to one side or the other. What the various chirping sounds meant, only the Boy and the Blind Horse knew. But the Horse seemed to understand them and, without being touched, he followed the Boy closely as if he'd been on a lead rope.

"A strange thing," the Horsebreaker remarked after a while. "The Horse can't see, and neither one can talk, yet they seem really to understand each other."

"Yeah," the Ranch Owner agreed. "And I'd have been willing to bet that the Boy would never be able to get a hand on that Horse, spooked like he was."

They watched a while longer, then climbed down the

outside of the fence and went away.

One evening the Boy brought the old horse into the corral with his saddle still on. While the Blind Horse nuzzled his hands and sniffed at his pockets, the Boy started taking the saddle off. At the first rattle of the loosened cinch buckle, the Blind Horse snorted and backed away. The Boy paid no attention, but went on making some unnecessary adjustments to the stirrup leathers before pulling the saddle off and dragging it to the fence.

But after a few nights, he began to lose his fear of the sounds and, before long, would stand unconcernedly sniffing the Boy's pockets all the while he was dealing with the saddle. Even when the dragging cinch brushed his leg one night, he paid it no attention.

And now when the Boy climbed to his place on the top rail to work a while at his leather braiding, the Horse would come to stand close by the fence just below him. And instead of spending the nights at the far side of the corral, he now slept, standing, close by the Boy's bed.

The Blind Horse hadn't completely shed his rough winter coat, and the ragged patches of long winter hair mixed with dirt and dried mud gave him a scruffy, unkempt look. So one evening the Boy brought an old

curry comb and brush into the corral and let the Horse smell them after he'd eaten the pieces of jelly bread he'd brought from the house. After he had carefully sniffed and nibbled at the tools, the Horse let the Boy begin lightly brushing the side of his jaw and his forehead.

That first evening the Boy worked gently, brushing only the Horse's head and the sides of his neck. When the brush or the currycomb pulled hairs out, along with patches of dried mud, the Horse would flinch or reach around to nibble at the Boy's hands. But by the time his head and neck had been brushed until they were sleek and shiny, he seemed to be enjoying the attention.

When he'd done that much, the Boy cleaned the currycomb and brush, fed the Horse a piece of brown sugar, and climbed to the top of the fence to work a while at his leather braiding.

But each night, he spent some time on the grooming, standing on a box to reach the Horse's back and rump. Even the gentlest horse will object to the touch of the brush on his flanks and legs but, as the Blind Horse became more and more accustomed to the feel of the Boy's hands on his skin, those places, too, were brushed and curried.

It was some time, however, before he would let his

feet be picked up and examined without snorting and backing away. But the Boy continued his coaxing and chirping and, in the end, the Horse stood without objection even when the Boy took a hoof between his knees and started smoothing and trimming the rough broken edges with an old rasp.

By now the Blind Horse had begun to take on a smooth, well-groomed look. But his long mane and tail, matted with mud and cockleburs, still had to be dealt with. So one night instead of using the brush, the Boy took his pocketknife and, standing on the box, started pulling and cutting away the tangles in the Horse's forelock.

With no rope or halter to hold him, the Horse was free to back out of reach at any time. But though he sometimes stamped a foot, or swung his head to nibble gently at the Boy's shirt or hands as the knife was tugged through an unusually tough tangle, he seemed not to object to the trimming.

Night after night, the little pile of coarse horse hair by the fence grew larger as the Blind Horse lost his ragged range horse appearance. And by the time the Boy had finished, the Outlaw was as neatly trimmed and groomed as any saddle horse on the ranch.

6

The Horse Escapes

A day or two after he'd finished grooming and
trimming the Horse, the Boy was feeding him some dried
apricots he'd taken from the kitchen after dinner when
he looked up and saw a tall, yellow-gray column of
smoke boiling up from beyond the ridge to the south.

For weeks the weather had been hot, dry, and
windy—and prairie fires in ranch country were even
more feared than tornadoes. One running out of control
might destroy thousands of acres of grass as well as
buildings in its path. So at the first sign of smoke, men
from all parts of the range dropped whatever they were
doing and rode out to fight the dreaded flames.

On most ranches and homesteads, the buildings were
protected by a wide fireguard—a strip of plowed ground
that, ordinarily, the creeping flames could not cross. But

even so, there was always danger that blowing sparks and brands might set new fires inside the protected islands. So when the men had gone, the women and children left behind filled water barrels, washtubs, and buckets, and put wet sacks, rags, and hoses in handy places. Fighting fire, in that country, was everybody's business.

So within minutes after the Boy had given the alarm, everyone on the ranch was busy. The team was quickly hitched to the wagon, while water barrels were loaded, along with shovels, pieces of canvas, and old grain sacks. As soon as those things had been done, and the water barrels filled at the windmill, the Ranch Owner drove the wagon out the gate, followed by the others on their horses.

With the fire moving away from the ranch, nobody needed to stay behind, so the Boy, on his potbellied old horse, rode with them. The Blind Horse had been standing at the corral gate, poking his muzzle between the planks, sniffing the air and listening to the unfamiliar sounds. As the Boy rode away, he nickered softly, but got no answer.

After several miles they came in sight of the fire, already burning in a great arc a mile or more across, leaving behind it a broad band of blackened, smoking ground. On the dry flats where grass was short, the flames crept slowly but steadily ahead but, in the swales and occasional patches of high grass, they roared up to great heights, into boiling clouds of greasy black smoke. Sparks and burning brands, picked up by the wind, swirled high in the air, then fell to the ground, starting new blazes in the unburned grass ahead.

The men quickly unhitched the team, well upwind from the burned ground, and tied them and the saddle horses to the wheels. Then after wetting their neckerchiefs and tying them over their noses, they moved to the line of fire, beating at the flames with pieces of canvas and sacks they'd soaked in the water barrels.

Following them, others worked with rakes and shovels to cover the smoldering spots before they could break into flames again.

Two riders from another ranch were already riding their snorting, protesting horses at a gallop along the line of fire, dragging a water-soaked tarpaulin over the flames by ropes tied to their saddle horns.

Little by little the advancing line was broken into smaller sections, somewhat reducing the intense heat. As men on foot moved into these gaps with their sacks and

shovels, others went on to smother and beat out the scattered fires set by blowing sparks.

It was hot, dirty work, with the thick acrid smoke making the eyes smart and breathing difficult. Flying ash and sparks burned holes in men's clothing and raised small blisters on their skin.

But as more and more men arrived from the more distant ranches, the fire was gradually brought under control. By late afternoon the last of advancing flames had been beaten down, and the newcomers moved back and forth over the blackened ground, shoveling dirt on smoldering sagebrush roots and the occasional small islands of still burning grass.

These latecomers would stay until the wind went down in the evening, making sure no hidden spark was fanned into flame again. So at last the men from the ranch shouldered their tools and started the long walk back to where they'd left the wagon and horses. On the way, a man from a ranch farther to the north joined them. He'd arrived late and left his horse tied to their wagon. Beyond saying a courteous "Howdy," they were all too tired for talk.

It wasn't until they had thrown their shovels and tattered sacks into the wagon and were standing about pouring water over their heads and checking their blisters, that the Stranger spoke up.

"I'm sorry," he told the Ranch Owner, "but I accidently let a horse out of your corral when I came through."

"Probably one of the old workhorses," the Ranch Owner answered. "He'll be hanging around when we get back."

"I dunno," the Rider said. "He was plenty spooked.

"I came down the trail between your wing fences," he went on. "Didn't seem to be any horses in the corrals, and I was in a hurry, so I left the big gate open, and the one into the next corral, too. I was just about to open the gate on the far side when this horse I hadn't seen busted out through the gate behind me. For some reason or other, he missed the far gate and crashed straight into the fence instead. Then he tried to climb over and fell back. While he was down I shook down my rope and, as he got up that time I dabbed a loop over his head to keep him from getting out the gate.

"But when that rope tightened on him, he went plumb loco! Before I could dally my end off around the saddle horn, he'd jerked it out of my hands and taken off, straight through your big gate. The last I saw of him, he

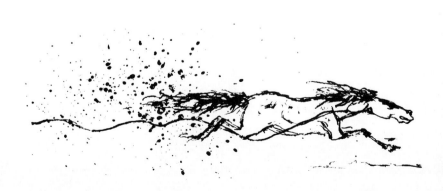

was heading for the ridge, dragging my best rope with him."

For a while nobody said anything. Then after looking at the Boy, who had made a sudden sound, the Ranch Owner spoke up.

"Wasn't your fault," he said to the Rider. "The Horse is blind, and an outlaw to boot. He goes crazy at the touch of a rope."

"I couldn't do anything with him," the Horsebreaker remarked. "Lately the Boy here had been working him in his spare time, trying to gentle him."

"I'm really sorry," the Rider said. "But I'll be glad to help you get him back."

"It's really the Boy's Horse," the Ranch Owner answered. "He'll probably have better luck catching him than any of us would. But thanks anyway."

Then turning to the silent Boy, who looked close to tears, he went on. "When we get back to the ranch, you leave your chores. We'll take care of them. You go and look for the Horse if you want."

After that nothing more was said and, after hitching the team to the wagon, the tired men mounted their horses for the long ride back to the ranch.

7

The Search

It was almost suppertime when the Boy and the rest of
the men rode over the last ridge and down through the
ranch yard gate. While the horses were being unhitched
from the wagon, the Boy went to the kitchen and
quickly made himself a sandwich and put some dried
apples in his pocket for the Blind Horse, in case he
found him.

Then after watering the old horse at the windmill, he
rode out to start his search. The Stranger offered again to
help him, but the Boy only raised a hand and shook his
head.

He had no trouble following the Horse's tracks and the
mark of the trailing rope in the deep dust of the wide
stock path to the top of the ridge. But just over the top,
the path swung sharply to the left to avoid a deep gully,

and the tracks showed that the Horse, instead of turning to follow it, had plunged straight ahead and over the bank.

Sorting out the signs in the torn-up dirt in the bottom of the washout, the Boy found where the Horse had rolled, struggled to his feet again, and scrambled up the farther bank. But after that the tracks disappeared in the grass and there was no way of telling which way he had gone.

So the Boy rode on, stopping at the top of every ridge to look around. Twice he saw lone horses in the distance, but both were grazing quietly so he didn't bother to go closer. He was sure that even after the Horse's first panic had passed, he would still be trying to get away from the trailing rope.

The sun went down and, before long, the deepening dusk made more search impossible, so at last he turned back toward the ranch.

The next morning the Boy was at daybreak to do his chores before riding out to continue his search. Starting again at the place where the Horse had climbed the bank of the washout, he rode back and forth in wider and wider arcs, examining each dusty stock path and

every patch of bare ground for some sign that would tell him which way the Horse had run.

Now and again he found a hoofprint or two and once a patch of trampled ground and a fresh hole where a clump of sage had been pulled up by the roots. It looked to the Boy as if the Horse's trailing rope had become entangled in the bush, and he'd struggled for some time before managing to pull free.

But these small signs were of little help, for the Horse seemed to still be running only to escape the dragging rope, veering off in a new direction each time it touched his legs or caught for a moment on bushes or clumps of high grass.

So there was nothing the Boy could do but ride at random, stopping on the top of every ridge or small hill to look about. He looked into any gully or washout big enough to hide a fallen horse, and carefully read the tracks in the mud around each spring and water hole.

There were small thickets of wild plum and box elder in almost every draw and, if the Blind Horse had blundered into one of these, he might easily have gotten entangled and be unable to escape. So the boy looked carefully into those places also.

But although he rode until sundown before turning back toward the ranch, he had still found no sign to tell him which way the Horse had gone.

It was near noon the next day when the Boy, searching the rocky country at the head of Cedar Creek, found a few faint hoofprints in patches of soft ground in the bottom of a little draw leading up to the rimrock above.

There was no way the Boy could be sure that the tracks had been made by the Blind Horse, and the draw appeared to end at the base of the rock cliffs above. But as nearly as he could tell the tracks led upwards, so, walking and leading his old horse, he followed them.

The head of the draw was partly blocked by a thicket of wild plum and choke cherry, but an old stock path led through it and around a rocky outcropping that concealed the entrance to a little box canyon. Except for the gap where the Boy now stood, the floor of the place was surrounded on all sides by overhanging rocky cliffs. Thick grass grew on the level ground, and water seeped from a little spring under the rocks at one side.

Backed against the rocky wall beyond the spring stood the Blind Horse.

The rope was still around his neck, and his hide was

smeared with mud, and skinned and scratched in places. But otherwise he seemed unharmed. He had heard the old horse and the Boy coming along the stock path, and now he shifted his feet, snorting and snuffing softly, but made no other move.

For a bit the Boy simply stood where he was, talking softly to the Horse in his wordless way. At the sound of the Boy's voice, the Blind Horse stretched his neck far forward, cocking his ears and widening his nostrils, listening and delicately testing the air for the familiar scent. When the Boy still made no move toward him, the Horse took a short, hesitant step forward, then stopped. It was plain that he was still badly spooked from his experience with the rope, and still fearful even though he seemed to recognize the Boy's scent and voice.

The Boy, moving quietly and without hurry, turned to the old horse, took off the saddle, and turned him loose. After shaking himself, the Horse walked toward the Blind One, touched muzzles with him, then started cropping the green grass growing around the spring.

After putting the saddle neatly down, the boy squatted on his heels, his back against a rock, chirping and crooning to himself while he thought about what to do next.

The young coyote, who had been lying under a bush, panting, got to his feet and began to explore. As he sniffed inquisitively under the scraggly bushes or poked his sharp nose into the grass tussocks and small holes in the rocks, the Horse started, then listened, attentively to the little rustlings and snufflings, but showed no sign of alarm. And when the pup came to where he stood and sniffed daintily at his forefeet, the Horse dropped his head and nuzzled the soft fur.

At any sound of movement from the Boy's direction, the Horse threw up his head and snorted softly. So the Boy continued to simply sit there against the rock, watching the Horse and making his soft reassuring sounds.

For a while the little box canyon was quiet except for the Boy's soft voice going on and on, and the small rustlings from where the young coyote went about his explorations among the rocks. Then the boy untied a package from the saddle beside him and began to eat his lunch.

At the first rattling of the paper bag, the Horse shifted his feet nervously and, turning his head from side to side, listened and sniffed for the meaning of the sound. But as the Boy went on with his eating, making coaxing sounds between bites, the Horse began moving toward him, a short cautious step at a time. Between steps he'd stop to listen, stretching his neck to catch the scent and sound of the Boy, then come slowly forward again. He held his head to one side to keep the rope away from his feet, but otherwise seemed not to be bothered by it.

As the Horse came closer, the Boy got quietly to his feet, chirping softly, and held out part of a brown-sugar sandwich. At the sound of his movement, the Horse stopped and backed up a step or two. But catching the sweet smell of the bread and sugar, he came slowly forward again until he could stretch his neck far enough to snatch it from the Boy's fingers.

Still making his soft chirping noises, the Boy took another piece of sandwich from the bag. But this one he held inside his closed fingers so that the Horse could not snatch it as he had done with the first. Still standing where he could reach the Boy's hand only by stretching his neck to the utmost, he gently nuzzled the closed fingers with his soft lips, trying to get at the bread. When he was able to get only a few crumbs, he finally seemed to overcome his fear and stepped closer,

impatiently nudging the Boy's arm with his muzzle.

Stepping back a little, the Boy chirped again and opened his hand. The Horse followed him with hesitation and took the bread. Then after nibbling and blowing his warm breath on the Boy's palm as he searched for the last sweet bits, he rubbed his forehead against the Boy's shirt and sniffed his pockets, looking for more.

Unhurriedly the Boy gave the Horse the last scraps of his lunch, rubbing his soft muzzle and ears between bits.

For a while the Boy made no move to take the rope from the Horse's neck, but when he tugged it lightly to see that the noose was not too tight, the Horse only tossed his head, then went on sniffing at the empty lunch bag. Gathering the dragging end of the rope into a loose coil, the Boy let the Horse smell it, then chirped to him and started walking away. The Horse followed him as he'd done in the corral at the ranch, rubbing his head against the Boy's shoulder as he walked.

For a while the Boy and the Horse moved this way and that inside the box canyon, starting, stopping, and turning as the Boy gave the little signals the Horse seemed to remember and understand. Later he carefully

took the noose from around the Horse's neck and
fastened the coil to his saddle. Then he caught and
saddled the old horse and rode out of the canyon with
the Blind Horse following close behind.

When they were out in the open, the Horse trotted a
few steps to catch up, then walked close alongside the
old horse, rubbing his head against the Boy's knee from
time to time as they went without hurry toward the ranch.

8

The Saddle Horse

For the first few days back at the ranch, the Horse seemed nervous and uneasy when the Boy was out of sight. He'd start and fling his head up at any sudden sound or, if the Ranch Owner or any of the men came near the corral, he'd back into a corner and stand there trembling.

But when the Boy and the small animals appeared, he met them at the gate, rubbing his muzzle against the Boy's shirt and sniffing at his pockets. And he seemed to no longer object to the tickling of the magpie's sharp claws when the bird flew up to perch on his back.

The Horse had lost his well-groomed look, and the Boy spent several evenings standing on the box, brushing dried mud from his coat and pulling away the cockleburs and tangles in his mane and tail.

The Horse seemed to enjoy these sessions, cocking his

ears back and forth, listening to the Boy's voice going on
and on. When he felt the sharp sting of the salve being
rubbed into deep scratches and skinned places, he'd shift
his feet and snort a little or reach around to nibble
lightly at the Boy's hands or the back of his shirt, but
that was all.

The young rabbits were nearly grown and had already
moved into the high grass somewhere in the big pasture,
but the small coyote and the magpie still followed the
Boy as he went about his chores. And sometimes now,
he opened the corral gate and let the Horse join the
little procession.

In the corral there had been nothing for the Horse to
avoid except the water trough and the fence itself. But in
the yard there was the windmill and the big water tank
as well as the woodpile, wagons, hayracks, and the
mowing machine to be looked out for.

Although the Horse could easily tell where the
windmill stood by listening for the squeak and rattle of
the pump rods, the other things gave no warning and
were more difficult to avoid. But after a few painful
bumps, he learned to sniff them out, and followed the
Boy without too much trouble.

For some time the Boy had been busy with his leather

strings, braiding a fancy noseband and making a
hackamore for the Horse and, one evening after supper,
he put it on him. At the first touch of the leather
around his muzzle, the Horse flung up his head to shake
the thing off. But as the Boy went on making his
coaxing sounds, he quickly quieted and stood still while
the headstall was slipped over his ears, and the throat
latch tied. No rope was fastened to the hackamore yet,
but the Boy took a light hold on one of the cheek pieces
and led the Horse this way and that for a while to get
him accustomed to the feel.

The Horse was still uneasy when he heard or smelled
the Ranch Owner or any of the cowboys who often came
to see how the Boy was getting along with his Outlaw.
As time went on, however, he paid less and less
attention, even when they came inside the corral itself.
But still he would snort and back away if any of them
tried to touch him.

One night the Boy carried a piece of old rope with
him when he came into the corral. After petting and
scratching the Horse for a while, he quietly laid the rope
over his back. At the first touch of the rope, the Horse
bowed his back and crowhopped a time or two to shake
it off. But the Boy went on making coaxing noises to

him while he scratched his neck and ears, then chirped
for the Horse to follow and walked away, leaving the
rope in place.

When the Horse moved, the rope across his back
shifted a little, and at first he made a startled side step
each time it happened. But by the time the lesson was
over, he no longer took any notice even when the
dangling ends swung against his sides and legs.

Later when the Boy brought his old saddle blanket
from the fence and dropped it on the ground at his feet,
the Horse sniffed it curiously but seemed unafraid. So
after a while the Boy dragged the box up and set it
beside the Horse and, standing on it, he carefully laid
the blanket over his back, chirping and crooning as he
smoothed out the wrinkles with his hands. The Horse
snuffed softly, turning his head to sniff and nibble at the
blanket's edge, but stood where he was.

When the Horse had relaxed and started nuzzling the
Boy's pockets for some bits of apple he was carrying, the
Boy fed them to him one at a time, rubbing his head and
muzzle between bites.

From then on the Blind Horse's training went ahead at
a faster pace. Getting the big saddle in place the first
time took several tries. No matter how carefully the Boy

moved, the cinch rings rattled a little, or the stirrup straps creaked, startling the Horse so that he'd move away from the box the Boy was standing on. But after a little coaxing he would come close again, and at last he stood without moving while the Boy set the saddle carefully in place on his back.

Each evening, for a while, the Boy put the saddle on the Horse, but without fastening the cinch, and led him around the corral until he no longer objected to the weight on his back or the sounds of the swinging buckles.

One night when the Ranch Owner and the Horse-breaker came to the corral, they found the Boy in the saddle, riding the Blind Outlaw slowly around inside the fence without bridle or hackamore. How he guided the Horse they could not tell. But while they watched, the two started, stopped, and turned this way or that as if avoiding unseen obstacles.

"Well! What do you know!" the Ranch Owner remarked after a while. "It looks like the Boy's got himself a Horse!"

"I didn't believe it could be done, but it sure looks like he's got that Horse gentled," the Horsebreaker agreed.

The Boy had been listening but, as usual, saying

nothing. Now he grinned a big grin and chirping softly to the Horse, urged him toward where the men sat on the top rail and stopped him directly below them. The Horse, with his neck stretched to sniff uneasily at the men, snorted and backed away when the Ranch Owner reached down to touch his muzzle, then stood quietly just beyond the man's reach.

"Looks like he's going to be a one-man horse," the Horsebreaker said, watching as the Boy coaxed the Horse back to where they sat.

For a while longer they watched while the Boy made birdlike sounds to the Horse as he unsaddled him.

"Well, he's your Horse, Boy," the Ranch Owner told him. "I'll give you a bill of sale whenever you want."

Then after watching the Horse a little longer, he and the Horsebreaker climbed down from the fence and went off into the deepening dusk. When the men were gone, the Boy fed the Horse some bits of dried apple, then after a while he took off his boots and got into his bedroll.

The Horse came up to blow his warm breath softly on the Boy's face, then after cocking his ears to catch the magpie's sleepy complaints from the top of a corral post, settled down to sleep where he stood.

9

The Roundup

Even though the Boy had gentled the Blind Outlaw and could ride him around the corral either bareback or with the saddle, the Horse still had much to learn before he would be a useful saddle horse. So night after night, when the days' chores were finished, the lessons went on.

Each evening when the Boy came to the corral after supper, he found the Blind Horse waiting for him at the gate. At the first sound of the Boy's voice and footsteps, he'd nicker softly and poke his nose between the planks to nuzzle the Boy's hands as he unfastened the heavy latch.

While the Horse sniffed and nudged his pockets, the Boy would make soft conversational sounds and scratch and stroke his head and neck. And when he'd given him

the last crumb, he'd saddle the Horse or simply ride him
bareback, and lessons would begin.

As he rode at a slow walk around the corral, the sound
of the Boy's soft voice went on and on. Without a
bridle, he apparently guided the Horse only by the little
chirps and clucks or the light pressure of one knee or the
other against his sides. It was impossible for a bystander
to tell what the signals were, but the Horse was rapidly
learning to understand what was wanted.

At first he occasionally misunderstood a signal to stop
or turn, and bumped into the corral or the water trough.
But as time went on, this happened less and less often.

Then one night, after he saddled the Horse, the Boy
scattered some buckets and a box or two on the ground
inside the corral. Mounting, he rode slowly toward the
nearest bucket. When they were close, he used a slight
pressure of his knee to guide the Horse around it. But
the Blind Horse's attention had apparently wandered
and, instead of making the slight turn, he took another
step forward and struck the thing with his hoof. At the
sound he snorted sharply, throwing up his head and
stepping back.

The Boy petted and soothed him, then urged him

gently forward until he was close enough to stretch his neck forward and sniff the thing he'd stumbled against. When he'd satisfied himself that it was harmless, he walked safely around it, guided by the Boy's small signals.

From then on the Horse seemed to pay closer attention and, before the evening was over, the Boy could ride him straight to the fence and stop him just before his head touched it, or turn him inches before his hoof touched one of the scattered boxes or buckets.

For several nights, the Boy seemed content to simply repeat that first night's lessons, riding in zigzags among the scattered boxes and buckets in the corral. But as the Horse's confidence increased, the lessons were moved out into the big stable yard. Constantly chirping and crooning to the Horse, the Boy rode him slowly among the wagons and machinery, around the woodpile, and finally to the big water tank beside the windmill. As the Horse sensed each new obstacle before him, the Boy let him stop and sniff it thoroughly before guiding him past.

And when the Horse would go without hesitation through the narrow space between a hayrack and mowing machine, or even through the alleyway down the center of the horse stable, the Boy began taking him out into

the horse pasture where the saddle horses were kept.
Here there were small patches of buckbrush, and deep-
worn stock paths to be avoided, and a little creek to be
crossed and recrossed.

Up to now the Horse's habit had been to travel at a
careful walk except when frightened, carefully sniffing
and testing the ground in front of him before each step.
But as he learned to trust the Boy's voice and touch to
warn him of things in his way, he became more
confident. And sometimes on flat ground, the Boy could
even urge him to a trot for a short distance.

By late summer the Boy was regularly riding the Blind
Horse instead of the old one when he wrangled the
saddle horses in the mornings or rode about the range
checking water holes and springs. And by that time the
Horse had become somewhat of a pet around the ranch.
The cowboys, even the Ranch Owner and the
Horsebreaker, had gotten in the habit of carrying bits
and pieces from the kitchen for him. He'd take these
things from their hands and sniff and nuzzle their pockets
looking for more—but still would let no one but the Boy
put a hand on him.

When time came for the fall roundup it was decided

that the Boy would go along to help the Horse Wrangler and the Cook. So the morning the crew was to leave the ranch, he threw his bedroll into the chuck wagon with the others, then saddled the Blind Horse and rode out to help the Wrangler with the extra horses.

When they reached the first camping place, he helped unhitch the team from the chuck wagon and turn them into the remuda. Then, while the Wrangler took them out to graze, he went to help the Cook.

After carrying water, filling all the empty buckets, he got on his Horse and rode along the creek looking for firewood. Looping his old throw rope around dry branches and dead small tree trunks, he dragged them to a pile close to where the Cook was setting up his kettles and Dutch ovens.

At first the Horse snorted and skittered away from the feel of the rope over his haunches and the sound of the wood dragging behind. But he soon quieted, and after that made no objections.

When the pile seemed big enough, the Boy took the ax from the wagon and started chopping wood for the cook fire. But the Horse insisted on following him around, kicking dust into the Cook's Dutch ovens and upsetting his kettles, so the Boy got a picket pin and staked him out on a patch of good grass nearby.

As the roundup went on, both the Boy and the Blind Horse more than earned their keep. When the wagon was moved every day or two, as different parts of the range were combed for cattle, the Boy helped the Wrangler with the remuda. And always there was wood to be dragged for the Cook's fires, and water to be carried. When the Boy wasn't riding the Blind Horse, he still kept him picketed on some patch of good grass instead of turning him out with the loose horses, but otherwise there seemed to be nothing unusual about either of them.

In the beginning the men from other ranches were surprised to find that the Boy couldn't talk, and that his Horse was blind. But they soon got used to the idea and no longer seemed to feel that they were anything out of the ordinary. However, being expert horsemen themselves, they were impressed when they heard that the Horse had been an outlaw, and in the evenings one after another told stories of outlaw horses they'd known. But few if any had ever heard of anyone dealing with a horse that was both outlaw and blind.

10

To Oklahoma

After the roundup was over, the work around the ranch settled back to the usual routine. Besides his daily chores, the Boy helped the Roundup Cook clean his kettles and Dutch ovens and put the big chuck wagon box away for the winter.

Some days he worked with the crews cutting and stacking wild hay on the flats across the river, or helped repair and strengthen the miles of barbwire fence. But wherever he went now, he rode the Blind Horse.

He spent much of his spare time making small repairs on his old, almost unrepairable saddle. The Horse would stand over him interestedly listening to the soft crooning that went on and on, or reaching his head down to nuzzle the Boy's hands and the straps he was working on.

The young coyote had been disappearing for a few days at a time, and now seemed to have gone away for good.

But the tame magpie was still around. He'd perch a while on the Boy's shoulder, apparently listening to his voice, then fly up to a higher lookout on the Horse's back. A few minutes later, they might hear him up by the ranch house, squalling at the dogs as he picked up scraps from around their feed pans.

The feel of the fall was in the air and, at the first faint sound of the wild geese flying in their great wavering vees high overhead, the Boy would stop his work and watch until they were out of sight, beyond the ridge to the south.

"The Boy's getting restless," the Horsebreaker remarked to the Ranch Owner one morning when flock after flock of the geese were flying overhead in almost endless procession.

"I recognize the signs," the Ranch Owner agreed. "He's about ready to start drifting again."

A few days later a Horse Buyer in a spring wagon, with two riders driving a small bunch of loose horses behind him, drove into the ranch. After some talk with the Ranch Owner, the horses were turned into the big pasture and the riders threw their bedrolls into the bunkhouse.

The strangers stayed for several days while the Horse

Buyer visited nearby ranches, looking at horses. Evenings the Boy listened to their talk of places they'd been, and of Oklahoma where they would probably go to sell their horses. When they brought in new ones the Horse Buyer had bought, the Boy always managed to be on hand to help corral them, and to see that the big water trough at the windmill was full.

After the strangers had gotten used to his strange ways and the magpie that was always with him, they found that in spite of his small size, the Boy was very knowledgeable about handling range stock. So it was not surprising that, when the Horse Buyer began talking of moving on, he asked the Boy if he'd like to go along and help with the horses.

The Boy grinned and nodded. And later, after the Horse Buyer had talked to the Ranch Owner, it was decided. During the winter there wouldn't be much for him to do around the ranch and, if he wanted to see more of the country, this was as good a chance as any.

The Ranch Owner, the Horsebreaker, and the Horse Buyer discussed the difficulty of writing a Bill of Sale for an unbranded horse to a boy who had no name. But in the end they decided that the fact that the Horse was blind and the Boy couldn't speak was identification enough to satisfy any reasonable stock inspector. And so

it was done. When finally written out the paper read:

SOLD THIS DAY, ONE UNBRANDED BLIND HORSE, BLUE-
GRAY IN COLOR AND ABOUT FIVE (5) YEARS OLD, TO
A BOY OF SMALL SIZE WHOSE NAME AND AGE ARE
UNKNOWN BECAUSE OF THE FACT THAT HE CANNOT
SPEAK.

(*signed*) THE RANCH OWNER
Witness . . . THE HORSEBREAKER
Witness . . . THE HORSE BUYER

"There's your Bill of Sale, Boy," the Ranch Owner
said. "The Horse is all yours."

The Boy grinned, folded the paper without reading it,
and stuck it in his pocket.

Since the Boy had simply stayed on when the Old
Buggy Salesman left, there had never been anything said
about wages. So now the Ranch Owner gave him a ten-
dollar bill and five silver dollars besides the Bill of Sale.
Then looking at the torn-up old saddle on the Blind
Horse, he said, "Why don't you leave that old hull here
and take that spare one hanging in the stable? Some
grub-line rider left it a year ago and has never come
back."

That saddle was not new, but it was a Furstnow from

Miles City, and in much better condition than the Boy's old one, and did much to improve the appearance of the Blind Horse when the change had been made. And while the Boy was shortening the stirrups to fit him, the Horsebreaker was rummaging through his war sack in the bunkhouse and brought out a somewhat ragged sheepskin coat and a well-worn but still serviceable blue flannel shirt.

"They ain't new," he said. "But they'll come in handy on the way to Oklahoma."

The boy grinned and put them in his skimpy bedroll, along with the well-used Indian blanket another of the riders had given him.

So at daybreak one morning the Boy threw his bedroll into the Horse Buyer's spring wagon and put his new saddle on the Blind Horse. Then with the magpie on his shoulder, and driving the old potbellied horse ahead of him, he rode out to help bunch the ones he would help drive south, perhaps all the way to Oklahoma.

At the top of the ridge to the south, the boy turned in his saddle and raised a hand to the Ranch Owner and the cowboys still standing by the gate. And that was the last they saw or heard of either the Boy or the Blind Outlaw.

But there are grizzled old-timers in that country who still remember the unnamed Boy who couldn't speak, and the Blind Outlaw Horse he gentled during that summer so long ago.

Meet the Author/Illustrator: **Glen Rounds**

One day in 1935, a young man wearing a Stetson hat carried a portfolio of his drawings into the offices of Holiday House, a small publishing company in New York. The stories he told enchanted the editors as much as his drawings did, so they suggested that he write down some of the stories and illustrate them. *Ol' Paul, the Mighty Logger* by Glen Rounds was published in the spring of 1936. The young man with the cowboy hat had a new career.

Rounds grew up on a ranch in South Dakota, studied art, and traveled throughout the United States holding various jobs including those of muleskinner, cowboy, sign painter, railroad hand, baker, carnival medicine man, and textile designer. He called on the experience he had at these jobs and his memories of the characters he met along the way to make his books about lumberjacks, miners, cowboys, and other workers realistic.

Rounds insists that he does not write for children. He says that he just likes to write simple, direct stories. Yet children have read and loved his many books for fifty years.

Responding to Literature

1. Do you enjoy reading animal stories such as *Blind Outlaw?* Why or why not?

2. Many stories and legends of the old West were told and retold around the campfire at night for entertainment. Suppose you were sitting around a campfire one dark night and someone said, "The only thing you can do with a blind outlaw is shoot it." How would you retell the story of the Boy who couldn't talk and the Blind Outlaw?

3. Why does the Boy seem to have a magical effect on the Horse?

4. The Boy can't use words to tell how he feels. How does the author reveal the Boy's desires and feelings?

5. Author Glen Rounds wants us to learn something about disabilities as we read *Blind Outlaw.* What is one important point the author makes about physical disabilities?

6. *Blind Outlaw* is not a tall tale as many cowboy stories are. The author includes details of everyday life to show us what the range and ranches of the west were like. Find four details that Rounds uses to make his story realistic.

The Runaway

Once when the snow of the year was beginning to fall,
We stopped by a mountain pasture to say, "Whose colt?"
A little Morgan had one forefoot on the wall,
The other curled at his breast. He dipped his head
And snorted at us. And then he had to bolt.
We heard the miniature thunder where he fled,
And we saw him, or thought we saw him, dim and gray,
Like a shadow against the curtain of falling flakes.
"I think the little fellow's afraid of the snow.
He isn't winter-broken. It isn't play
With the little fellow at all. He's running away.
I doubt if even his mother could tell him, 'Sakes,
It's only weather.' He'd think she didn't know!
Where is his mother? He can't be out alone."
And now he comes again with clatter of stone,
And mounts the wall again with whited eyes
And all his tail that isn't hair up straight.
He shudders his coat as if to throw off flies.
"Whoever it is that leaves him out so late,
When other creatures have gone to stall and bin,
Ought to be told to come and take him in."

Robert Frost

Appreciating Author's Craft

Thinking About Theme

A work of fiction may have several themes, or important ideas. Many times these themes are woven together like the strands of a spider's web. Among these themes, there may be one or more that are central to the underlying meaning of the work.

Here is how one theme in *Blind Outlaw* is expressed by author Glen Rounds:

> "A strange thing," the Horsebreaker remarked after a while. "The Horse can't see, and neither one can talk, yet they really seem to understand each other."

The theme of the growth of trust between the Blind Outlaw and the Boy is shown in many ways in the story. Other themes are also woven into the novel.

Writing About Theme

One effective way to tell other people about *Blind Outlaw* is to write a book review. In a book review you can give information about the book and tell why you like or dislike it. (For more ideas about writing, look at your Writer's Handbook.)

Prewriting To begin, read the themes on the chart. Then skim *Blind Outlaw* and pick out one or several sentences that illustrate each of the three themes.

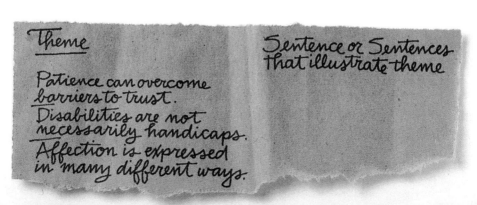

Theme

Patience can overcome barriers to trust.
Disabilities are not necessarily handicaps.
Affection is expressed in many different ways.

Sentence or Sentences that illustrate theme

Writing Now you are ready to write a book review in which you explain how one of the themes of *Blind Outlaw* is expressed in the novel.

Begin your book review by telling the name of the book and its author. Then tell in a sentence or two what *Blind Outlaw* is about. In the next paragraph briefly describe the setting and main characters. Then write a paragraph that discusses a theme from the novel and shows how the theme is expressed by the author. In the last paragraph, tell why you would or would not recommend the book to other people.

Revising Reread the draft of your book review carefully. Does your introductory paragraph include the book's title and author? Have you described the setting and main characters? Have you discussed a theme from the novel? Have you included your opinion of the work? Go over your review with a partner to make sure your paper is complete. Proofread your draft, adding any information you may have forgotten. Then write your final copy.

Presenting Take your book review home. Read it to a family member. Ask that person whether your review has made her or him want to read the book. Then read that person some of your favorite passages from *Blind Outlaw*. Has the person changed his or her mind about the novel?

Extending Your Reading

Expressing Yourself
Choose one or more of these activities:

Tame a Wild Animal How would you go about taming a wild animal? Choose an animal you would like to tame. Think of some good ideas and tell your plan to the class.

Research Breeds of Horses Find out about the various breeds of horses. Learn how they differ physically and to which tasks the various breeds are best suited. Make a written or oral report.

Make Up a Short Story How might the Blind Outlaw have lost his vision? Make up a story about the Horse's early life. Then read *The Blind Colt* by Glen Rounds.

Make an Old West Corner Work with a committee to set up a display of books about horses and cowboys for the class library. Include both fictional and non-fictional books. Display pictures classmates have drawn and collected, and, if possible, include equipment used with horses and clothing worn by cowboys.

Have a Class Debate What should be done with the wild horses that exist in the United States today? Have a class debate on this subject.

Sing Cowboy Songs Choose some favorite cowboy songs and sing them in class. If you like, dress in western clothing for inspiration.

Read Poems by Robert Frost If you enjoyed the poem "The Runaway" on page 505, read other poems by this famous poet. One collection to consider is *A Swinger of Birches: Poems of Robert Frost for Young People* published by Stemmer House.

More Books About People and Animals

The Horse in the Attic by Eleanor Clymer. Bradbury Press. Twelve-year-old Caroline loves horses. So, when she moves to the country with her family, she is thrilled to discover a painting of a race horse in the boarded-up attic of their house. She cannot imagine who painted the picture, why it is in the attic, and who the beautiful horse is. Caroline's questions are answered most unexpectedly.

Thing by Robin Klein. Merrimack Publishing Circle. Emily certainly would never disobey her landlady's rule forbidding pets, but when her pet rock cracks open to reveal a loveable dinosaur, Emily hopes to keep her animal a well-behaved secret. What can she do to save the dinosaur from a life in a zoo or museum?

The Midnight Fox by Betsy Byars. The Viking Press. Tommy begins his summer on his aunt and uncle's farm reluctantly, but soon his interest is sparked by the astonishing appearances of a black fox. Fascinated by this beautiful creature, Tommy tracks the fox to her den. The day comes when Tommy learns that there are others who know about the black fox, and *they* have no wish to protect her.

Misty of Chincoteague by Marguerite Henry. Macmillan Publishing Company. At a yearly roundup, some of the wild ponies of Assateague Island are caught and sold. Young Paul and Maureen have set their hearts and their savings on a mare named Phantom and her colt Misty. Their hearts' desire is not simply fulfilled because other people want to buy Phantom, and Phantom's own spirit must be reckoned with.

Handbook of Literary Terms

Pages 511–519

Animal fantasy
Biography
Characterization
Conflict
Fantasy
Fiction
Figurative language
Folk tales
Free verse
Historical fiction
Hyperbole
Lyric

Modern realistic fiction
Nonfiction
Personification
Plot
Point of view
Rhyme
Setting
Simile
Style
Theme
Time-travel fantasy
Tone

Guide to Literature

Pages 520–525

Mysteries
High fantasy

Sports stories
Historical fiction

Writer's Handbook

Pages 526–533

Glossary

Pages 534–543

Animal fantasy

a type of fantasy in which animals talk, think, and act like people

In *Babe: The Gallant Pig*, for example, notice that the author has invented a conversation between Babe and Fly to reveal the human feelings of loneliness and love.

"Well, what did your mother call you, to tell you apart from your brothers and sisters?" said Fly and then wished she hadn't, for at the mention of his family the piglet began to look distinctly unhappy. His little forehead wrinkled and he gulped and his voice trembled as he answered.

Well-written fantasy like this makes us believe that another world exists where animals can put their thoughts and feelings into words. Which part of Babe's world do you like better—how the puppies act with Babe or how Babe becomes a sheep-pig? Choose one and explain why you especially enjoyed this part of the fantasy.

Biography

the account of a person's life

Biographies include not only the events of a person's life, but also discuss the individual's personality.

The biographer tells a story based on facts found in various records and documents. Some things the biographer may not be able to find out, such as exact conversations or how a person may have really felt about certain incidents. In such instances, a biographer finds out so much about the subject that he re-creates incidents and feelings as they might have been.

Readers can imagine how Scott Joplin felt when he approached his future teacher for the first time. The biographer tells us how Joplin *might* have felt and what he *thinks* Joplin would have observed.

The man who greeted him was small and soft-spoken. He had white hair, and seemed older than any of the adults Scott had ever seen. He shook Scott's hand and Scott noticed his long, tapering fingers. He wore a rumpled, gray suit, and in his pocket was a small gold chain attached to a stopwatch.

Look back at the biography of Scott Joplin. Can you find other incidents where the author has made Joplin's personality or ideas particularly clear? Choose an incident in the biography and tell how it helped you get to know Joplin's thoughts or feelings.

Characterization

the methods an author uses to reveal the personality of a character in a literary work

An author may develop a character by describing the character's physical appearance, speech, actions, and inner thoughts, or by revealing attitudes and reactions of other characters.
(For information about animals as characters, see Appreciating Author's Craft, page 42. For information about characters and plot, see Plot in this Handbook.)

Conflict

occurs when the main character struggles against an opposing force

Tension, friction, force, excitement, suspense, discovery, and resolution are parts of conflict. There are four types of conflict in literature: person-against-self, person-against-person, person-against-society, and person-against-nature.
(For more information about character conflict and plot, see Plot in this Handbook.)

Fantasy

a type of literature in which the author creates another world

Authors may choose to make one or more of the elements—characters, setting, or events—fantastic while other elements are realistic.
(For more information, see Animal fantasy and time-travel fantasy in this Handbook.)

Fiction

a type of literature in which the author creates a story

Modern realistic fiction, historical fiction, and science fiction and fantasy are types of fiction.

Figurative language

the use of words beyond their usual or everyday meaning

Figurative language can also be referred to as figures of speech. An example of figurative language is referring to a heavy rainstorm as "raining cats and dogs."
(For more on Figurative language, see Hyperbole and Personification in this Handbook.)

Folk tale

traditional stories told by ordinary people in all countries, retold for generations before being written down

Folk tales often express the similarities of human wishes and needs around the world. Frequently good conquers evil. Folk tales have fast-paced narration (events happen quickly), flat characters (you learn only one or two major character traits), stock characters (such as a fairy godmother), and incidents often occurring in threes or fours.

In the play *The Wise and Clever Maiden*, the author has based the story on more than one folk tale. The tale about the trickster farmer is told in Argentina and countries in Africa. Sometimes it is told with animals as characters, sometimes people.

A farmer and a young maiden appear before the royal court of a young king to settle a dispute concerning a plot of land they own together. The farmer wants the maiden to marry him, but the maiden refuses until they strike a fair bargain concerning farming the land. The bargain is that the farmer keeps everything that grows above or below the ground, depending on what the maiden decides when she plants. For the past three years, the maiden has planted vegetables which allow her the benefit of the harvest. The bargain is never fair.

Read the tale on pages 214–217. See what elements of folk tales you can find in this tale.

Notice that the characters are not very fully developed and that it is the action of the story that is most important. Notice that the story is based on three incidents of planting different crops. A clever trickster, in this case the maiden, is a common character found in folk tales.

Locate a folk tale and tell it to your class. After telling the folk tale, point out the elements that make it a folk tale.

Free verse

poetry that follows no set patterns of rhyme, rhythm, or line length

"The Laughing Faces of Pigs" on page 41 is an example of free verse.

Historical fiction

a type of fiction which occurs in the past, and in which the time and place in the past determine setting

Details about clothing and language, for example, must fit the time and place. The setting is important to the story because it shows how the characters live. Since the characters are caught in the events of the time, setting influences plot. In order to turn historical facts into fiction, the writer combines imagination with fact.

In *In The Year of the Boar and Jackie Robinson,* we learn something about life in America at an earlier period through the eyes of Shirley Temple Wong, a Chinese immigrant. Parts of this story could happen to any family at any time, but many details root that story to a definite time and place—Brooklyn, New York, in 1947, the year Jackie Robinson was named Rookie of the Year.

Reread the selection and look for details that place this story in a specific time and place. Would Shirley receive thirty cents for baby-sitting for three children today? Do you know what it means to do the jitterbug? Who is Red Barber, and why was he so important to baseball fans?

Can you find a newspaper in your public library that tells about life in the United States in 1947? If you met someone who traveled in time from the year 1947, what are some of the important changes and discoveries you would relate?

Hyperbole

a figure of speech which uses great exaggeration

Like other types of figurative language, we use hyperbole in our everyday conversations. When we say to someone, "I've told you a million times," we're using hyperbole.

Hyperbole is often used in folk tales for comic effect. Look at the following examples of hyperbole from Carl Sandburg's poem, "Yarns."

"They have yarns . . .
   Of a mountain railroad curve
      where the engineer in his cab
      can touch the caboose and
         spit in the conductor's eye."

What image of a railroad curve does this hyperbole create in your mind?

"They have yarns. . .
   Of the herd of cattle
      in California getting lost
      in a giant redwood tree
         that had been hollowed out."

By using hyperbole, what image of this redwood does the speaker create?

What is humorous in each of these hyperboles?

Now try writing an original hyperbole. You might write an exaggerated description of something you see every day.

a short poem expressing a basic, personal emotion such as grief, happiness, love, or gloominess.

"The Piper" on page 163, with its emotions of happiness and joy, is a lyric.

Modern realistic fiction

a type of fiction in which the events and characters resemble real-life occurrences and people

Realistic stories have several characteristics in common. They are fictional narratives with characters. The characters are involved in some kind of action that holds our interest, and the story is set in some realistic place and time. In modern realistic fiction, the main character's real-life problem is the source of plot and conflict.

In *The Agony of Alice*, Alice is suffering the problems of growing up. She is looking for someone to help her cope with life. She believes that if she only had a mother or someone acting as a mother in her life, her problems would be solved.

> I wanted Miss Cole for my adopted mother more than I wanted anything else in the world. I wanted her to dress me in a green and yellow kimono and show me how to wear flowers in my hair. I wanted someone to make a fuss over me and teach me how to walk in tiny little steps and bow the way Miss Cole was bowing to some of her students.

In well-written realistic fiction the character and the conflict are closely related. We can identify with Alice's goal and the way she goes about handling her situation. Everything that happens in this story could actually happen in real life.

How would you describe Alice? If you were her best friend what advice would you give her? Since you can put yourself in Alice's place, she is a believable and a sympathetic character.

Nonfiction

a type of literature based on facts and information

Informational books, autobiographies, and biographies are types of nonfiction.

a figure of speech in which human characteristics are given to nonhuman things, or life is attributed to nonliving objects

We use personification every day when we refer to a weeping-willow tree, the hands or face of a clock, or the arms or legs of a chair. Can you think of other examples of person- ification that we use every day?

Poets use personification because it helps them to make descriptions of things more vivid and understandable.

In "Echo" (page 281), the poet uses personification to help the reader experience the sound of the echo as it is carried on the wind. Read the following stanza from the poem, and look for examples of personification.

> The leafy boughs on high
> Hissed in the sun;
> The dark air carried my cry
> Faintingly on:

How does the poet personify the boughs of the trees? the dense air? How do these descriptions help us to experience the sound of the echo?

If you were writing a poem about nature, how would you personify the wind? the waves of a calm sea on the shore? the branches of trees in a forest during a storm?

a series of related events that make up a story

In a carefully constructed plot, events are arranged in a pattern, with each incident forming a link that involves conflict and leads to a climax and a conclusion. Most plots consist of a character's attempts to reach a goal and the outcome of those attempts. (For information about character conflict and plot, see Appreciating Author's Craft, page 234.)

the author's choice of narrator, or the teller of the story

(For more information on point of view, see Appreciating Author's Craft, page 322.)

Rhyme

the repetition of syllable sounds (*grain* and *train*, for example)

End words that share a particular sound are called *end rhymes*. The pattern of end rhymes in a poem is called a *rhyme scheme*.

Poets use rhyme for different reasons. Rhyme gives a poem a musical sound that is pleasant to listen to when the poem is read aloud. Rhyme can add humor to a poem. It can also help to unify a poem when the same rhyming sound or rhyme scheme is repeated in more than one stanza of a poem. As you read the stanza from "Abigail" (page 321), listen for the end rhymes.

Abigail knew when she was born
Among the roses, she was a thorn.
Her quiet mother had lovely looks.
Her quiet father wrote quiet books.
Her quiet brothers, correct though pale,
Weren't really prepared for Abigail
Who entered the house with howls and tears
While both of her brothers blocked their ears
and both of her parents, talking low,
Said, "Why is Abigail screaming so?"

How often does the poet repeat the same end sounds in this stanza? What pattern does this create? Turn back to "Abigail" and determine the rhyme scheme for the second and third stanzas.

Setting

the time, place, and general environment in which the events of a narrative occur

Details of setting may be either stated or suggested. Although setting in modern fiction serves primarily as background for the action, it can also be used to reveal character and to help develop plot.
(For information on multiple settings, see Appreciating Author's Craft, page 74.)

Simile

a comparison between two unlike things signaled by the word *like* or *as*

In a simile, an author compares two things which we don't usually think of as being similar. What two unlike things are being compared in the following sentence?

The boy was as brave as a lion as he traveled through the dark woods.

Ordinarily, a boy wouldn't be compared to a lion, but in this sentence the writer wants to explain how brave this boy was.

Read the following lines from "Rebels from Fairy Tales" (page 233).

Men are so up and down, so thin they look like walking trees.
Their knees seem stiff . . .

What two things are being compared in these lines? Pretend that you're the frog speaking in the poem. What similarities do you find between men and trees?

We frequently use similes without even noticing them. Make a list of similes that we use in everyday speech.

Style

the manner in which writers use words and sentences to fit their ideas

Style involves many choices on the part of the writer: types of words, placement of words in a sentence, the purpose of the written work, tone, mood, imagery, figurative language, sound devices, and rhythm.

Theme

the message or the meaning behind the things that happen in a literary work

A theme may be directly stated, but more often it is implied. While plot answers the question, "What happens?" theme answers the question, "What does it all mean?" (For more information on theme, see Appreciating Author's Craft, page 126.)

Time-travel fantasy

Tone

a type of fantasy in which the author takes the characters back to the past or forward to the future

Time-travel fantasies contain a device by which the characters move through time. In *Time Cat*, the author gives Gareth the power to propel himself and Jason from the present back through four centuries of time to ancient Peru where they encounter the Great Inca:

> Jason had never seen a man so brilliantly dressed. Over a long tunic the Inca wore a brightly decorated cape; around his forehead were colored braids, with tassels and bits of gold. From his ears hung enormous disks of pure gold. The Inca turned a handsome, bronzed face toward Jason—a face that was severe, commanding, and at the same time filled with deep sadness.

The reader sees the magnificence of the ancient Incas in this time-travel fantasy. What might the Great Inca find magnificent if he could travel through time to your world?

an author's expressed attitude toward the subject in a literary work

Tone is conveyed through the author's choice of words and details in describing setting, portraying characters, and presenting events. Tone should not be confused with mood, which is the atmosphere or feeling within a work of art.
(For more information on tone in nonfiction, see Appreciating Author's Craft, page 200.)

519

How Can I Find a Book I Will Like?

- Look for more of what you know you like, such as other books in a popular series, more books by a favorite author, or books on your special interest. Use the subject, title, and author indexes of the card catalog to develop a personal file of books you would like to read.

- Talk to friends, family, teachers, or librarians about books they like. Make a list of the books they suggest, and take it with you to the library.

- Find out if there is a book about a movie or a television show you enjoyed. After reading it, decide which is better, the book or the show.

- Look at books recommended as "Children's Choices" by other young people. Ask your teacher or librarian for a copy of the list. Read what it says about the books for your age level and choose one that sounds good to you.

- Browse in the library and pick up a book whose cover appeals to you. Read the information on the book jacket, but don't stop there. Read the opening paragraphs of the first few chapters. Thumb through the remaining pages, noticing pictures, size of print, and overall length. Decide if the book is one you might enjoy.

What characteristics do good mystery stories have?

- In good mystery stories, the plot carries the story and the story moves quickly with little description and much dialogue and action.

- Carefully crafted mystery stories show strong characterization.

- Effective mystery stories have a mysterious tone. Suspense builds from what seems like unexplained events and actions which, by the story's end, are all resolved by reasonable and carefully detected discoveries.

What makes mysteries fun to read?

- You can try to outwit the author by putting together the bits of information to predict the outcome before it is revealed.

- You can feel the tension and suspense build up chapter after chapter.

- You can enjoy being frightened knowing you are really safe.

- You can read fast to find out who did it.

What are some mystery stories I might like?

Choose one or more of the following books. Look for the characteristics that make them good mysteries and fun to read.

The Case of the Baker Street Irregular, Robert Newman. Atheneum.

The Mysterious Disappearance of Leon (I Mean Noel), Ellen Raskin. Dutton.

A Nose for Trouble, Marilyn Singer. Holt, Rinehart and Winston.

The Turquoise Toad Mystery, Georgess McHargue. Delacorte.

What characteristics does good high fantasy have?

* The make-believe world of a good high-fantasy story is believable because the customs, characters, and events are consistent and logical within that setting.

* In high fantasy, an imaginative plot usually involves a conflict between good and evil.

* Realistic central characters in well-written high fantasy are concerned about people, and, although humorous incidents occasionally take place, the tone of the story is serious.

What makes high fantasy fascinating?

* You can escape to an imaginary but believable world.

* You can enjoy impossible adventures that seem real.

* You can meet creatures and objects with supernatural powers.

* You can travel through time and space.

* You can participate in a battle between good and evil, knowing that good will eventually win.

What are some high-fantasy books I might like?

Consider reading one or more of the following books. Look for the characteristics that make them good high fantasies that are fascinating to read.

The Foundling, Lloyd Alexander. Holt, Rinehart and Winston.

The Gammage Cup, Carol Kendall. Harcourt Brace Jovanovich Inc.

The Search for Delicious, Natalie Babbit. Farrar, Straus and Giroux.

Dragon's Blood, Jane Yolen. Delacorte Press.

What characteristics do exciting sports stories have?

- In good sports stories, the action centers around a specific sport, and the vocabulary and events for that sport are authentic.

- The characters in well-constructed sports stories react to situations in a realistic manner, so you can identify with them.

- The plot of effective sports stories often involves a central character who overcomes some obstacle that interferes with athletic success.

What makes sports stories fun to read?

- You can feel the action in a fast-moving story.

- You can read about a sport that interests you.

- You can pick up terms and techniques to help you improve your game.

- You can use what you learn about winning and losing to help you be a good sport.

- You can imagine that you are a sports hero.

What sports stories might I like to read?

You might want to consider reading one or more of the following sports books. Look for the characteristics that make them good sports stories and fun to read.

Skinnybones, Barbara Park. Avon Books.

Nutty Can't Miss, Dean Hughes. Atheneum.

The Year Mom Won the Pennant, Matt Christopher. Little, Brown and Company.

The Rascals from Haskell's Gym, Frank Bonham. Dutton.

What characteristics does good historical fiction have?

- Good historical fiction combines imagination and facts into an entertaining story that shows how the events of the past affected people.

- The plot of an effective historical-fiction book focuses on events or values that were important during the past that are still important today.

- Carefully crafted historical fiction includes authentic details of life during the past and does not exaggerate either the good or the bad qualities of life in those times.

What makes historical fiction memorable?

- You can learn about past times and people as you read a good story.

- You can discover that young people in days gone by thought and felt very much like young people do today.

- You can experience history through the eyes of someone living in another time or place.

- You can meet the people behind historical events and find out how they really lived.

- You can begin to realize why events in history happened as they did.

What are some books of historical fiction I might like?

Try reading one or more of the following books. Look for the characteristics that make them good historical fiction that is memorable for you.

All-Of-A-Kind Family, Sydney Taylor. Dell Publishing Company.

All This Wild Land, Ann Nolan Clark. Viking Press.

Trouble River, Betsy Byars. Viking Press.

A Gathering of Days, Joan Blos. Scribner's.

How Can I Share a Book That I Enjoy?

- Talk to a friend about your book. Tell why you liked the book and why you think your friend would like it too.

- Write a short news story about your book. As a good reporter, try to include the "who," "what," "when," "where," and "why" in your lead sentences.

- Create a poem to describe the main character. Start by writing the name of the character down the side of a piece of paper. Use each of the letters as the first letter of the lines of your poem. When you have finished, others can discover the character's name by reading vertically down the lines of your poem.

- Plan a meal that could have been served to the characters in your book. Be sure the foods you choose are appropriate for the time and place.

- Develop an advertisement that will make others want to read your book. Look in magazines to get ideas of how advertisers make their products appealing.

- Choose an incident from your book that would appeal to a younger child. Tell that incident as a story to a group of younger children.

- Compose one of the following items, pretending to be a character from your book:
  a diary or journal entry
  a twelve-word telegram
  an invitation to a party
  a letter to the editor of a newspaper
  a thank-you note

- Rewrite an exciting episode from your book in play form. Act out the episode, and encourage others to read the book to find out what happened next.

This handbook will help you write well in response to the literature you have been reading. It answers the kinds of questions that you might ask when you are doing your writing assignments for Appreciating Author's Craft in this book as well as when you are doing other writing assignments. It is divided into four parts, one part for each stage of the writing process: prewriting, writing, revising, and presenting. The handbook also explains four types of writing: descriptive, narrative, explanatory, and persuasive.

Prewriting

1. I know the topic I'm going to write about, but how can I organize my ideas and narrow my topic?

There are many ways to organize ideas. One way is to use a chart, such as the one on page 43. One way to narrow a topic is to use a web, or cluster diagram. A cluster diagram is a visual map showing how a main topic, subtopics, and details are related to one another. To make a cluster diagram, first write a main topic and circle it. Then write related subtopics around it. Circle them and draw lines to connect them to the main topic. Last, list details related to the subtopics.

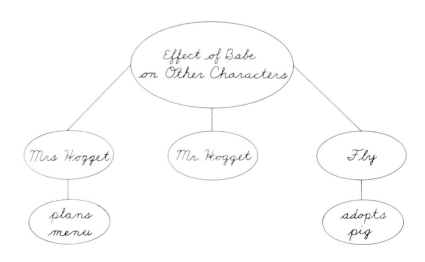

2. When I'm given a writing assignment, what is my first task?

When you are given a writing assignment, your first task is to determine your purpose for writing and your audience. Your audience is the people whom you want to read your work. They may be your teachers, classmates, friends, writing partners, family, perhaps even people you don't know. To determine your purpose, ask yourself, "What *type* of writing am I being asked to do?" Different types of writing have different purposes. Study the following chart to help you better understand your purpose for writing.

Type of Writing	Purpose	Examples
descriptive	• to paint a picture in words by using details that help the reader see, hear, feel, taste, or smell what you describe	• description of a character • comparison/contrast paragraph • description of a scene • description of setting
narrative	• to tell a story (real or imaginary) about something that happened to you or someone you know or a character you've read about • to tell the events in the order in which they happened	• story ending • journal entry • story patterned after folk tale • biographical paragraph
explanatory	• to tell how something is made or done • to request information • to explain similarities and differences	• feature story • instructions
persuasive/ analytical	• to state your opinion and give reasons in order to convince others to share your opinion • to analyze facts and reach a conclusion • to interpret a poem or a story	• persuasive paragraph • book review

1. Sometimes when I sit down, I just can't get started. What can I do then?

There are several ways to get started. Here are some suggestions.

<u>Review</u> Review what you did in Prewriting. Look for a specific fact or idea that could be used in an opening paragraph or sentence.

<u>Tune Out</u> Tuning out means concentrating on your writing assignment. For many people this means no television, radio, food, or phone calls. Experiment to see when and under what conditions you write best.

<u>Push Ahead</u> Sit down and pick up a pencil. Push your ideas out of your head and get them down on paper.

2. What is a first draft?

A first draft is like a trial run or a rehearsal. The purpose of a first draft is to get your ideas down. Don't stop writing even if you feel you don't like everything you are saying. When you are writing a first draft, don't worry about perfect spelling, punctuation, or capitalization. If you stop to correct these types of errors, you may lose your train of thought.

Revising

1. I have just written my first draft. What do I do next?

It is helpful to pause, read over your first draft, and "listen" to yourself. Think about your big point. Is it clear? Will it make sense to your audience? Also think about the overall direction your writing is taking. Does your draft reflect the criteria for the specific type of writing you have been asked to do? The chart below offers some information on what makes a specific type of writing good.

Type of Writing	What Makes It Good
descriptive	• keeping to one main idea • choosing words that help the reader see, feel, hear, smell, taste what you describe • being sure the words support the main idea • using spatial order—describing your topic as an observer from a particular position such as top to bottom—to organize the paragraph
narrative	• keeping to one main idea • telling events in time order • using signal words such as *first, next, then,* and *last* to make the order clear
explanatory	• beginning with a topic sentence that tells what will be explained • following the topic sentence with detail sentences that support the main idea • telling steps in order • using examples to clarify or illustrate the steps • using signal words such as *first, next, then,* and *last* to make the order clear
persuasive	• keeping your audience in mind so you choose ideas and language that will appeal to them • stating your opinion in your topic sentence • using facts to support your opinion • putting the most persuasive reasons last

2. What should I do when I revise?

First, revise your content. Have a writing conference by getting together with a partner, a small group, your teacher, or a friend. Read your draft aloud and ask for comments on what is good about your paper and about how it could be made even better. Take notes on the comments to help you make changes.

3. How do I make changes?

There are four kinds of changes to make when revising: adding, taking out, reordering, and proofreading which are explained below. Remember that you can use the information you gathered in Prewriting as well as your conference notes as you work through these changes.

Adding Information Reread your draft and check to see if you left out any important information, such as an event in a narrative paragraph or an important fact that supports your opinion in a persuasive paragraph.

Taking Out Unnecessary Information Check to see that you have kept to your topic. Take out any sentences that don't keep to your topic. Also examine your paper for any unnecessary words. Can you say the same thing in fewer words?

Moving Words, Sentences, and Paragraphs The order of your words, sentences, and paragraphs determines how clear and logical your writing is. Ask yourself if you have told things in the right order. Is anything out of place? You may have to move a sentence or two, or even entire paragraphs.

Proofreading Your final task in revising is to check your paper for mistakes in spelling, punctuation, capitalization, and form. Use the proofreading marks at the top of the next page to help you make these changes.

Proofreader's Marks	
≡ Make a capital.	⌒→ Move something.
⊙ Add a period.	(sp) Correct spelling.
∧ Add something.	¶ New paragraph.
ℯ Take out something.	

4. How can I be sure I've done a thorough job of revising?
You can use this Revision Checklist to check yourself.

Revision Checklist

Content

- ✔ Did I say what I wanted to say?
- ✔ Are my details in order?
- ✔ Does my composition have a beginning, a middle, and an end?
- ✔ Is each paragraph about one main idea? Is the main idea expressed in a topic sentence?
- ✔ Have I taken out all unnecessary words and replaced all dull, overused, or inexact words?
- ✔ Are all facts and figures correct?

Mechanics

- ✔ Are any of the pronouns confusing?
- ✔ Do subjects and verbs agree?
- ✔ Did I keep the correct verb tense throughout?
- ✔ Is each sentence correctly punctuated?
- ✔ Is other punctuation correct?
- ✔ Have I avoided fragments and run-on sentences?
- ✔ Did I capitalize the first word of each sentence?
- ✔ Did I capitalize proper nouns and adjectives?
- ✔ Did I check the spelling and meaning of unfamiliar words?
- ✔ Is my handwriting clear and easy to read?

1. What are some ways I can present my writing to others?

There are many ways to share your writing. Here are some suggestions.

<u>Read Aloud</u> Read your paper aloud to your audience. Invite discussion by asking such questions as, "What did I describe?" "Were you able to predict that my story would end like it did? Why or why not?"

<u>Display</u> Mount your paper on some colored construction paper or create illustrations for it. Then display your work on the bulletin board in your classroom.

<u>Make a Book</u> You can make a book easily by stacking sheets of blank paper. Use a paper punch to make three holes in the stack. Punch three holes in cardboard for front and back covers. Thread yarn through the holes to hold your book together. Write your name and the title of your book on its cover.

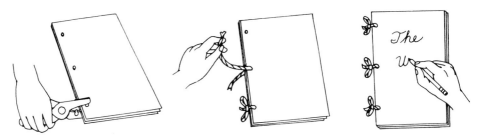

Once your book is made, put it in the class or school library. Encourage your classmates and friends to read your book.

<u>Give a Speech</u> After writing your paper, make notes or an outline if you need to. Then present your paper as a speech or an oral report.

2. How can our class work together to present our writing?
Here are some ways your class can work together.

Hold a Young Author's Conference Follow these steps:
a. Organize a special day for presenting and honoring the writing of students in your class.
b. Before the conference, choose the best pieces of writing from your class.
c. On the day of the conference, meet with classmates to share writing, talk about writing problems, listen to guest speakers, and give awards for writing.
d. Students or teachers can collect the best pieces and publish them in a school magazine.

Start a Class Newspaper Follow these steps:
a. Choose a small group to be in charge of the newspaper.
b. As a class, think of a name for your newspaper. Then discuss the types of news stories, features, cartoons, and other information you could include.
c. Decide when and how often you will publish.
d. Work in teams to revise and proofread all pieces.
e. Distribute your newspapers in and outside the school.

Present a Class Play Turn a story into a play. Work with a few of your classmates to assign parts and rehearse. Put on the play for your classmates or other classes.

How to Use the Pronunciation Key

After each entry word in this glossary, there is a special spelling called the **pronunciation.** It shows how to say the word. The word is broken into syllables and then spelled with letters and signs. You can look up these letters and signs in the **pronunciation key** to see what sounds they stand for.

This dark mark (′) is called the **primary accent.** It follows the syllable you say with the most force. This lighter mark (′) is the **secondary accent.** Say the syllable it follows with medium force. Syllables without marks are said with least force.

Full Pronunciation Key

a	hat, cap	**i**	it, pin	**p**	paper, cup	**ə**	stands for:
ā	age, face	**ī**	ice, five	**r**	run, try		a in about
ä	father, far			**s**	say, yes		e in taken
		j	jam, enjoy	**sh**	she, rush		i in pencil
b	bad, rob	**k**	kind, seek	**t**	tell, it		o in lemon
ch	child, much	**l**	land, coal	**th**	thin, both		u in circus
d	did, red	**m**	me, am	**ŦH**	then, smooth		
		n	no, in				
e	let, best	**ng**	long, bring	**u**	cup, butter		
ē	equal, be			**ů**	full, put		
ėr	her, learn	**o**	hot, rock	**ü**	rule, move		
		ō	open, go				
f	fat, if	**ô**	order, all	**v**	very, save		
g	go, bag	**oi**	oil, toy	**w**	will, woman		
h	he, how	**ou**	house, out	**y**	young, yet		
				z	zoo, breeze		
				zh	measure, seizure		

A

ac·com·mo·date (ə kom′ə dāt),
1 have room for; hold comfortably.
2 supply with a place to sleep or live for
a time: *Tourists are accommodated
here. v.,* **ac·com·mo·dat·ed,
ac·com·mo·dat·ing.**

a hat	i it	oi oil	ch child	ə stands for:
ā age	ī ice	ou out	ng long	a in about
ä far	o hot	u cup	sh she	e in taken
e let	ō open	u̇ put	th thin	i in pencil
ē equal	ô order	ü rule	ŦH then	o in lemon
ėr term			zh measure	u in circus

accommodate—The bobsled was long
enough to **accommodate** fifteen riders.

ad·ver·tise·ment (ad′vər tīz′mənt,
ad vėr′tis mənt), a public notice or announcement recommending some product or service, or informing of some
need: *The furniture store has an advertisement in the newspaper for a
special sale. n.*

ag·i·tate (aj′ə tāt), disturb or excite
very much: *He was agitated by the unexpected news of his friend's illness. v.,*
ag·i·tat·ed, ag·i·tat·ing.
—**ag′i·tat′ed·ly,** *adv.*

ag·o·niz·ing (ag′ə nī′zing), **1** causing
very great suffering. **2** painful. *adj.* —
ag′o·niz′ing·ly, *adv.*

ag·o·ny (ag′ə nē), very painful suffering; very great anguish: *the agony of
family problems. The loss of their child
filled them with agony. n., pl.* **ag·o·nies.**

ap·pren·tice (ə pren′tis), **1** person
learning a trade or art. In return for instruction the apprentice agrees to work
for the employer a certain length of time
with little or no pay. **2** bind or take as
an apprentice: *Benjamin Franklin's father apprenticed him to a printer.* **1** *n.,*
2 *v.,* **ap·pren·ticed,
ap·pren·tic·ing.**

B

be·rate (bi rāt′), scold sharply; upbraid.
v., **be·rat·ed, be·rat·ing.**

be·wil·der (bi wil′dər), confuse completely; puzzle: *The child was bewildered by the crowds. v.*

bitch (bich), a female dog, wolf, or fox.
n., pl. **bitch·es.**

blin·tze (blin′tsə), a thin, rolled pancake
filled with cheese, fruit, etc. *n.*

borscht (bôrsht), a Russian soup consisting of meat stock, cabbage, and
onions, colored red with beet juice and
served with sour cream. *n.*

bro·cade (brō kād′), **1** an expensive
cloth woven with raised designs on it,
used for clothing or upholstery: *silk
brocade, velvet brocade.* **2** weave or
decorate with raised designs. **1** *n.,* **2** *v.,*
bro·cad·ed, bro·cad·ing.

C

can·ter (kan′tər), **1** gallop gently: *The
horse cantered across the meadow.* **2** a
gentle gallop. **1** *v.,* **2** *n.*

car·cass (kär′kəs), body of a dead animal. *n., pl.* **car·cass·es.**

cha·os (kā′os), very great confusion;
complete disorder: *The tornado left the
town in chaos. n.*

chit·ter·lings (chit′linz, chit′ər linz),
parts of the small intestines of pigs,
calves, etc., cooked as food. *n. pl.*

cir·cuit (sėr′kit), **1** a going around; a moving around: *It takes a year for the earth to make its circuit of the sun.* **2** route over which a person or group makes repeated journeys at certain times: *Some judges make a circuit, stopping at certain towns along the way to hold court.* **3** the district through which such journeys are made. *n.*

col·on·nade (kol′ə nād′), series of columns set the same distance apart. *n.*

colonnade

com·mis·sion (kə mish′ən), **1** a written order giving certain powers, rights, and duties: *She held a commission as United States ambassador to Italy.* **2** a written order giving rank or authority in the armed forces: *A captain in the United States Army has a commission signed by the President. n.*

con·ceit·ed (kən sē′tid), having too high an opinion of oneself or of one's ability; vain. *adj.*

con·se·quence (kon′sə kwens), **1** a result or effect: *The consequence of the fall was a broken leg.* **2** importance: *The loss of her ring is a matter of great consequence to her. n.*

cor·ral (kə ral′), **1** pen for horses, cattle, etc. **2** drive into or keep in such a pen: *The cowhands corralled the herd of wild ponies.* 1 *n.*, 2 *v.*, **cor·ralled, cor·ral·ling.**

coun·ter·point (koun′tər point′), **1** melody added to another as an accompaniment. **2** art of adding melodies to a given melody according to fixed rules. *n.*

cur·ry·comb (kėr′ē kōm′), a comb or brush with metal teeth for rubbing and cleaning a horse. *n.*

cu·ti·cle (kyü′tə kəl), the hard skin around the sides and base of a fingernail or toenail. *n.*

D

de·scend (di send′), **1** go or come down from a higher to a lower place: *We descended the stairs to get to the basement.* **2** be handed down from parent to child: *This land has descended from my grandfather to my mother and now to me.* **3** come down or spring from: *He is descended from pioneers. v.*

di·lem·ma (də lem′ə), situation requiring a choice between two evils; difficult choice: *She was faced with the dilemma of either telling a lie or betraying a friend. n., pl.* **di·lem·mas.**

E

eb·on·y (eb′ə nē), **1** the hard, black wood of a tropical tree, used for the black keys of a piano, for the backs and handles of brushes, and for ornamental woodwork. **2** like ebony; black; dark. 1 *n.*, 2 *adj.*

em·a·nate (em′ə nāt), come forth; spread out: *Light and heat emanate from the sun. v.*, **em·a·nat·ed, em·a·nat·ing.**

en·tou·rage (än′tü räzh′), group of attendants; people usually accompanying a person: *a queen and her entourage. n.*

ewe (yü), a female sheep. *n.*

F

fan (fan), **1** instrument or device with which to stir the air in order to cool or ventilate a room, remove odors, cool one's face, etc. **2** stir (the air) with a fan. **3** (in baseball) to strike out. 1 *n.*, 2, 3 *v.*, **fanned, fan·ning.**

flam·boy·ant (flam boi′ənt), **1** gorgeously brilliant; flaming; showily striking: *Some tropical flowers have flamboyant colors.* **2** given to display; showy: *a flamboyant person. adj.* —**flam·boy′ant·ly,** *adv.*

flank (flangk), **1** side of an animal or person between the ribs and the hip. **2** get around the far right or the far left side of. 1 *n.*, 2 *v.*

fo·rage (fôr′ij), **1** hay, grain, or other food for horses, cattle, etc. **2** hunt or search for food: *Rabbits forage in our garden.* **3** get by hunting or searching about. **4** search about; hunt: *The boys foraged for old metal.* 1 *n.*, 2-4 *v.*, **fo·raged, fo·rag·ing.**

G

gal·lant (gal′ənt), **1** noble in spirit or in conduct; brave: *King Arthur was a gallant knight.* **2** grand; fine; stately: *A ship with all of its sails spread is a gallant sight.* **3** very polite and attentive to women. *adj.* —**gal′lant·ly,** *adv.*

gar·de·nia (gär dē′nyə), an evergreen shrub or small tree bearing fragrant, white flowers with smooth, waxy petals. *n., pl.* **gar·de·nias.** [*Gardenia* was formed from the name of Alexander *Garden,* 1730-1791, an American botanist.]

gar·ri·son (gar′ə sən), **1** group of soldiers stationed in a fort, town, etc., to defend it. **2** place that has a garrison. *n.*

a hat	i it	oi oil	ch child	ə stands for:
ā age	ī ice	ou out	ng long	a in about
ä far	o hot	u cup	sh she	e in taken
e let	ō open	u̇ put	th thin	i in pencil
ē equal	ô order	ü rule	ᴛʜ then	o in lemon
ėr term			zh measure	u in circus

gul·den (gu̇l′den), any of several gold coins once current in a number of European countries. *n.*

H

hack·a·more (hak′ə môr, hak′ə mōr), halter, especially one used in breaking horses. *n.*

har·mo·ny (här′mə nē), **1** an orderly or pleasing arrangement of parts; going well together. **2** the sounding together of musical tones in a chord. **3** study of chords in music and of relating them to successive chords. *n., pl.* **har·mo·nies.**

her·ald (her′əld), **1** person who carries messages and makes announcements; messenger. **2** In former times, an official who made public announcements, carried messages, and supervised public ceremonies. *n.*

Hin·du·stan·i (hin′du̇ stan′ē), **1** of India, its people, or their languages. **2** the commonest language of northern India. 1 *adj.*, 2 *n.*

hock (hok), joint in the hind leg of a horse, cow, etc., corresponding to the human ankle. *n.*

hog·back (hog′bak′, hôg′bak′), (in geology) a low, sharp ridge with steep sides. *n.*

hos·pi·tal·i·ty (hos′pə tal′ə tē), friendly reception; generous treatment of guests or strangers. *n.*

hu·mil·i·a·tion (hyü mil′ē ā′shən), a lowering of pride, dignity, or self-respect; a making or a being made ashamed. *n.*

I

im·per·i·al (im pir′ē əl), **1** of an empire or its ruler: *the imperial palace.* **2** supreme; majestic; magnificent. *adj.*

im·pro·vise (im′prə vīz), make up (music, poetry, etc.) on the spur of the moment; sing, recite, speak, etc., without preparation: *We improvised a play for our parents. v.,* **im·pro·vised, im·pro·vis·ing.**

im·pu·dent (im′pyə dənt), shamelessly bold; very rude and insolent: *The impudent child made faces at us. adj.* —**im′pu·dent·ly,** *adv.*

in·au·gu·ra·tion (in ô′gyə rā′shən), act or ceremony of installing a person in office. The inauguration of a President of the United States takes place on January 20. *n.*

in·dis·tin·guish·a·ble (in′dis-ting′gwi shə bəl), not able to be told apart; not able to be recognized as distinct. *adj.*

in·tox·i·cate (in tok′sə kāt), **1** to make drunk: *Too much wine intoxicates people.* **2** excite emotionally; exhilarate: *The music was intoxicating. v.,* **in·tox·i·cat·ed, in·tox·i·cat·ing.**

i·ron·i·cal (ī ron′ə kəl), contrary to what would naturally be expected: *It was ironical that the man was run over by his own automobile. adj.* —**i·ron′i·cal·ly,** *adv.*

ir·ri·ta·ble (ir′ə tə bəl), easily made angry; impatient: *When the rain spoiled her plans, she was irritable for the rest of the day. adj.* —**ir′ri·ta·bly,** *adv.*

i·tin·er·ant (ī tin′ər ənt, i tin′ər ənt), **1** traveling from place to place, especially in connection with some employment or vocation. **2** person who travels from place to place. 1 *adj.,* 2 *n.*

J

jit·ter·bug (jit′ər bug′), **1** lively dance for couples, with rapid twirling movements and acrobatics. It was especially popular in the 1940s. **2** dance the jitterbug. 1 *n.,* 2 *v.,* **jit·ter·bugged, jit·ter·bug·ging.**

K

ki·mo·no (kə mō′nə), **1** a loose outer garment held in place by a sash, worn by Japanese men and women. **2** a woman's loose dressing gown. *n., pl.* **ki·mo·nos.**

kimono

L

lar·der (lär′dər), **1** place where food is kept; pantry. **2** supply of food. *n.*

lar·va (lär′və), **1** the wormlike early form of an insect. A caterpillar is the larva of a butterfly or moth. A grub is the larva of a beetle. **2** an immature form of certain animals. A tadpole is the larva of a frog or toad. *n., pl.,* **lar·vae** (lär′vē), **lar·vas.** [*Larva* comes from Latin *larva,* meaning "a ghost, a mask." It was called this because this stage of an insect's life was thought to be "a mask" of its later form.]

leg·horn (leg'ərn), a rather small kind of domestic fowl which produces large numbers of eggs. *n.*

lin·e·age (lin'ē ij), **1** descent in a direct line from an ancestor. **2** family or origin. *n.*

lin·i·ment (lin'ə mənt), a soothing liquid which is rubbed on the skin to relieve the pain of sore muscles, sprains, bruises, etc. *n.*

liv·er·y (liv'ər ē), any uniform provided for servants, or adopted by any group or profession: *a chauffeur in green livery. n., pl.* **liv·er·ies.**

lou·ver (lü'vər), **1** any of several overlapping horizontal boards or strips of wood set at a slant in a window or other opening, so as to keep out rain, but provide ventilation and light. **2** window or other opening covered with these boards. *n.*

louvers
left def. 1;
right def. 2

lux·ur·i·ous (lug zhùr'ē əs, luk shùr'-ē əs), **1** lavish beyond what is necessary: *a luxurious way of life.* **2** very comfortable and beautiful: *Some theaters are luxurious. adj.*

M

mag·is·trate (maj'ə strāt), **1** a government official who has power to apply the law and put it in force. **2** judge in a minor court. *n.*

a hat	**i** it	**oi** oil	**ch** child	**ə** stands for:
ā age	**ī** ice	**ou** out	**ng** long	a in about
ä far	**o** hot	**u** cup	**sh** she	e in taken
e let	**ō** open	**ù** put	**th** thin	i in pencil
ē equal	**ô** order	**ü** rule	**ŧH** then	o in lemon
ėr term			**zh** measure	u in circus

ma·ha·ra·ja (mä'hə rä'jə), formerly, a ruling prince in India, especially one who ruled a state. *n., pl.* **ma·ha·ra·jas.**

mem·o·ran·dum (mem'ə ran'dəm), **1** a short written statement for future use; note to aid one's memory: *Make a memorandum of the things we need for the trip.* **2** an informal letter, note, or report. *n., pl.* **mem·o·ran·dums** or **mem·o·ran·da.**

mul·ti·tude (mul'tə tüd, mul'tə tyüd), a great many; crowd: *a multitude of difficulties, a multitude of enemies. n.*

N

nat·ur·al·ist (nach'ər ə list), person who makes a study of animals and plants. *n.*

noc·turne (nok'tėrn'), a musical composition appropriate to the night or evening, especially of a dreamy character. *n.*

nom·i·nate (nom'ə nāt), **1** name as candidate for an office; designate: *William Jennings Bryan was nominated three times for President, but he was never elected.* **2** appoint to an office or duty: *In 1933 Roosevelt nominated the first woman cabinet member in U.S. history. v.,* **nom·i·nat·ed, nom·i·nat·ing.**

539

O

ob·e·lisk (ob′ə lisk), a tapering, four-sided shaft of stone with a top shaped like a pyramid. *n.*

obelisk

o·bliv·i·ous (ə bliv′ē əs), forgetful; not mindful; not attentive: *The book was so interesting that I was oblivious to my surroundings. adj.*

oc·cu·pant (ok′yə pənt), **1** one that takes or fills up space, time, etc.: *The occupants of the car stepped out as I approached.* **2** person in actual possession of a house, office, etc. *n.*

om·i·nous (om′ə nəs), unfavorable; threatening: *Those black clouds look ominous. adj.* —**om′i·nous·ly,** *adv.*

or·der·ly (ôr′dər lē), **1** in order; with regular arrangement, method, or system: *an orderly arrangement of dishes on shelves.* **2** soldier who attends a superior officer to carry orders and perform other duties. 1 *adj.,* 2 *n., pl.* **or·der·lies.**

P

parch·ment (pärch′mənt), **1** the skin of sheep or goats, prepared for use as a writing material. **2** manuscript or document written on parchment. *n.*

phe·nom·e·non (fə nom′ə non), **1** fact, event, or circumstance that can be observed. **2** something or someone extraordinary or remarkable: *The Grand Canyon is a phenomenon of nature. n., pl.* **phe·nom·e·na** (or **phe·nom·e·nons** for 2).

pop·u·lace (pop′yə lis), the common people; the masses. *n.*

pro·long (prə lông′), make longer; extend; stretch; lengthen out in time: *prolong a visit. v.*

pro·vi·sion (prə vizh′ən), **1** statement making a condition: *A provision of the lease is that the rent must be paid promptly.* **2** care taken for the future; arrangement made beforehand: *There is a provision for making the building larger if necessary. n.*

R

rab·bi (rab′ī), teacher of the Jewish law and religion; leader of a Jewish congregation. *n., pl.* **rab·bis** or **rab·bies.** [*Rabbi* comes from Hebrew *rabbī,* meaning "my master."]

ra·jah (rä′jə), ruler or chief in India, Java, Borneo, etc. *n.*

ra·zor·back (rā′zər bak′), kind of thin, half-wild hog with a ridged back, common in the southern United States. *n.*

re·bel·lious (ri bel′yəs), **1** defying authority; acting like a rebel; mutinous: *a rebellious army.* **2** hard to manage; disobedient: *a rebellious child. adj.* —**re·bel′lious·ly,** *adv.* —**re·bel′-lious·ness,** *n.*

reck·on·ing (rek′ə ning), **1** method of computing; count; calculation: *By my reckoning we are miles from home.* **2** bill, especially at an inn or tavern. *n.*

re·mu·da (ri müd′ə), the herd of horses from which are chosen those to be used for the day by ranch hands. *n.*

re·proach·ful (ri prōch′fəl), **1** full of blame or censure. **2** expressing blame or disapproval. *adj.* —**re·proach′-ful·ly,** *adv.*

re·sem·ble (ri zem′bəl), be like; have likeness to in form, figure, or qualities. *v.,* **re·sem·bled, re·sem·bling.**

rig·a·ma·role (rig′ə mə rōl′), foolish talk or activity; words or action without meaning; nonsense. *n.*

row·el (rou′əl), a small wheel with sharp points, attached to the end of a spur. *n.*

rowel

S

sa·chet (sa shā′ *or* sash′ā), **1** a small bag or pad containing perfumed powder, placed among articles of clothing. **2** perfumed powder. *n.*

san·i·tize (san′ə tīz), **1** make sanitary; disinfect. **2** make more desirable or acceptable by removing unpleasant or offensive elements. *v.,* **san·i·tized, san·i·tiz·ing.**

scribe (skrīb), **1** person who copies manuscripts. Before printing was invented, there were many scribes. **2** a public clerk or secretary. *n.* [*Scribe* is from Latin *scriba,* meaning "an official writer," which came from *scribere,* meaning "to write."]

scru·ti·nize (skrüt′n īz), examine closely; inspect carefully: *The jeweler scrutinized the diamond for flaws. v.,* **ru·ti·nized, scru·ti·niz·ing.**

a hat	**i** it	**oi** oil	**ch** child	**ə** stands for:
ā age	**ī** ice	**ou** out	**ng** long	a in about
ä far	**o** hot	**u** cup	**sh** she	e in taken
e let	**ō** open	**ù** put	**th** thin	i in pencil
ē equal	**ô** order	**ü** rule	**ŦH** then	o in lemon
ėr term			**zh** measure	u in circus

skit·tles (skit′lz), game in which the players try to knock down nine wooden pins by rolling balls or throwing wooden disks at them. *n.*

snubbing post, a short post to which a line may be attached to check the movement of a boat, horse, etc.

stan·dard (stan′dərd), **1** anything taken as a basis of comparison; model: *Your work is not up to the class standard.* **2** flag, emblem, or symbol: *The dragon was the standard of China. n.*

stol·id (stol′id), hard to arouse; not easily excited; showing no emotion; seeming dull. *adj.* —**stol′id·ly,** *adv.*

sus·pi·cious (sə spish′əs), **1** causing one to suspect or think likely: *a suspicious manner.* **2** feeling suspicion; suspecting: *Our dog is suspicious of strangers. adj.* —**sus·pi′cious·ly,** *adv.*

syn·co·pate (sing′kə pāt), (in music) begin (a tone) on an unaccented beat and hold it into an accented one. *v.,* **syn·co·pat·ed, syn·co·pat·ing.**

syn·co·pa·tion (sing′kə pā′shən), **1** a syncopating or a being syncopated. **2** music marked by syncopation, such as jazz or ragtime. *n.*

T

tap·es·try (tap′ə strē), fabric with pictures or designs woven in it, used to hang on walls, cover furniture, etc. *n.,* *pl.* **tap·es·tries.**

tem·pes·tu·ous (tem pes′chü əs), **1** stormy: *It was a tempestuous night.* **2** violent: *a tempestuous fit of anger. adj.* —**tem·pes′tu·ous·ly,** *adv.* —**tem·pes′tu·ous·ness,** *n.*

thought·less (thôt′lis), **1** without thought; doing things without thinking; careless: *Thoughtless drivers cause many automobile accidents.* **2** showing little or no care or regard for others. *adj.* —**thought′less·ly,** *adv.* —**thought′less·ness,** *n.*

trac·er·y (trā′sər ē), ornamental work or designs consisting of lines. Stonework, carving, and embroidery often have tracery. *n., pl.* **trac·er·ies.**

tracery

trot·ter (trot′ər), **1** horse that trots, especially one bred and trained to trot in a race. **2** a pig's foot used as food. *n.*

truss (trus), tie or fasten; bind: *truss up a prisoner hand and foot.* *v.*

tus·sock (tus′ək), a tuft of growing grass or the like. *n.*

U

u·nan·i·mous (yü nan′ə məs), **1** in complete accord or agreement; agreed. **2** characterized by or showing complete accord: *She was elected by a unanimous vote.* *adj.* [*Unanimous* is from Latin *unanimus,* which comes from *unus,* meaning "one," and *animus,* meaning "mind."]

V

vaude·ville (vôd′vil, vô′də vil), theatrical entertainment featuring a variety of acts such as songs, dances, acrobatic feats, short sketches, trained animals, etc. *n.*

veg·e·tar·i·an (vej′ə ter′ē ən), person who eats only vegetables but no meat, fish, or other animal products. *n.*

vic·ar (vik′ər), the minister of a parish or a clergyman who has charge of one chapel in a parish. *n.*

W

wal·low (wol′ō), roll about; flounder: *The pigs wallowed in the mud.* *v.*

wane (wān), **1** lose size; become smaller gradually. **2** lose strength or intensity: *The light of day wanes in the evening.* **3** draw to a close: *Summer wanes as autumn approaches.* *v.,* **waned, waning.**

way·far·er (wā′fer′ər), traveler, especially one who travels on foot. *n.*

wran·gle (rang′gəl), **1** argue or dispute in a noisy or angry way: *The children wrangled about who should wash the dog.* **2** (in the western United States and Canada) to herd or tend (horses, cattle, etc.) on the range. *v.,* **wran·gled, wran·gling.**

wrap·per (rap′ər), **1** a covering or cover: *Some magazines are mailed in paper wrappers.* **2** a woman's long, loose garment to wear in the house. *n.*

wretch·ed (rech′id), **1** very unfortunate or unhappy. **2** very unsatisfactory; miserable: *a wretched hut.* *adj.* —**wretch′ed·ly,** *adv.*

Z

zwie·back (swī′bak′, zwī′bak′), kind of bread or cake cut into slices and toasted dry in an oven. *n.* [*Zwieback* is from German *Zwieback,* meaning "a biscuit," which comes from *zwie-,* meaning "twice," and *backen,* meaning "to bake."]

Word List

The following words all appear in the glossary. Those followed by an asterisk are introduced optionally in the Teacher's Edition.

**Babe:
The Gallant Pig**
bitch
canter*
chitterlings
ewe*
flank*
forage*
gallant*
hock
skittles
vicar

Time Cat
commission*
garrison
imperial*
impudent
memorandum*
orderly*
parchment
scribes
standard*
trussed

Zeely
carcass
descended
ebony*
larva
leghorn*
louvered
ominously*
razorback*
sachet
wallow*

**Scott Joplin
and the Ragtime
Years**
counterpoint*
flamboyant
harmony*
improvise*
intoxicate
itinerant
nocturne*
syncopation*
tempestuous
vaudeville

**Our Nation's
Capital**
agonize
circuit
inauguration
ironic*
naturalist
nominate*
obelisk
provision*
scrutinize*
unanimous*

**The Wise and
Clever Maiden**
apprentice
conceit*
herald
lineage*
livery
magistrate
oblivious*
reckoning
rigamarole*
stolid*

The Secret Garden
agitate*
brocade
consequence
Hindustani
rajah
rebellious*
reproachfully
tapestry*
wrapper*
wretched*

The Agony of Alice
advertisement*
agony*
cuticle
gardenia
humiliation*
kimono
maharaja
occupant*
vegetarian*
zwieback

**Three Stories by
I.B. Singer**
berate*
bewilder*
blintze
borscht
dilemma*
gulden
larder
luxurious*
rabbi
resemble*

**In the Year of the
Boar and Jackie
Robinson**
chaos*
emanate*
fanned
indistinguishable*
jitterbug
multitude
phenomenon
prolong*
sanitize
thoughtlessly*

**The Dragons of
the Queen**
accommodate*
colonnade
entourage*
hospitality
irritable*
populace
suspiciously*
tracery
waning*
wayfarer

The Blind Outlaw
corral*
currycomb*
hackamore
hogback
liniment*
remuda
rowel
snubbing post
tussock*
wrangle*

Page 370: from *In the Year of the Boar and Jackie Robinson* by Bette Bao Lord. Illustrated by Marc Simont. Text copyright © 1984 by Bette Bao Lord. Illustrations copyright © 1984 by Marc Simont. Reprinted by permission of Harper & Row, Publishers, Inc. and Irving Paul Lazar Agency.

Page 385: "We Have Our Moments" *Sports Pages*, by Arnold Adoff. Copyright © 1986 by Arnold Adoff. Reprinted by permission of Harper & Row Publishers, Inc.

Page 394: Complete text of *The Dragons of the Queen* by Mary Stolz. Copyright © 1969 by Mary Stolz. Reprinted by permission of Harper & Row, Publishers, Inc. and Roslyn Targ Literary Agency.

"Travel" by Edna St. Vincent Millay from *Collected Poems*, Harper & Row. Copyright 1921, 1948 by Edna St. Vincent Millay. Reprinted by permission.

Page 432: *Blind Outlaw* by Glen Rounds. Copyright © 1980 by Glen Rounds. Reprinted by permission of Holiday House.

Page 505: "The Runaway" by Robert Frost from *The Poetry of Robert Frost* edited by Edward Connery Lathem. Copyright 1923, © 1969 by Holt, Rinehart and Winston, Inc. Copyright 1951 by Robert Frost. Reprinted by permission of Henry Holt and Company, Inc. and Jonathan Cape Ltd.

Artists

Section 1: Mary Rayner, 8, 9, 41; Robert Wahlgren, 10, 11, 14, 20, 22, 23, 28, 30, 32, 34, 38, 43, 44

Section 2: Ben Otero, 46, 47, 52, 54, 55, 57, 62, 63, 64, 68; Charles Hughes, 72, 73

Section 3: Janet LaSalle, 80, 81, 125, 127, 128

Section 6: David Small, 204–207, 211–213, 218, 219, 224, 228, 229, 231, 232

Section 7: Joel Spector, 238–279; Robert Wahlgren, 281, 283

Section 8: Don Madden, 286–289, 294, 302, 310, 316, 320, 321, 323, 324

Section 9: Ralph Creasman, 328–330, 339, 345, 358–361, 363

Section 11: Ann Grifalconi, 390, 391, 394, 399, 405, 412, 416, 423; Charles Hughes, 423

Section 12: Robert Wahlgren, 428, 429, 505

Freelance Photography

Photographs not listed were shot by Scott, Foresman and Company.
William Sladcik, 130–131, 161
Allan Landau, 369, 382

Pictures

Positions of pictures are shown in abbreviated form as follows: top (t), bottom (b), center (c), left (l), right (r).

Page 39: Photo by Michael Dyer. Courtesy Crown Publishing Company.

Pages 48, 50: National Museum of Archeology and Anthropology, Lima. Loren A. McIntyre.

Page 49: Mujica Gallo Museum. Loren A. McIntyre.

Page 71: Photo by Alexander Limont. Courtesy E. P. Dutton, Inc.

Page 76: Art Institute of Chicago, Buckingham Fund.

Page 123: Cox Studios. Courtesy William Morrow & Co.

Page 139: Florida State Archive, Tallahassee.

Page 147: Texarkana Museums and Historical Society.

Page 153: New York Public Library. Schomburg Center for Research in Black Culture.

Page 156: Missouri Historical Society.

Page 159: Courtesy The Historical New Orleans Collection Museum Research Center.

Page 160: Courtesy of the author.

Page 163: Brian Brake/Rapho/Photo Researchers.

Pages 168, 169: Library of Congress.

Page 171: Courtesy District of Columbia.

Page 172(t): Robert Skenco/FPG International.

Page 175: Culver Pictures.

Page 177: Library of Congress.

Page 182: © Peter Gridley/FPG International.

Page 186(l,r): National Archives.

Page 187(l,r): Library of Congress.

Page 188: Library of Congress.

Page 190: © Peter Gridley/FPG International.

Page 191: Bettmann Newsphotos.

Page 192: © Chip Clark.

Page 192 (inset): Library of Congress.

Page 195: Smithsonian Institution.

Page 196(l): © Charles H. Phillips.

Page 196(c): Smithsonian Institution, From the book *The National Museum of Natural History* by Philip Kopper. Published by Harry N. Abrams, Inc.

Page 196(r): Photograph by Chip Clark.

Page 279: Mary Evans Picture Library.

Page 319: Courtesy Atheneum Publishers.

Pages 326, 327: Chagall, Marc. *Over Vitebsk*, 1914. Art Gallery of Ontario, Toronto. Gift of Sam and Ayala Zacks, 1970. Copyright ARS NY/ADAGP 1988.

Page 357: © 1982 Jerry Bauer. Farrar, Straus & Giroux, Inc.

Page 383: © 1981 Jim Kalett. Courtesy Harper & Row Publishers, Inc.

Page 421: Courtesy Harper & Row Publishers, Inc.

Page 503: Courtesy Holiday House, Inc., NY.

Glossary

Unless otherwise acknowledged, all photos are the property of Scott, Foresman and Company.
Page 535: Culver Pictures; Page 540: Walter S. Clark, Jr.

Cover Artist

Joel Spector